RELIGION AND PUBLIC LIFE
IN THE PACIFIC REGION:
FLUID IDENTITIES

RELIGION BY REGION

Religion by Region Series
Co-published with the Leonard E. Greenberg Center for the
Study of Religion in Public Life at Trinity College
Mark Silk and Andrew Walsh, Series Editors

The United States is a nation of many distinct regions. But until now, no literature has looked at these regional differences in terms of religion. The Religion by Region Series describes, both quantitatively and qualitatively, the religious character of contemporary America, region by region. Each of the eight regional volumes includes overviews and demographic information to allow comparisons between regions. But at the same time, each volume strives to show what makes its region unique. A concluding volume looks at what these regional variations mean for American religion as a whole.

1. Religion and Public Life in the Pacific Northwest: *The None Zone*
   Edited by Patricia O'Connell Killen (Pacific Lutheran University) and Mark Silk

2. Religion and Public Life in the Mountain West: *Sacred Landscapes in Tension*
   Edited by Jan Shipps (Indiana University–Purdue University, Indianapolis) and Mark Silk

3. Religion and Public Life in New England: *Steady Habits, Changing Slowly*
   Edited by Andrew Walsh and Mark Silk

4. Religion and Public Life in the Midwest: *America's Common Denominator?*
   Edited by Philip Barlow (Hanover College) and Mark Silk

5. Religion and Public Life in the Southern Crossroads Region: *Showdown States*
   Edited by William Lindsey (Philander Smith College) and Mark Silk

6. Religion and Public Life in the South: *In the Evangelical Mode*
   Edited by Charles Reagan Wilson (University of Mississippi) and Mark Silk

7. Religion and Public Life in the Middle Atlantic Region: *The Fount of Diversity*
   Edited by Randall Balmer (Columbia University) and Mark Silk

8. Religion and Public Life in the Pacific Region: *Fluid Identities*
   Edited by Wade Clark Roof (University of California, Santa Barbara) and Mark Silk

9. Religion by Region: *Religion and Public Life in The United States*
   By Mark Silk and Andrew Walsh

RELIGION AND PUBLIC LIFE IN THE PACIFIC REGION: FLUID IDENTITIES

Edited by

Wade Clark Roof

and

Mark Silk

Published in cooperation with the Leonard E. Greenberg
Center for the Study of Religion in Public Life at
Trinity College, Hartford, Connecticut

ALTAMIRA
PRESS

A Division of
ROWMAN & LITTLEFIELD PUBLISHERS, INC.
Walnut Creek • Lanham • New York • Toronto • Oxford

Published in cooperation with the Leonard E. Greenberg Center for the Study of Religion in Public Life at Trinity College, Hartford, Connecticut

ALTAMIRA PRESS
A division of Rowman & Littlefield Publishers, Inc.
A wholly owned subsidary of The Rowman & Littlefield Publishing Group, Inc.
4501 Forbes Boulevard, Suite 200
Lanham, MD 20706
www.altamirapress.com

PO Box 317
Oxford
OX2 9RU, UK

British Library Cataloguing in Publication Information Available

Library of Congress Cataloging-in-Publication Data

Religion and public life in the Pacific region : fluid identities / edited by
    Wade Clark Roof and Mark Silk.
        p. cm. — (Religion by region)
    Includes bibliographical references and index.
    ISBN 0-7591-0638-X (cloth: alk. paper) — ISBN 0-7591-0639-8 (pbk. : alk. paper)
    1. California—Religion. 2. Nevada—Religion. 3. Hawaii—Religion.
    4. Religion and politics—California. 5. Religion and politics—Nevada.
    6. Religion and politics—Hawaii. I. Roof, Wade Clark. II. Silk, Mark.
    III. Series.

    BL2527.C2R45 2005
    200'.979—dc22   2005020714

Printed in the United States of America

♾™ The paper used in this publication meets the minimum requirements of American National Standard for Information Sciences—Permanence of Paper for Printed Library Materials, ANSI/NISO Z39.48–1992.

CONTENTS

PREFACE

Geographical diversity is the hallmark of religion in the United States. There are Catholic zones and evangelical Bible Belts, a Lutheran domain and a Mormon fastness, metropolitan concentrations of Jews and Muslims, and (in a different dimension) parts of the country where religious affiliation of whatever kind is very high and parts where it is far below the norm. This religious heterogeneity is inextricably linked to the character of American places. From Boston to Birmingham, from Salt Lake City to Santa Barbara, even the casual observer perceives public cultures that are intimately connected to the religious identities and habits of the local population.

Yet when the story of religion in American public life gets told, the country's variegated religious landscape tends to be reduced to a series of monochrome portraits of the spiritual state of the union, of piety along the Potomac, of great events or swings of mood that raise or lower the collective religious temperature. Whatever the virtues of compiling such a unified national narrative—and I believe they are considerable—it obscures a great deal. As the famous red-and-blue maps of the 2000 and 2004 presidential votes make clear, region has not ceased to matter in national politics. Indeed, in this era of increasing federalism regions are, state by state, charting ever more distinctive courses.

To understand where each region is headed and why, it is critical to recognize the place of religion in it. Religion by Region, a project of the Leonard E. Greenberg Center for the Study of Religion in Public Life at Trinity College in Hartford, represents the first comprehensive effort to show how religion shapes, and is being shaped by, regional culture in America. The project has been designed to produce edited volumes (of which this is the seventh) on each of eight regions of the country. A ninth volume will sum up the results in order to draw larger conclusions about the way religion and region combine to affect civic culture and public policy in the United States as a whole.

The purpose of the project is not to decompose a national storyline into eight separate narratives. Rather, it is to bring regional realities to bear, in a systematic way, on how American culture is understood at the beginning of the twenty-first century. In line with the Greenberg Center's commitment to enhance public understanding of religion, these volumes are intended for a general audience, with a particular eye towards helping working journalists make better sense of the part religion plays in the public life—local, statewide, regional, and national—that they cover. At the same time, I am persuaded that the accounts and analyses provided in these volumes will make a significant contribution to the academic study of religion in contemporary America.

The project's division of the country into regions will be generally familiar, with the exception of what we are calling the Southern Crossroads—a region roughly equivalent to what American historians know as the Old Southwest, comprising Louisiana, Texas, Arkansas, Oklahoma, and Missouri. Since we are committed to covering every state in the Union (though not the territories—e.g., Puerto Rico), Hawaii has been included in a Pacific region with California and Nevada, and Alaska in the Pacific Northwest.

Cultural geographers may be surprised to discover a few states out of their customary places. Idaho, which is usually considered part of the Pacific Northwest, has been assigned to the Mountain West. In our view, the fact that the bulk of Idaho's population lives in the heavily Mormon southern part of the state links it more closely to Utah than to Oregon and Washington. To be sure, we might have chosen to parcel out certain states between regions, assigning northern Idaho and western Montana to the Pacific Northwest or, to take another example, creating a Catholic band running from southern Louisiana through south Texas and across the lower tiers of New Mexico and Arizona on into southern California. The purpose of the project, however, is not to map the country religiously but to explore the ways that politics, public policies, and civil society relate—or fail to relate—to the religion that is on the ground. States have had to be kept intact because when American laws are not made in Washington, D.C. they are made in statehouses. To understand what is decided in Baton Rouge, Louisiana's Catholic south and evangelical north must be seen as engaged in a single undertaking.

That is not to say that the details of American religious demography are unimportant to our purpose. That demography has undergone notable shifts in recent years, and these have affected public life in any number of ways. To reckon with them, it has been essential to assemble the best data available on the religious identities of Americans and how they correlate with voting patterns and views on public issues. As students of American religion know, however, this is far from an easy task. The U.S. Census is prohibited by law from asking questions about religion, and membership reports provided by religious bodies to non-governmental researchers—when they are provided at all—vary greatly in accuracy. Most public opinion polling does not enable us to draw precise correlations between respondents' views on issues and their religious identity and behavior.

In order to secure the best possible empirical grounding, the project has assembled a range of data from three sources, which are described in detail in the Appendix. These have supplied us with, among other things, information from religious bodies on their membership; from individuals on their religious identities; and from voters in specific religious categories on their political preferences and opinions. (For purposes of clarity, people are described as "adherents" or "members" only when reported as such by a religious institution. Otherwise, they are "identifiers.") Putting this information together with 2000 census and other survey data, the project has been able to create both the best available picture of religion in America today and the most comprehensive account of its political significance.

Religion by Region does not argue that religion plays the same kind of role in each region of the country; nor does it mean to advance the proposition that religion is the master key that unlocks all the secrets of American public life. As the tables of contents of the individual volumes make clear, each region has its distinctive religious layout, based not only on the numerical strength of particular religious bodies but also on how those bodies, or groups of them, function on the public stage. In some regions, religion serves as a shaping force; in others it is a subtler conditioning agent. Our objective is simply to show what the picture looks like from place to place, and to provide consistent data and a framework of discussion sufficient to enable useful contrasts and comparisons to be drawn.

A project of such scope and ambition does not come cheap. We are deeply indebted to the Lilly Endowment for making it possible.

Mark Silk
Hartford, Connecticut
January 2005

INTRODUCTION

RELIGION IN THE PACIFIC REGION

Phillip E. Hammond

K evin Starr, the California State Librarian and professor of history at the University of Southern California, begins the first volume of a remarkable series entitled *Americans and the California Dream*[1] thus:

> The unfolding of California as a regional culture in the nineteenth century is a rich and colorful chapter in American history ... From the beginning, California promised much. While yet barely a name on the map, it entered American awareness as a symbol of renewal. It was a final frontier: of geography and of expectation ...

> Reaching its maturity sometime in the decade before World War I, provincial California, its population a bare fraction of what it is today, possessed an intimacy now impossible. Artists and intellectuals knew one another and tended to share certain hopeful assumptions regarding the region where they lived and worked. They were hopeful because, although many opportunities had been squandered, all was not lost. California yet ached with promise. In this more complicated time, when hope is not so certain and the promise is unclear, the faith of those years must come to our aid. Although Californians of today inhabit a civilization and grapple with problems only dimly dreamed of in the nineteenth century, the struggle of previous generations, the emergence of provincial California, deserves scrutiny. It was, after all, the founding time, when, for good and for evil, what it meant to be a Californian was first probed and defined. That past act of definition is part of a present identity. That California continues, in part, to live ...

Of course, the dream outran the reality, as it always does. California experienced more than its share of social problems because its development was so greedy and so unregulated. No evocation of imaginative aspiration can atone for the burdens of the California past, especially the violence and the brutality. Acknowledging the tragedy, however, Californians must also attune themselves to the hope. The struggle for corrective action in the face of history put earlier generations in touch with their best selves. What they attained, attained in the struggle and the dreaming, deserves our respect—and our most sincere celebration.

Arranged chronologically, the volumes show how the hope and optimism expressed at the time of California's entry into the Union in 1850 continues to this day, embattled though it has been at times. California, Starr thinks, embodies the American dream as well as its own.

There was, of course, the Gold Rush, which brought countless hopeful miners, but it also brought others hoping to capitalize on miners and mining. Levi Strauss, for example, may have dreamed of gold, but he made his fortunes selling sturdy trousers to men who panned for it. Indeed, not a single fortune from gold itself survived the Gold Rush, though it made possible the fortunes of those who built railroads, founded banks, or sold chocolates.

California was a land of opportunity for many, if not all. It still is, and people keep migrating there, though not in the huge numbers of earlier decades. Thus, for example, the 2000 census reports that 68 percent of California residents were born in that state, a rate slightly higher than the national average of 60 percent. Thirty years earlier, however, the rate was 47 percent, meaning the majority of Californians then were immigrants. That was the case from 1849 until well after World War II.

People have also been migrating to Nevada and Hawaii, the other two states in the Pacific region. Nevada's bulging population is quite recent, dating from the middle of the twentieth century. The 2000 census reports that only 25 percent of its current residents were born in Nevada, by far the lowest rate in the United States. (Florida, at 39 percent, is next lowest.) Most of Nevada's immigrants are drawn by the tourist and gaming industries or from the ranks of retirees.

Hawaii's migration history is different, spurred first by the need for laborers in the pineapple and sugar cane industries. People were "imported" from China, Japan, and Portugal; later from Korea and the Philippines. World War II, followed by jet air travel, changed the Hawaiian economy. The military retained a large economic role after the war, but tourism increased greatly—the University of Hawaii, Manoa, now has a School of Tourism Management. Like California, therefore, Hawaii has become less a society of immigrants; in 2000, 69 percent of its residents had been born there.

Because of its location the region has been, and still is, a crossroads of global encounters. Migration to the region—East and West, North and South—has led to a mix of traditions unlike any found elsewhere in the country. These encounters have intensified in the years since World War II as a result of the disruptions of war in South Asia; political unrest in Africa, the Middle East, and elsewhere; and the movement of people resulting from a growing network of multinational corporations. Also, passage of the 1965 Immigration Reform Act eliminated restrictions favoring European immigrants and opened the doors to those caught up in these global shifts or otherwise choosing to migrate to the United States. For all these reasons, the Pacific region is at the forefront of what has been called an "exaggerated America," mirroring ever more closely the religious makeup of the world and signaling what the future will look like.

Especially in large cities such as Honolulu, Los Angeles, Las Vegas, and San Francisco, religious and cultural pluralism is visible. It also takes on a double meaning. Aside from the more obvious boundaries separating, say, Catholics, Protestants, Muslims, and Buddhists are those *within* the large religious constituencies based upon ethnicity, race, and national background. No region in the country hosts so many varieties of Buddhism, Christianity, or Islam, literally dozens in each instance. The result is a richly textured tapestry of overlapping religious and ethnic identities that are at once colorful and complex, and a challenge to anyone trying to make sense of the scene.

Despite their considerable differences, these three states share a culture of openness to change, coupled with an optimism that such change will be for the better. Perhaps nothing symbolizes this feature better than the fact that California, Hawaii, and Nevada appear prominently in written fiction, television, and movies. Just as Kevin Starr regards California as embodying "the American Dream," so do Hawaii and Nevada exist similarly in the American imagination.

Other evidence supports the joining together of these three states, as diverse as they certainly are in many respects. About nine of every 10 Nevadans live within a few miles of California, 72 percent in Clark County (Las Vegas) and 18 percent in Washoe County (Reno). Of the 2,034,890 domestic visitors to Hawaii in 2002, 35 percent came from California, far more than from any other region. Since California has 12 percent of America's population, this means that Californians are three times more likely than other U.S. citizens to visit their neighboring state in the mid-Pacific. The "mountain region," including Nevada, comes in second with 12 percent of Hawaii's visitors in 2002.

Needless to say, Californians also dominate tourism to Nevada, with special bus and plane travel from major population centers to both Las Vegas and Reno. Hawaiians, too, flock to Nevada; not only are there numerous daily flights through Los Angeles and San Francisco to Las Vegas but no less than three direct flights daily from Honolulu or Kahului (Maui).

These and other modes of transportation make all three states meccas for tourists. While California and Nevada, like Hawaii, count on the military and agriculture as key elements in their economies, tourism also plays a major role. In Nevada tourism is the dominant share.

Openness and Fluidity

Diverse populations high in hope and high in tourism are populations high in openness to the new. Mobility involves more than just moving around physically, however; it also means breaking ties in one place and forging ties in a new place. Soon after World War II, Margaret Mead, visiting Levittown—an early mass-produced suburb on Long Island—remarked on the absence of cemeteries, a sure sign, she said, of a sense of impermanence. Something of this restlessness and fluidity characterizes the states of the Pacific Region; not just there, but notice-ably there.

A 1988 random survey of the adult population in four states—Massachusetts, North Carolina, Ohio, and California—asked about strength of people's "local ties" (closeness to other people in the neighborhood; number of one's close friends living in the local area). On the basis of answers to these two questions, one can say Californians had significantly weaker ties to their localities than people in the other three states.[2] We can surmise that, had those questions been asked in Nevada and Hawaii, similar results would be found.

As Wade Clark Roof's demographic chapter points out, only the Pacific Northwest and Mountain West regions surpass the Pacific region in the per-cent disclaiming any religious identification or affiliation. Individuals lacking in "attachments" to others are less inclined toward traditional behaviors like church-going and more inclined toward "experimental" behaviors. One way to experiment religiously is to practice a religion with roots in a foreign culture. Such practices, to the degree they are in tension with the dominant culture, can be called cults.

The Pacific region fits this pattern. Nevada, Hawaii, and California rank forty-fifth, forty-sixth, and forty-eighth, among the 50 states in percentage of church members. Oregon and Washington have lower percentage than all three states in the Pacific Region, and Alaska, in forty-seventh place, has a lower percentage than Nevada or Hawaii.[3] However, considering that Utah (836 church members per 1,000 population) and Louisiana (814) are highest in rates of church mem-bership, the differences among the six far-Western states—from 394 to 331—are insignificant; the whole area west of the Pacific range of mountains is less tradi-tional in religious behavior. As Tamar Frankiel points out in this volume, most counties in California have more religiously unaffiliated than affiliated residents, reaching a high of 81 percent in Calaveras County. Storey County in Nevada exceeds that rate with 93 percent. People move in and out of organized religion, check out spiritual movements, and switch from one faith community to another or to none, all with considerable ease.

Frankiel also notes the limited influence of Puritan or Anglican religion in the modern founding of California. Catholic Spaniards came via Mexico to establish settlements and neutralize the Native Americans already there. Gaining independence from Spain in 1821, however, Mexico showed little interest in Alta (upper) California. By the time of the Gold Rush, the series of missions were in disrepair and the number of clergy was only a dozen in the entire area that was to become California. When, in 1846, the Bear Flag War occurred, little effort was made by Mexico's officials in California to keep the North Americans from taking charge.

Despite the changeover, visitors to California were struck by how "Catholic" it seemed, vestiges no doubt of the Spanish/Mexican missionaries' success in instituting rituals, holidays, festivals, and pageants, if not high rates of church-going. It is true that the Reverend Thomas Starr King was prominent in the state during the middle of the nineteenth century, but as Frankiel points out, King was a Unitarian and, while dynamic, preached a message Frankiel labels "personalist"—socially engaging, perhaps, but leaning in the direction of the literary salon. Nonetheless, the California legislature selected him in 1931 to be, along with Junipero Serra, the state's representative in the National Hall of Fame.

It is correct to say that until the last decades of the nineteenth century, California life centered on San Francisco and the Bay area. Southern California retained the pattern of land-grant days with huge ranches, many cattle, and few people. It also retained more of the earlier Spanish/Mexican influence. This all changed, however, beginning in the 1870s when serious—and effective—plans were put into place for bringing water into the area. In rather quick order, institutions such as newspapers, libraries, schools, and hospitals developed in the area.

Included were colleges, at the time chiefly sponsored by immigrants who were significantly Protestants from the Midwest. Chapman College was established in 1861 in Orange, California by the Disciples of Christ. Methodists built the University of Southern California (USC) in Los Angeles in 1879, followed by Congregationalist Pomona College in Claremont and Presbyterian Occidental College in Los Angeles, both established in 1887. Only USC grew into a major graduate research university, and, until the University of California built its Southern Branch (later the University of California at Los Angeles {UCLA}), USC was the single major source of southern California's doctors, lawyers, musicians, and other professionals.

But this Protestant influence could not be sustained in California's fluid and increasingly secular culture. Instead, so-called "mainline" Protestants had to contend with secular forces, along with cults, with sectarian evangelicalism, and with restored Catholicism.

More than just this, however, boundaries among religions are remarkably fluid within the region, and people mix and match religious teachings and practices from many sources with considerable ease. Christian churches incorporate yoga classes, absorb New Age teachings, and blend notions of reincarnation with the doctrine of eternal life. Neo-evangelical megachurches adapt to the consumer culture, offering a variety of small groups and programs to choose among, popular music and drama to appeal to a seeker mentality, and informal worship services. They drop ties to old-style denominational loyalties and call themselves community congregations so as to appeal to a broader audience. The region leads the country in religious adaptability.[4]

Even immigrant populations with beliefs and practices dating back thousands of years re-style themselves to fit the new context, and do so relatively quickly. Buddhists, Sikhs, Hindus, Muslims, and others from Asia, Africa, the Middle East, and elsewhere adopt new institutional forms, creating American-styled congregations that emphasize greater lay participation in decision-making, organizing Sunday schools for children, planning fellowship and coffee hours after worship services, and engaging in capital campaigns for building temples and mosques much like their friends in nearby Catholic and Protestant churches.

Cults

Church-going is traditional and associated with strong local ties to the community. Joining a cult is experimental by definition, if by cult it is meant a religious tradition that has not long been part of the American culture. This difference is variable to be sure, with Buddhism in Hawaii, as practiced by Japanese immigrants or their children, having more in common in this respect with Christian churches than with, say, the Zen Center in San Francisco or the Soka Gakkai Center in Los Angeles. Japanese-American Buddhists in Hawaii are being traditional; many Buddhists elsewhere in America are being experimental.

Unfortunately, national surveys are not subtle enough to allow this distinction to be confirmed. We have surveys that employ the vague category of "Asian religions," however, which show that the Pacific region has nearly four times the number of Asian religion adherents as the average of the other seven regions—2.8 percent compared with 0.75 percent. Only the Mid-Atlantic and Pacific Northwest also reach over 1.0 percent.

We gain confidence in this finding by referencing a quite different finding. Rodney Stark and William Bainbridge have noted the location of cult headquarters state-by-state. They argue that cult leaders are inclined to put their headquarters where their membership figures are large, not a perfect correlation perhaps, but based on a reasonable assumption. In the "cult-headquarters per million population" ranking, Nevada is first, California is third, and Hawaii seventh. These three states also rank high in Theosophy and Spiritualism cults, coming in behind only New Mexico, Arizona, and Florida.[5] Put another way, California had three times the number of cult headquarters as its closest competitor, New York (167 vs. 59). Because of its population size, one expects more of lots of things in California, but it—along with Nevada and Hawaii—are also three of the top seven states in "cults per one million residents."[6]

None of this comes as a surprise regarding California, long known for its fluidity and openness to the novel and innovative, even the bizarre. But it is significant to note that these characteristics are shared by Nevada and Hawaii, even dwarfed as they are by California's 34 million population. Other authors in this book give more and different detail on novel religions, especially Anderson, Frankiel, and Machacek.

Sectarian Evangelicalism

In its early years, the United States was a society that did little to regulate religions, and churches made little effort to seek government sponsorship. Initially, of course, Protestantism was informally the "established" American religion, but massive Catholic immigration led to the erosion, bit by bit, of Protestantism's privileges. It was inherent in the Establishment Clause that such privileges would be found unconstitutional, so either by legislation or court decision, they chiefly disappeared. Laws against blasphemy, Sunday closing laws, and state laws prohibiting Catholic office-holding were erased. Devotional Bible-reading in public schools was outlawed.

Another factor in this increasing neutrality between church and state, and among churches themselves, was the relative paucity of politically aggressive religion. Until recently, religious groups that advocated an intolerant political agenda were small in number, largely without clout, and effectively marginalized. Religious groups that might have been politically effective kept within the bounds of democratic procedures, and, in any event, were kept in check by the dynamics of pluralism. Mainline Protestant churches (i.e., those that had digested the religious implications of the Enlightenment) were joined by the Reform and Conservative branches of Judaism and, on some matters, by Roman Catholicism to create a peaceful religious climate.

After the 1960s this situation changed. The Moral Majority, followed by the Christian Coalition, James Dobson's Focus on the Family, and other groups sharing a varying "evangelical" world view emerged with decided political aims.[7]

The American Religious Identification Survey (ARIS) data for the Pacific region reflect the religious tension created by this politicized world view. With

15.1 percent affiliated with an evangelical non-denominational church and another 7.1 percent Baptist (most of whom are Southern Baptist), the Pacific Region leads even the Pacific Northwest (with 16.2 percent evangelical and 5.8 percent Baptist) in people associated with a conservative religio-political point of view. Moreover, the Pacific region has significantly fewer people (9.4 percent) affiliated with historic "mainline" Protestant denominations, compared with a national average of 15 to 20 percent. The imbalance is palpable.

The situation is politically explosive because the Pacific region also leans left politically, especially on the sex-related moral issues most vexing to the Religious Right. From presidential elections to sex education in the public schools, this religio-political divide can be—and is—mobilized. Anderson's chapter is especially sensitive on this issue, though both Frankiel and Tanabe also have trenchant comments on the matter.

Restored Catholicism

Catholic missionaries had some success in Hawaii and Nevada that continues today, but nothing compared to the once-dominant missions in California. As already noted, the formal aspects of this dominance evaporated early in the nineteenth century. But the discovery of gold by mid-century set in motion the restoration of Catholicism in the state. Today more than half of those religiously affiliated are Roman Catholic.

This turnaround came about because of immigration. First came the Irish and the Italians. Many settled in or around San Francisco, but many farmed and others fished. The Irish moved into political offices, entered the police and fire departments, and gave San Francisco a flavor that remains noticeably "Irish," as in many street names. The Italians raised fruits (e.g., Gallo) and vegetables (e.g., Del Monte) and provided 90 percent of the fish consumed in San Francisco. A visit to Fisherman's Wharf today suggests that the pattern may still hold.

By 1885 the San Francisco diocese had 177 priests, 93 churches, six colleges (including Santa Clara University, California's first college, founded by Italian Jesuits in 1851), four hospitals, and 200,000 members. Sacramento had 40 priests and two colleges.

The Spanish influence disappeared before the Gold Rush, and the few Mexican nationals in California chose not to take up the cultural slack left behind. How, then, did Mexican-Americans become the largest ethnic group in California Catholicism? One answer is found in the tumult in Mexico, especially the Revolution from 1910 to 1920. From 1900 to 1930 fully 10 percent of Mexico's population moved to the American Southwest. Another answer is found in the need for industrial laborers during World War II and farm laborers later. The migration that continues to this day waxes and wanes with economic conditions and the border regulation. All Mexicans who come, however, are at least nominally Catholic.

Pluralism and the Reorganization of Religion

Pluralism has another consequence when it goes beyond simply multiple Protestant denominations, beyond Christianity, and all western religions—even beyond what is generally regarded as religion. When diversity expands all the way to the very definition of "religion"—as in the current popularity of the word "spirituality"—one can anticipate some confusion and doubt in people's minds about what is and is not religion. Courts, for example, have had difficulty seeing Native American religions as "real," given the centrality of land rather than a building in their worship.[8]

Into this setting there emerges what David Machacek calls here the "niche" religion—the religion that makes no claim to universality but appeals only to one kind of ethnicity, one kind of sexual orientation, one age group, etc. Certainly this bodes ill for any renewed call for ecumenism, and may even make interfaith efforts daunting. The implications for religion's public involvement are enormous.

Another way in which religion gets reorganized is through defection. Defection by switching denominations has been common among Protestants, chiefly through inter-denominational marriages. Rather than attend two different—but not that different—churches, a couple would typically agree to attend one, together with their children. Such was not regarded as defection but as accommodation. The notion of religious identity as "inherited" was not disrupted by this pattern.

Things are now greatly changed. A 1986 study, using data from the General Social Surveys of 1973-80, found a remarkable development. Respondents were divided into three categories: those born in 1931 or before, those born during 1932-46, and those born since 1947. The percentage of Protestants who did not share their parents' religious affiliation was essentially unchanged across the three age groups. The defection rate was 35, 37, and 33 percent, largely because of intermarriage. The Catholic defection rate, however, rose from 13 to 17 to 22 percent, nearly doubling. The Jewish rate more than doubled, from 10 to 16 to 25 percent.

Even more remarkable is the increase during this time of the percentage of respondents who, having defected from their "inherited" religion, departed from a religious affiliation altogether. For Protestants, the increase was from 6 to 34 percent (a figure essentially found in all the major denominations); for Catholics, the increase was from 26 to 55 percent; and for Jews, from 50 to 64 percent.[9] Both kinds of defection are associated not just with religious intermarriage but also with mobility, both geographic and socio-economic. And the Pacific region has high rates of all three of these phenomena.

Native-American Religion

Eric Mazur writes about a Native American who, in 1992, was on trial having been caught with carcasses of several birds protected under the Endangered Species Act. He argued that his actions were justified on religious grounds. In a plea bargain that gave him probation instead of prison, he promised to stop killing protected birds. "I will obey your law," he told the judge.[10]

Notice the word "your." It was not "the" law he would obey but a law he did not believe applied to him. Complicating matters is the fact that Native American religion is territorial in nature, and most of the legal disputes involving Native Americans revolve around the use of land. In the only land-use case brought by Native Americans to reach the U.S. Supreme Court (*Lyng v. Northwest Indian Cemetery Protective Association*, 1988 [485 U.S. 439]) the Native-American religious claims were summarily dismissed. A road was to be constructed to assist in logging in a mountainous region in northwest California, a region that Native Americans regard as sacred and thus would be desecrated if the road were built.

That is the way most such claims have been treated; not only are the claims not upheld but they are often seen as unworthy of debate. This dilemma lies behind George Tanabe's discussion of the on-going disputes in Hawaii over the religious rights of the Hawaiian people. These disputes are intense in that state, but similar kinds of tension exist elsewhere in the Pacific region, especially in California over the building of casinos on reservations that may be close to urban areas.

Church-State Jurisprucence is Challenged

The rights of Native Americans to practice a religion markedly at odds with what most Americans imagine religion to be is not confined to the Pacific region. As Robert Michaelsen says, this religion is "more hampered and threatened than is the practice of any other traditional religion in the country."[11] It was a free exercise case coming out of Oregon, for example, where the U.S. Supreme Court denied unemployment benefits to two Native Americans who were fired after admitting that they participated in the peyote ritual in a Native American Church service. Because Oregon had peyote on its list of "controlled substances," the two men had broken the law. There was no need, said Justice Antonin Scalia, even to discuss Oregon's reasons for having such a law (*Employment Division v. Smith*, 1990 [494 U.S. 872]).

This decision, especially the reasoning behind the decision, was profoundly alarming to many people and groups across the political spectrum. By 1993 Congress passed, by an overwhelming vote, the Religious Freedom Restoration Act, which stated that government may not "substantially burden" a person's exercise of religion without identifying a "compelling" governmental interest. Four years later the U.S. Supreme Court declared the 1993 Act an unconstitutional usurpation by Congress of a power rightfully belonging to the Judicial branch.

Unlike the legal battle over Native-American casinos, the controversy involving Native Americans in Hawaii has a large religious component, which Tanabe covers well. Whether this religious component will factor into the eventual outcome for this issue is hard to predict; the fluidity of life in the Pacific region, its optimism and openness to change, suggest one answer, but the secularism associated with lowered traditionalism suggests another.

Endnotes

1. Kevin Starr, *Americans and the California Dream, 1850-1915* (New York: Oxford University Press,1973), vii, viii. The other volumes are: *Inventing the Dream: California Through the Progressive Era* (New York: Oxford University Press, 1985); *Material Dreams: Southern California Through the 1920s* (New York: Oxford University Press, 1990); *Endangered Dreams: The Great Depression in California* (New York: Oxford University Press, 1996); *The Dream Endures: California Enters the 1940s* (New York: Oxford University Press, 1997); *Embattled Dreams: California in War and Peace, 1940-1950* (New York: Oxford University Press, 2002); and *Coast of Dreams: California on the Edge, 1990-2003* (New York: Alfred A. Knopf, 2004). Much of the material in the present chapter was drawn from these volumes, especially the first and second.
2. Phillip E. Hammond, *Religion and Personal Autonomy* (Columbia, SC: University of South Carolina Press, 1992), 39-40.
3. Rodney Stark and William Bainbridge, *The Future of Religion* (Berkeley, CA: University of Californian Press, 1985), 75. These data are from 1974. No doubt newer data would be different, but there is no reason to expect much shift in the rankings.
4. Thirty percent of Californians say they believe in reincarnation, more so than in North Carolina, Ohio, or Massachusetts. See Hammond, *Religion and Personal Autonomy*, 131. In this same survey, 71 percent of boomer-age Californians said that it was better to "explore teachings from other religions"

than to "stick to a faith"—higher than for the other states. Summary data are presented in Wade Clark Roof, *A Generation of Seekers: The Journeys of the Baby Boom Generation* (San Francisco: Harper San Francisco, 1993), 71.

5. Stark and Bainbridge, *The Future of Religion*, 200.

6. Stark and Bainbridge, *The Future of Religion*, 192, 200.

7. Citing both a Harris poll and a Gallup poll, Nikolas Kristof stated in his August 15, 2003 *New York Times* column that while only 28 percent of Americans believe in evolution, 83 percent believe in the virgin birth of Jesus. The fact that 47 percent of non-Christians are part of that 83 percent suggests how far the politicization of religion has gone. President Bush himself, asked about evolutionary theory, said the jury is "still out."

8. Eric Michael Mazur, *The Americanization of Religious Minorities* (Baltimore, MD: The Johns Hopkins University Press, 1999).

9. See Phillip E. Hammond, "The Extravasation of the Sacred and the Crisis in Liberal Protestantism," in R. M. Michaelsen and W. C. Roof, eds., *Liberal Protestantism: Problems and Prospects* (New York: The Pilgrim Press, 1986), 61-62.

10. Eric Michael Mazur, *The Americanization of Religious Minorities*, 96.

11. Robert Michaelsen, "American Indian Religious Freedom Litigation: Promise and Perils," *Journal of Law and Religion* 3 (1985): 50.

RELIGIOUS AFFILIATION IN THE
PACIFIC REGION AND THE NATION

The charts on the following pages compare two measures of religious identification: self-identification by individuals responding to a survey and adherents claimed by religious institutions. The charts compare regional data for the Mountain West and national data for both measures. The sources of the data are described below.

On page 22
Adherents Claimed by Religious Groups

The Polis Center at Indiana University-Purdue University Indianapolis provided the Religion by Region Project with estimates of adherents claimed by religious groups in the Mountain West and the nation at large. These results are identified as the North American Religion Atlas (NARA). NARA combines 2000 Census data with the Glenmary Research Center's 2000 Religious Congregations and Membership Survey (RCMS). Polis Center demographers supplemented the RCMS reports with data from other sources to produce estimates for groups that did not report to Glenmary.

On page 23
Religious Self-Identification

Drawn from the American Religious Identification Survey (ARIS 2001), these charts contrast how Americans in the Mountain West and the nation at large describe their own religious identities. The ARIS study, conducted by Barry A. Kosmin, Egon Mayer, and Ariela Keysar at the Graduate Center of the City University of New York, includes the responses of 50,283 U.S. households gathered in a series of national, random-digit dialing, telephone surveys.

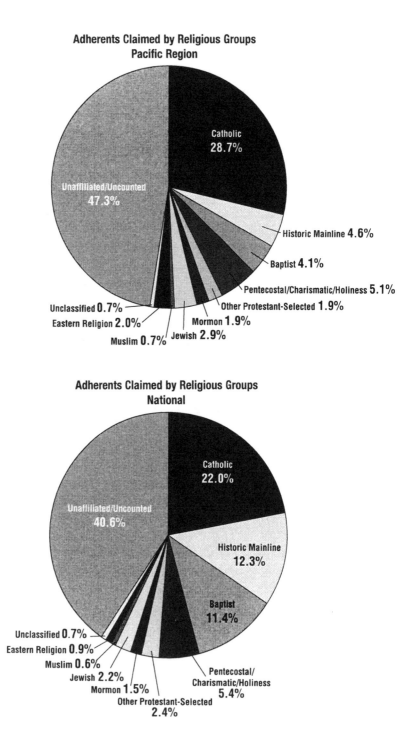

Adherents Claimed by Religious Groups
Pacific Region

Catholic
28.7%

Unaffiliated/Uncounted
47.3%

Historic Mainline 4.6%

Baptist 4.1%

Pentecostal/Charismatic/Holiness 5.1%

Unclassified 0.7%   Other Protestant-Selected 1.9%
Eastern Religion 2.0%   Mormon 1.9%
Muslim 0.7% Jewish 2.9%

Adherents Claimed by Religious Groups
National

Catholic
22.0%

Unaffiliated/Uncounted
40.6%

Historic Mainline
12.3%

Baptist
11.4%

Unclassified 0.7%
Eastern Religion 0.9%
Muslim 0.6%
Jewish 2.2%   Pentecostal/
Mormon 1.5%   Charismatic/Holiness
Other Protestant-Selected   5.4%
2.4%

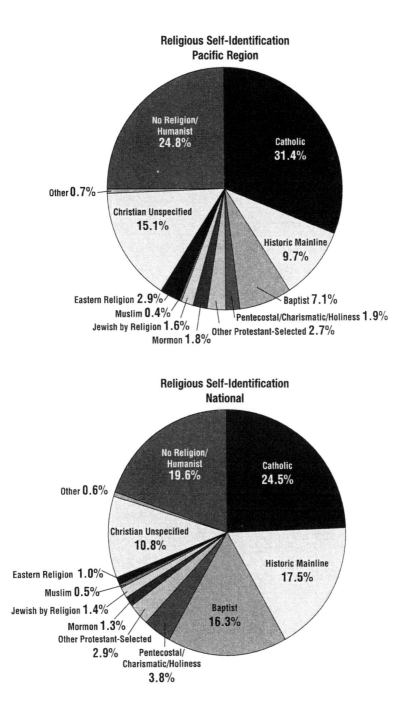

Religious Self-Identification
Pacific Region

No Religion/ Humanist 24.8%

Catholic 31.4%

Other 0.7%

Christian Unspecified 15.1%

Historic Mainline 9.7%

Eastern Religion 2.9%

Baptist 7.1%

Muslim 0.4%

Pentecostal/Charismatic/Holiness 1.9%

Jewish by Religion 1.6%

Other Protestant-Selected 2.7%

Mormon 1.8%

Religious Self-Identification
National

No Religion/ Humanist 19.6%

Catholic 24.5%

Other 0.6%

Christian Unspecified 10.8%

Historic Mainline 17.5%

Eastern Religion 1.0%

Muslim 0.5%

Jewish by Religion 1.4%

Baptist 16.3%

Mormon 1.3%

Other Protestant-Selected 2.9%

Pentecostal/ Charismatic/Holiness 3.8%

CHAPTER ONE
RELIGION IN THE PACIFIC REGION:
DEMOGRAPHIC PATTERNS

Wade Clark Roof

The Pacific region consists of three states—California, Nevada, and Hawaii. On first glance this might seem like an odd grouping, yet on reflection it makes some sense. A history of continuous migrations of diverse peoples and cultures, an open and fluid religious environment, and a borderland consciousness born out of the region's location on, or proximity to, the Pacific Rim and/or highly charged geographical borders make for a distinctive religious environment.

The Big Picture

California is, of course, the demographic giant of the three states, with 91.3 percent of the region's population in 2000. Forty-one percent of the entire Pacific region's population (and 45 percent of California's residents) live in the dense coastal megalopolis of southern California formed by the three contiguous counties of Los Angeles, Orange, and San Diego. In both California and Hawaii populations are concentrated on the coast, leaving vast areas of mountainous and desert lands sparsely populated; Nevada's cities are surrounded by a similar physical environment. Over 90 percent of the population in all three states lives in urban areas, making the region the most urbanized in the United States, as shown in **Figure 1.1**.

According to the 2000 census, the Pacific region's population is 37,081,442— 13 percent of the nation's total population. Over the past century, the region's population has increased at an astounding rate. Even in the period from 1950 to the present, a time generally of declining growth rates, the region's growth exceeded that of the nation in every decade. Only in the 1990s was there a noticeable convergence of regional and national trends.

The Pacific region has the youngest population of any region. There is a large cohort of adults age 25-44, many of whom have recently migrated into the region in search of employment. In some of the densely populated coastal counties of California, one-third or more of the population are in this age range. Fewer in the region are married than in the country as a whole, reflecting again the large number of young migrants. Though the level of divorce is the same as the national average, the region has a higher level of separation among those who are married. With respect to these basic demographics—age and marital status—the region stands in marked contrast to the rest of the country.

Various demographics point to a fluid, rapidly changing environment. Forty-six percent of the Pacific region's population report living in a different house in 2000 than they did five years earlier; only two other regions, the Pacific Northwest and the Mountain West, have more residential movement. Among those now living in a different house than in 1995, the region has the smallest proportion compared with anywhere else in the country having moved from another state (12.9 percent), which means that it has a huge in-flow of people moving into the region from other countries.

More than a fourth of the Pacific region's current population are foreign-born, far greater than any of the other regions. Of these, over half (54.6 percent) are from Latin America, 33.7 percent from Asia, 7.9 percent from Europe, 1.7 percent from North America, 1.3 percent from Africa, and 0.8 percent from Oceania. Sixty percent of the foreign-born population are not citizens, and their frequent moves back and forth across national boundaries add to the region's demographic flow.

Overall, the region's racial and ethnic makeup—particularly in California and Hawaii—is extraordinarily diverse and ever-evolving. The region is less white than the country as a whole—in fact, it has the lowest Caucasian population of any region. The 2000 census revealed that a majority of Californians (53.3 percent) now identify as non-white. The region also has a much lower proportion of African Americans (6.5 percent) than the country as a whole, though a somewhat larger proportion than several other regions. The Asian population is the highest of any region, 11.6 percent (Filipino, Chinese, Japanese); the Native-American population, 1.0 percent; and the Hawaiian/Pacific-Islander population, 0.6 percent.

The region has the highest level of any region belonging to "Other Races" (15.7 percent) and identifying as "Multi-Racial" (5.2 percent). Hawaii tops all states in this respect with 21.4 percent claiming a multiracial heritage; California follows at 4.7 percent; Nevada has 3.8 percent. The size of the population identifying as multiracial is rapidly growing; in California alone in 2000, 27.1 percent of children (including Latinos) under the age of 10 report descending from two or more races, as compared with only 7.4 percent of those who are 80 years of age and over.

The percentage identifying as Latino in the Pacific region is more than double

Figure 1.1   Population Characteristics of the Pacific Region Compared to the Nation (U.S. Census 2000)

	Pacific Region	Nation
Population Count	37,081,442	281,421,906
Land Base (square miles)	285,206	3,537,440
Population Density (per square mile)	130.0	79.6
Percent living in a different state in 1995	12.9	19.5
Percent living in a different house in 1995	45.9	43.0
Percent living in urban areas	94.2	79.0
Percent that are		
Less than age 18	27.1	25.7
18 - 44	41.5	39.8
45 - 64	20.7	22.0
65 and over	10.7	12.4
Percent Male	49.9	49.1
Percent that are		
Married	54.9	56.5
Never married	29.8	27.0
Divorced	9.7	9.7
Widowed	5.6	6.6
Separated	4.4	3.8
Percent that are		
Caucasian	59.2	75.1
Other Race	15.7	5.5
Asian	11.6	3.6
African American	6.5	12.3
Multi-racial	5.2	2.4
American Indian	1.0	0.9
Hawaiian/Pacific Islander	0.6	0.1
Non-Hispanic	69.1	87.5
Hispanic	30.9	12.5
Percent foreign born	25.3	11.0
Of foreign born, percent that are		
Not a citizen	60.4	59.5
Born in Latin America	54.6	51.7
Born in Asia	33.7	26.4
Born in Europe	7.9	15.8
Born in North America	1.7	2.7
Born in Africa	1.3	2.8
Born in Oceania	0.9	0.5
Percent over age 25		
Without a High School Degree	22.7	19.6
At least a Bachelor's degree	26.1	24.4
Percent employed in		
Management/Professional	35.3	33.6
Sales/Office	26.9	26.6
Service	15.5	14.8
Production/Transportation	12.5	14.6
Construction/Maintenance	8.6	9.4
Farming/Fishing/Forestry	1.3	0.7
Percent living in poverty	13.6	12.3
Median Household Income		$42,148
By State:		
California		$46,802
Nevada		$44,755
Hawaii		$48,026

that of the nation and the largest of any region. This partly explains the region's growth rate: the birthrate for Latino immigrants from Mexico and Central America averages more than three children per mother, which is considerably higher than for non-Latinos. Latinos in the region are overwhelmingly Mexican (77 percent), yet the diversity of ethnic cultures among Latinos catches any observer's eye: 5.2 percent are of Central American origin (mainly Salvadoran and Guatemalan), 1.6 percent of Puerto Rican origin, 1.5 percent of South American origin, 0.7 percent of Cuban origin, and 14.5 percent of other origins. In terms of languages spoken, the region has the greatest diversity of all regions, with 21.3 percent of its households speaking Spanish and 15.5 percent speaking a language other than English or Spanish. In effect, more than a third of the population does not speak English.

As measured by graduation from high school, the region has the highest level of illiteracy in the country. Large numbers of uneducated, primarily Latino migrants, explain this situation. Yet the sector with a bachelor's degree or higher is also larger than the national average. This "bi-polar" educational distribution, in turn, contributes to a distinctive socio-economic structure: An expansive high-tech, corporate, business, and entrepreneurial sector ("white-collar") thrives in an economy that rests upon a large supply of available blue-collar laborers, operatives, machinists, and seasonal farm workers. The region's class structure is reflected in the occupational breakdown. A large proportion of the work force is employed in managerial and professional positions (35.3 percent) and in sales and office work (26.9 percent)—more so than for the country at large. Disproportionately fewer are employed in the blue-collar sectors of production and transportation (12.5 percent) and construction and maintenance (8.6 percent). The farming/fishing/forestry sector is small, though larger than in most other regions. As might be expected by the class structure, the region leads all others in the top income categories, yet has the second highest poverty level of any region. California's poverty level is especially high, at 14.2 percent.

The three states are distinctive in many ways:

Nevada

This state's population is only 1,998,257, but it grew very rapidly—by 66.3 percent—during the 1990s, which made it the fastest-growing state during that decade. Historically, migrant streams into the state have shifted from Utah exiles to pleasure-seeking Californians and Latino immigrants. It is also the least dense of the three states, with only 18.2 people per square mile.

Of the three states, it has:

- the largest divorced population
- more people living in a different house in 2000 than in 1995, due in great

part to a large proportion of in-migrants from other states (61.5 percent of its population was born elsewhere in the United States)

* the highest percentage of Caucasians (75.2 percent), mostly of German, English, and Irish ancestry
* one of the largest concentrations of Latin Americans among its foreign born
* the greatest number of grandparents claiming responsibility for grandchildren

* a disproportionately large portion of its labor force working in arts, entertainment, and recreation industries, as well as in education, health, and social services.

Only 11.7 percent of all businesses are minority owned, lower than in the other two states.

Much of the state's population is concentrated in the Las Vegas metropolitan area[1]—1,375,765, or 68.8 percent of the total. Metro Las Vegas was the fastest-growing metropolitan area in the country in the 1990s (increased by 83.3 percent). This city of mega-resorts, gambling, and entertainment has 174 people per square mile. Slightly fewer here hold a bachelor's degree or higher than for the state as a whole. Married couples make up 48.7 percent of the population; female-headed families, 11.8 percent; other family types, 5.8 percent; and non-family households, 33.7 percent. Of all the metropolitan areas in the Pacific region, Metro Las Vegas is the most white—60.2 percent.[2] Twenty-two percent identify as Latino (of which the vast majority are Mexican); 10 percent are African American; 6.6 percent are Asian; 1.5 percent are American Indian or Alaska Native; and 0.5 percent are Native Hawaiian/Pacific Islander.

The median household income is $44,616, and the median value of an owner-occupied home is $139,500—much the same as for the state as a whole. Fourteen percent of businesses here are minority owned, slightly more than for the state as a whole.

Hawaii

Hawaii's population is 1,211,537, and for the 1980s and 1990s Hawaii was the slowest-growing of the three states. It has 188.6 people per square mile, far greater than Nevada though fewer than California. Compared with the other two states, it has:

* the largest singles population
* the highest average household size
* a slightly higher median income ($56,961 compared to California's $53,025 and Nevada's $50,849)
* less residential mobility, as evident in the smallest proportion living in a different house in 2000 than in 1995

- the largest segment of its population born outside the United States, primarily Asian (83.3 percent)
- the largest multiracial population (21.4 percent)
- the highest level of American citizenship; and the greatest proportion of its labor force employed in government jobs.

The largest metropolitan area is Honolulu, with a population of 876,156.[3] It grew very slowly in the 1990s, by only 4.8 percent. It has 1,461 people per square mile. It has a median age of 35.7, with 13.4 percent of the population 65 years of age or above. A bachelor's degree or higher is held by 27.9 percent of the population, only slightly higher than for the state as a whole. Almost 20 percent claim to be multiracial, and 21.5 percent are foreign-born. The vast majority of the population is Asian—61.6 percent (of these, the majority are Japanese, then Filipino, Chinese, Korean, and Vietnamese, in that order—true for the state as well). The Native-Hawaiian and Other Pacific-Islander population accounts for 21.6 percent of the total population. The African-American population is small, at 3.4 percent; the American-Indian and Alaska-Native population even smaller, at 1.8 percent. Not surprisingly, 65.1 percent of all businesses are minority-owned. The median household income is $51,914.

California

The Golden State's population in 2000 was 33,871,648, the largest of any state in the country. The population grew by 13.8 percent in the 1990s, even though this was actually the slowest rate of growth for any decade since the 1950s. California is very densely populated, with 217.2 people per square mile. Among the three states it has:

- the largest proportion without a high-school diploma
- a slightly larger proportional urban population
- greater racial and ethnic diversity, according to reported ancestries
- more female-headed families
- more non-English-speakers (39.5 percent)
- a higher poverty rate, combined with a greater portion of its work force in management, professional, and related occupations
- a considerably greater proportion of adults owning three or more vehicles.

Metro Los Angeles has the largest metropolitan population in the state, with 12,365,627 residents; it has 2,550 people per square mile, concentrated more in Orange County than in Los Angeles County.[4] The population grew by 9.7 percent from 1990 to 2000. Los Angeles is a world trade center with its "Gateway to the Pacific Rim" port. Slightly more than a fourth of the residents (26.3 percent) hold a bachelor's degree or higher, just below the average for the state. Households are 49.5 percent married, 13.7 percent female-headed, 5.7 percent other family arrangements, and 31.1 percent non-family households.

Of the population, 4.7 percent identifies as multiracial and its population is 34.7 percent foreign born. Latinos make up 41.4 percent (of these, almost three-fourths are Mexican, less than 1 percent Puerto Rican and the same for Cuban, and almost one-fourth Other Latino). Other large constituencies are Asian (13.5 percent), consisting of Chinese, Filipinos, Koreans, Vietnamese, Japanese, and Asian Indians, in that order; African American (8.6 percent); American Indian and Alaska Native (1.4 percent); Native Hawaiian and Other Pacific Islander (0.5 percent). Racial and ethnic diversity generally is greater in Los Angeles County than in Orange County, which, as expected, correlates with median family incomes—$42,189 in the former and $58,820 in the latter. More than a third (35.6 percent) of businesses are minority-owned; 16.2 percent of the population lives below the poverty level, higher than for the state generally.

San Francisco's metropolitan-area population is the second largest, at 4,123,740, with 1,667 people per square mile.[5] The area grew by 11.9 percent in the 1990s. Thirty-nine percent of residents have a bachelor's degree or higher level of education. Households are 46.5 percent married, 11 percent female-headed; 4.3 percent other family arrangements; and 38.2 percent non-family households (56 percent in San Francisco County itself).

Of the total population, 4.7 percent claim multiracial back-grounds and 27.4 percent are foreign born. The Asian population is 19.2 percent, but it varies greatly by county (as high as 30.8 percent in San Francisco and only 4.5 percent in Marin), the largest groups being Chinese, Filipinos, Japanese, Vietnamese, and Koreans, in that order. Latinos account for 17.8 percent of the population—overwhelmingly Mexican, but there are also many Puerto Ricans, Cubans, and a sizable mix from other nationality backgrounds. Other populations include African American (9.6 percent); Native Hawaiian and Other Pacific Islander (0.6 percent); and American Indians and Alaska Natives (0.5 percent).

Median household incomes vary: $55,221 in San Francisco, $55,946 in Alameda, $63,675 in Contra Costa, $70,819 in San Mateo, and $71,306 in Marin. Over a quarter of businesses (28.3 percent) are minority owned, and the population living below the poverty line is 9.1 percent, less than for the state generally.

San Diego's metropolitan population in 2000 was 2,813,833, and is much less dense than its neighbors to the north, with only 670 people per square mile.[6] The area grew by 12.6 percent in the 1990s. It has a median age of 33.2, with 11.2 percent 65 years of age or older. Twenty-nine and a half percent hold a bachelor's degree or higher.

Households are 50.7 percent married couples, 11.6 percent female-headed, 4.4 percent other family types, and 33.3 percent non-family households. Slightly less than 5 percent report a multiracial identity. The population is 21.5 percent foreign born. Latinos are the largest ethnic population, accounting for 26.7 percent of the population (of these 83.7 percent are Mexican, 13.8 percent Other Latino, 2 percent Puerto Rican, and 0.5 percent Cuban). Other sizable constituencies include Asian (10.5 percent), mainly Filipinos, but also Vietnamese, Chinese, Japanese, and Koreans, in that order; African American, with 6.6 percent; American Indian and Alaska Native, with 1.6 percent; and Native Hawaiian and Pacific Islander, with 0.9 percent.

The median household income is $47,067. Slightly less than one-quarter (23.2 percent) of businesses are minority owned, and 12.4 percent of the population are below the poverty level.

Religious Adherence

As commentators point out, there is considerable freedom for people to believe and practice faith, or no faith, in the Pacific region. This freedom fits well with the region's optimism and openness, its individualism and mobility, and its fluid cultural life. Religion mirrors the culture with a continuing rise of new spiritual movements, exploration of alternative religions, the easy flow of people into and out of religious congregations, and a good deal of indifference to organized religion. This open religious environment is evident in the region's lower-than-average level of adherence to organized religion: 52.7 percent as compared to the nation's 59.5 percent in 2000, as shown in **Figures 1.2** and **1.3** (pgs. 34 and 35). It is the third most "unchurched" area within the United States, after the Pacific Northwest and the Mountain West regions.

Religious freedom is expressed in subtle ways. Many of the people within the region who are not adherents—that is, members of or participants in a faith community—choose nevertheless to *identify* with those communities and traditions. When asked "What is your religion, if any?" by the American Religious Identification Survey (ARIS), 75 percent in the Pacific region identified with a religious group. While we would not expect self-reported identities from surveys to yield comparable results with institutional records and estimates, still a gap of this magnitude (22.3 percent—75 percent minus 52.7) is sizable.

It means that many people in the Pacific region affirm a "weak" religious identity as measured by institutional loyalty. This is especially the case for the large Catholic and white mainline Protestant constituencies, where 57.4 and 73.9 percent respectively are classified in the Akron/Pew surveys as low-commitment (defined as attending worship less frequently than once a week). These figures are substantially higher than the national figures, 51.7 and 64.2 percent. Less a sign of outright rejection of faith, the figures suggest the region is characterized by a secular, accommodating religious style.

A secular ethos amounts to an "irreligious establishment" of sorts. This ethos encompasses the faith communities themselves, creating, as one commentator says, "a religious circus in the tents of secularity."[7] In other words, even religious people enjoy their independence in making choices about belief and practice, and the ease with which they define their religious identities is in keeping with personal choices. Given the region's frontier history, its high level of religious pluralism, and its continuing dynamic economy and rapid social change, its "tents of secularity" continue to leave a noticeable imprint on religious and spiritual styles.

Some attention to religious adherence and style for each of the three states is important.[8]

Nevada was admitted as a state within the Union in 1864, just 13 years after its first Mormon settlement. Prior to then it was, of course, claimed by Native Americans, Spain (until 1821), Mexico (until 1848), and then as a U.S. territory. Its great land mass—the Great Basin—is the setting of an East-West confrontation religiously, with Mormons dominating the eastern portion of the state and Christians (mainly Catholics) the western portion.

Mormons in the early years migrated into the territory from Utah; others came from elsewhere, including many who had been miners in California. Migrants from California into the state have steadily increased over the past half-century, prompting many old-timers to speak of their state as becoming "Californicated." A popular distinction is still drawn between "Saints" and "sinners," the latter of course associated with gambling, drinking, and other vices in places like Reno and Las Vegas. But it is a blurred distinction considering that some of today's Las Vegas Mormons are linked with—and often profit from—the city's gambling industry (legalized in 1931), its quickie marriages and divorces, and non-stop day and night activities as the "pleasure capital" of the world.[9]

In 1890, 26 years after becoming a state, there were only 5,877 "communicants" in small settlements across the state—just 12.8 percent of the population. There were 64 religious "organizations" (congregations, societies, and missions) and communicants distributed as follows: Catholic, 67.3 percent; Protestant Episcopal, 9.1 percent; Latter-day Saints, 8.9 percent; Methodist, 7.1 percent; Presbyterian, 4.7 percent; Baptist (Northern), 1.1 percent; Congregational, 0.9 percent; and Adventist, 0.9 percent.

By 1926, Latter-day Saints had pulled ahead of Protestant Episcopalians as the second-largest constituency. By 1936, there were 153 churches with 27,881 members. Catholics had declined proportionately but remained in the majority (43.2 percent). Latter-day Saints were second (27.8 percent), followed by Protestant Episcopal (12.8 percent). Other groups were relatively small: Baptists with 4.3 percent; Methodists with 3.3 percent; Presbyterians with 1.3 percent; Lutherans

Figure 1.2   Number of Adherents in the Pacific Region by
Religious Family (NARA)

Religious Family, Rank Ordered	# of Adherents	% of Total Population	% of all Pacific Region Adherents
Catholic	10,651,967	28.7	54.5
Historically African-Amer. Protestant	1,538,504	4.2	7.9
Jewish	1,078,100	2.9	5.5
Other Conservative Christian	1,060,709	2.9	5.4
Holiness.Wesleyan/Pentacostal	1,024,741	2.9	5.3
Baptist	911,558	2.5	5.3
Eastern Religion	744,804	2.0	4.8
LDS (Mormon)	689,258	1.9	3.8
Orthodox	289,103	0.8	1.5
Muslim	262,662	0.7	1.3
Confessional/Reformed Non-UCC	254,543	0.7	1.3
United Methodist	247,563	0.7	1.3
Presbyterian USA	238,875	0.6	1.2
Episcopalian	185,448	0.5	0.9
Lutheran (ELCA)	184,450	0.5	0.9
UCC	74,037	0.2	0.4
Christians (Disciples)	35,714	0.1	0.2
Other Mainline Protestant/Liberal Christian	35,535	0.1	0.2
Pietist/Anabaptist	22,537	0.1	0.1
Total Adherents	19,530,108	53.7	100.0
Unaffiliated	17,551,334	47.3	
Total Population	37,081,442	100.0	

with 2.4 percent; and a mix of still smaller denominations. From early on, Christian faiths rather easily assimilated Native-American folk teachings and spirituality.

By 1971, Nevada's adherence to organized religion was at 37.8 percent of the state's population. Catholics represented 49.9 percent of those religiously affiliated, somewhat more than in 1936, due in part to the influx of Mexicans. Latter-day Saints remained second, with 25.6 percent, down only slightly. Southern Baptists

Figure 1.3 Number of Adherents in the United States by Religious Family (NARA)

Religious Family, Rank Ordered	# of Adherents	% of Total Population	% of all Adherents
Catholic	62,035,042	22.0	37.0
Baptist	23,880,856	8.5	14.3
Historically African-Amer. Protestant	20,774,338	7.4	12.4
United Methodist	10,350,629	3.7	6.2
Other Conservative Christian	7,943,198	2.8	4.7
Holiness/Wesleyan/Pentecostal	7,764,756	2.8	4.6
Jewish	6,141,325	2.2	3.7
Lutheran (ECLA)	5,113,428	1.8	3.1
Confessional/Reformed Non-UCC	4,374,743	1.6	2.6
LDS (Mormon)	4,224,026	1.5	2.5
Presbyterian USA	3,141,566	1.1	1.9
Eastern Religion	2,560,243	0.9	1.5
Episcopalian	2,314,756	0.8	1.4
UCC	1,698,918	0.6	1
Muslim	1,559,294	0.6	0.9
Orthodox	1,449,274	0.5	0.9
Christians (Disciples)	1,017,784	0.4	0.6
Pietist/Anabaptist	698,897	0.2	0.4
Other Mainline Protestant/Liberal Christian	418,098	0.1	0.2
Total Adherents	167,425,161	59.4	100.0
Unaffiliated	114,165,080	40.5	
Total Population	281,590,322	100.0	

made major inroads with the white population (5 percent), and were now the third largest denomination. Lutherans had increased to 4.6 percent, Methodists to 4.1 percent. Episcopalians had declined proportionately to 3.5 percent. Presbyterians claimed 2.3 percent; American Baptists, 1.6 percent; Church of the Nazarene, 1.1 percent; and the remaining were mainly small evangelical Protestant denominations plus even fewer Unitarians and Quakers.

Today, Nevada's religious adherence is 38.6 percent, having increased only so slightly over the last 30 years of the twentieth century. Even after 110 years, the state's religious adherence is only 5.7 percentage points more than that characterizing the nation back in 1890 (32.9 percent). Catholics continue to dominate the state—making up 43 percent of the religiously affiliated—although their proportion has declined over time. Latter-day Saints are now at 15.2 percent and Jews at 10 percent. Historically African-American Protestants account for 8.5 percent. Conservative Protestants have grown: Baptists (mostly Southern Baptists), 6.5 percent; Holiness/ Wesleyan/ Pentecostal, 4.3 percent; and Other Conservative Protestants, 3.8 percent. Eastern Religions now account for 1.7 percent, which is greater than for many mainline Protestant denominations: Lutherans (ELCA) and United Methodists, each with 1.4 percent; Reformed/non-UCC Congregational, 1.3 percent; Presbyterians, 0.9 percent; Episcopalians, 0.7 percent; Orthodox, 0.6 percent; United Church of Christ, Christian (Disciples), and Other Mainline Protestants, each with 0.1 percent. Muslims now constitute 0.3 percent.

Hawaii bears the strong imprint of its Polynesian cultural and religious background with its emphasis upon nature worship and the four great gods—Kane, Ku, Lono, and Kanaloa—and numerous lesser deities. Traditional Hawaiian spirituality is closely linked to the land and the life force that resides in the land. Objects, animals, gods, and humans all have power, or *mana*, which can move from one being to another, and often does by means of ritual practices. Hence the Christian teachings of missionaries about the power of God meshed well with earlier views of a force that united and healed what is separated in the world. Congregational missionaries from New England arrived in the 1820s. Catholics arrived later and were followed by Mormons in the 1850s, and still later by Buddhists, Shintoists, and representatives of other faiths. Overlapping the religious diversity are the many differing ethnic and national backgrounds, with many immigrants coming to the islands from Europe (especially Portugal), the United States, China, Japan, the Philippines, and Samoa. But no matter their origins, people there are, as one commentator says, "practitioners of varied religions, but all are also practitioners of native Hawaiian spirituality."[10]

Reliable statistics on religion in Hawaii in the early years are incomplete, largely because they were compiled by Christian missionaries who did not count non-Western religions.[11] Protestant missionaries estimated that 80 percent of the population was Protestant in 1853, but by 1896 a more systematic study revealed that figure had "declined" to 41 percent. Aside from better record keeping, the proselytizing efforts of Catholics and Mormons help account for the Protestant decline. Focusing on church membership, the 1896 study reported a religious adherence rate of 50 percent—almost half of whom were reported as Catholic, almost as many as Protestant (but limited mainly to Congregationalists and a few other mainline churches), and a small proportion as Mormon. Later, during World War II, there was an expansion in the number of evangelical Protestant denominations and Mormon growth. Other-worldly and faith-healing sects grew especially during this period, as did Buddhist and Shinto splinter groups, particularly among the Japanese, who had experienced severe attacks upon their pride.

Using data supplied by the denominations, a 1954-55 study found an adherence rate of 63.9 percent, again with a huge majority of Catholics, followed by Buddhists, Protestants (with some 40 or more denominations), Shinto followers, and Latter-day Saints, in descending size. As elsewhere in the United States, Hawaii experienced a post-war religious revival, though it did not become a state until 1959. A 1972 membership study reported an adherence rate of 68.7 percent, even higher than that at mid-century; the religious distribution of major constituencies was roughly the same but with an expansion of traditional Holiness faiths, other small Christian groups, and new religious movements.

In 2000, religious adherence was 44.6 percent, down considerably from the earlier estimates. It is impossible to know how much of this decline is due to better record keeping, or to a shift of the religious mood in Hawaii. If the latter is the case, then Hawaii is clearly an exception to the general American trend toward increasing church membership. Catholics make up 44.6 percent of the religiously affiliated. Eastern religions (primarily Buddhists) account for 12.9 percent. Latter-day Saints constitute 7.9 percent. The single largest Protestant denomination is still the United Church of Christ (Congregationalist), with 4.2 percent. However, the striking trend here is the remarkable growth of Conservative Protestants: Baptists, Holiness/ Wesleyan/ Pentecostal faiths, and Other Conservative Christians combined now amount to almost 20 percent of all adherents. As elsewhere in the country, there was a significant shift in the composition of the Protestant faiths. Not unlike in California and Nevada, the dominant faiths mix easily with folk traditions and spiritual trends.

Turning to California, it differs from both Nevada and Hawaii in the scale and intensity of religious contacts. Early on, Spanish Catholics from the south came into contact with Russian Orthodox migrating from the north, both in contact of course with Native Americans. In the period between 1846, when the United States occupied the state, until the completion of the transcontinental railroad in 1869, there was remarkable growth both in the number and differing types of religions, as well as ethnic populations served by those traditions.

By 1890, California had 280,619 "communicants," representing 23.2 percent of the population. There were 1,996 religious "organizations," already quite diverse. Catholics were a majority, with 55.9 percent. They were also quite diverse—from Ireland, France, and Italy, as well as those of Spanish ancestry who had settled earlier in the southern portion of the state. Next were the Methodists, at 12.9 percent; then Presbyterians, at 6.7 percent; the Congregationalists, with 4.2 percent; the Baptists, with 4.1 percent; the Protestant Episcopalians, with 3.4 percent; and the Disciples of Christ, with 2.7 percent. Jews at that time constituted 2.2 percent.

Smaller groups included the Lutherans, at 1.5 percent; the Unitarians, at 1.4 percent; and the Adventists, at 1.1 percent. Even smaller, yet present, were Spiritualists, at 0.7 percent; Latter-day Saints, at 0.6 percent; Universalists, with 0.5 percent; Friends (Quakers), with 0.3 percent; Christian Scientists, with 0.3 percent; African Methodists, with 0.3 percent; Brethren, with 0.2 percent; the Evangelical Association, with 0.2 percent; Russian Orthodox, with 0.2 percent; Dunkards, with 0.1 percent; the Salvation Army, with 0.1 percent; the Theosophical Society, with 0.1 percent; and the Church of New Jerusalem, with 0.1 percent. At the time 41 Chinese temples and 178 shrines were also listed in the religious census.

By 1926, Jews had become the second-largest religious group following Catholics. The 1936 census showed the state to have 4,904 churches and 1,928,439 members. Of these, 50.8 percent claimed to be Catholics, 8 percent were Jewish, and 7 percent were Methodist. Other mainline Protestant denominations with sizable numbers were Presbyterians, at 4.8 percent; Episcopalians, at 3.7 percent; Lutherans, at 2.7 percent; Disciples, at 2.6 percent; Congregationalists, at 2.6 percent; and Northern Baptists, at 1.2 percent. Mormons had grown to 2 percent, Christian Scientists to 1.5 percent. The Historically African-American Protestant denominations (Baptists and Methodists) made up 1.6 percent.

Many conservative Protestant denominations now claimed sizable followings—the largest being the Adventists, followed by the Church of the Nazarene, the Four-Square Gospel Church, Churches of God, Churches of Christ, Holiness Churches, Christian and Missionary Alliance, Salvation Army, and others, whose combined memberships accounted for roughly 5.6 percent. Orthodox Christians made up less than 1 percent. The numbers of Buddhists, Baha'is, Mennonites, Brethren, Friends, Spiritualists, Universalists, Unitarians, Theosophists, and members of Vedanta Society had all increased or become present on the California scene; but proportionately of course, these bodies were all quite small.

In 1971, California's religious adherence was 33.5 percent, up somewhat from 1890. With growing numbers of Mexican immigrants moving into the state, the Catholic percentage of the religiously affiliated had increased to 58.9 percent. Jews remained in second position, followed by Mormons, United Methodists,

United Presbyterians, and Southern Baptists. Conservative Protestants generally continued to grow. By 2000, the state's religious adherence was 53.8 percent, considerably higher than it had been 29 years earlier. Catholics made up 55.3 percent. Jews and Other Conservative Christian groups each claimed 5.5 percent of the religious population. Combined Holiness/Wesleyan/Pentecostals and Conservative Protestant presence now totals 11 percent. All the mainline Protestant denominations have declined, each with less than 2 percent. Mormons account for 2.9 percent; Muslims, 1.4 percent; and Eastern religions, 3.6 percent.

The Two Californias

Aggregate statistics, however, fail to reveal the many interesting differences between California's southern and northern portions. Early on, Russian Orthodox migrants from Alaska settled in the northern area. Then, beginning with the Gold Rush in 1848, migrants swarmed into the area, especially into San Francisco and the surrounding towns and hamlets. Migrants came often as unattached individuals in search of fortunes and happiness. Soon behind them came missionaries organizing Protestant churches, particularly Methodists, Presbyterians, Congregationalists, and Baptists; and later Lutherans, Quakers, and Disciples of Christ.

Though Catholics were a majority, there were 22 Protestant congregations in San Francisco in 1850. By 1890 the city's total population was 298,997, of which 92,872 (31.1 percent) claimed a religious membership.[12] The 1890 census showed the city's religious membership to break down as follows: Catholics, 75.4 percent; Jews, 4.4 percent; Presbyterians, 3.7; Methodist Episcopal Church, 3.4 percent; Episcopalians, 2.6; Congregationalists, 2.3 percent; Lutherans, 2.3 percent; Baptists, 1.3 percent; Orthodox Christians, 0.5; and Miscellaneous, 4.1 percent. Eleven of the Protestant denominations had Chinese churches. By this time San Francisco was a point of entry to a growing number of Pacific Islanders and other Asians who, along with some Chinese, brought their own folk religions with them.

Disproportionate to their numbers, Protestants in northern California were visible in temperance crusades and in trying to keep the Sabbath free of vice-ridden activities. They had a strong sense of civic responsibility, owing no doubt to a Protestant heritage of custodianship over the culture. Because of widespread public indifference and lack of support from other religious and secular groups, however, their successes were limited. In 1883, California permanently repealed the Sabbath laws, becoming the first state in the country to do so. This added to perceptions back East that the place was one of free-thinkers and infidels, if not morally depraved. To an extent, that reputation remains associated with San Francisco.

By 2000, the San Francisco metropolitan area looked quite different. Relative to the others, the Catholic population had declined considerably, although it was still a strong plurality of the total religious population, at 41.9 percent. Jews were 6.6 percent, more than at the earlier time. All the denominations we now call "Mainline Protestants" had declined significantly as a proportion of the whole, often by as much as one-half: Presbyterians were now only 1.8 percent; Methodists 1.6 percent; Episcopalians, 1.2 percent; Congregationalists, or the United Church of Christ, 0.5 percent; Lutherans, 0.9 percent. The Historically African-American denominations did not show up in the 1890 census but now claim 12.1 percent of the total religious population.

Not surprisingly, Protestant conservatives grew in astounding numbers throughout the mid-to-late 1900s, and now account for almost 20 percent of the total: Baptists, 4.4 percent; Evangelical Protestants, 9.1 percent; Holiness/ Wesleyan/ Pentecostals, 2.5 percent; and Other Conservative Christians, 3.2 percent. Orthodox Christians had almost tripled in proportionate size, to 1.3 percent. Mormons now constitute 2.2 percent; Eastern religions, 7.1 percent; and Muslims, 2.5 percent. Small groups, such as the Reformed, Other Mainline, Disciples, and Pietist/Anabaptist, account for the remainder of the religious population.

In southern California, Catholicism was more laid-back, its missions having been "secularized," or transformed into parishes as early as 1854. Protestant denominations were also slower to organize. "For sixteen years after the beginnings in and around San Francisco," writes William H. Ferrier, "there was no established Protestant work south of Monterey along the coast, nor south of Visalia in the San Joaquin Valley."[13] But by the 1870s and 1880s the inflow of newcomers into southern California had picked up considerable momentum. Large numbers of Anglo-Protestants moved into the area—some from the South who had been dispossessed by the Civil War, but mostly from the Midwest. Compared to migrants into northern California, they were more family oriented and came as permanent settlers. All came in search of opportunities, health, a warm and comfortable place to retire, and with hopes of re-creating paradise. Southern California took on mythic significance as a place of new beginnings and fulfillment in life. In 1906, Los Angeles had a considerably higher level of reported church membership (74 percent) than did San Francisco (41.7 percent) or the state generally (41.2 percent).

By the 1920s, Los Angeles was the most automobile-oriented city in the world; indeed, this vehicle symbolized the city's vitality and fluidity. Anglo-Protestants wielded a good deal of political control over Los Angeles. But perhaps more significantly, they created a cultural climate unlike that of the state's northern tier.

"As the Gold Rush had given the San Francisco region an enduring cosmopolitan tone, a place for tourists and settlers alike," write Elden Ernst and Douglas Firth Anderson, the "migration to Los Angeles gave that city and its metropolitan region a persistent flavor of comfortable conservatism that was open to innovation in the pursuit of the good life."[14]

Other populations joined the Anglo-Protestants. Jews settled in Los Angeles and elsewhere in the state at an unprecedented rate during this period. By 2000, 61 percent of the state's Jews were living in Los Angeles County. Mexicans moved into the state in increasing numbers after 1920, disproportionately into the southern part. Today, Latinos make up more than 40 percent of the population in some southern counties (Imperial County, 72.2 percent; Los Angeles County, 44.6 percent). Over the years their presence has refashioned Catholicism with ethnic festivals, personal piety as expressed in prayer and Bible study, and family-based religious activities. Latin piety has not, however, led to greater church involvement; rather, its presence has meshed well with the easy-going religious environment that characterizes the state. The post-1965 "new immigrant" streams, of course, greatly expanded the faith traditions present in the area.

For all these reasons, southern California has undergone a demographic and cultural transformation on a scale that the earlier Anglo-Protestants (not to mention the Native Americans and Mexicans) would neither have envisioned nor probably desired. Within the sprawling urban space of Los Angeles, as the geographer Edward J. Soja says, "it all comes together" —people, ideas, information, commerce, and cultures representing "the world in connected urban microcosms."[15] What began in the twentieth century as the whitest, most Protestant big city in the nation with its own particular vision of utopia was by the beginning of the twenty-first century the most ethnically and religiously diverse city in the United States.

Religious Presence in the Region

Given its history and demographics, the religious economy of the region is quite peculiar. It has long had a distinctive ethos that influences faith communities as well as those who are religiously inactive or even oppose religion. Once again, data from the North American Religion Atlas (NARA) yield important insights. The two pie charts at the front of this book comparing religious adherents in the region with adherents claimed nationally offer a better grasp of the region's distinctive religious environment.

By far, the largest religious constituency within the region is Catholic (28.7 percent of the population), considerably greater than in the country at large (22 percent). The region has the third largest Catholic concentration of all the regions—17.1 percent of all Catholics in the country—after New England and the Middle Atlantic region. The Catholic majority has considerable liturgical dominance, and its numbers have gradually increased over the decades. Yet this demographic majority does not constitute a strong public religious presence for two reasons: one, because of its internal ethnic diversity, and two, because of the large number of nominal Catholics—those who are either marginal to the faith community or non-practicing (over half are described as "low-commitment" according to surveys by the political scientist John Green and his colleagues at the Bliss Center at the University of Akron).

The mainline Protestant presence in the region has been declining, and considerably so, over the past half-century. Mainline Protestant adherents account for 4.6 percent of the region's population—the lowest in the nation. By contrast, a much larger proportion of the population (9 percent) are Conservative Protestant. Over 70 percent of white Protestants (that is, excluding African-American denominations) belong to conservative religious bodies—the highest of any region outside the Southern Crossroads and the South. There are more Conservative Protestants than adherents of both the liberal/mainline Protestant and Historically African-American Protestant denominations combined, which is quite the reverse of what holds for the country as a whole.

And unlike in the South (and the Southern Crossroads) where Southern Baptists constitute an overwhelming Protestant majority, here there are far more conservative Pentecostals and independent, non-denominational Christians than Baptists. The largest category of Protestants for the Pacific region in the ARIS classification—15.1 percent—identify as "Protestant" or "Christian" but do not specify a particular denominational tradition. Some of them may not know their tradition well enough to name it, but most are likely to belong to non-denominational churches that choose to identify themselves simply as Christian or have a highly privatized faith cut loose from a religious community.

Other features of the Protestant presence should be noted. There are a large number of Latino Protestants (19.5 percent of all Protestants), the largest proportionally for any region of the country. Striking, too, is the racial division within Protestantism. Those belonging to the Historically African-American Protestant bodies constitute the second largest religious grouping within the Pacific region (4.1 percent of the population).

Eastern religions have a larger following in the region than elsewhere in the country (2 percent of the population). In fact, 29 percent of all Eastern religions followers in the United States reside within the region. Further breakdown on Eastern religions by the ARIS survey shows that the number that identify with Buddhism within the region are almost double that of Hinduism. But more striking is the fact that Eastern religions have more identifiers than any of the Liberal/Mainline Protestant denominations. Nowhere else in the country does this pattern hold (the Pacific Northwest comes closest, except that there Lutherans do still outnumber those who identify with Eastern religions). Eastern religions attract more followers within this region than does the Church of Jesus Christ of Latter-day Saints, which is striking considering the prominent role the latter has played historically in the region.

Jews, Mormons, and Muslims are over-represented in the region. The public presence of these smaller religious populations is reinforced by their disproportional representation—17.6 percent of the nation's Jews are in the region, 16.3 percent of Mormons, and 16.8 percent of Muslims.

There are also scores of small, non-conventional religious and spiritual groups, many having originated in this region, that either do not keep membership records or have followings too small to register in the broadly defined categories of the NARA classification.

Public perceptions of religion's presence are shaped also by the density of religious populations and the visibility of their edifices. A case in point is Nevada, where Catholics predominate in the four northwestern counties and Mormons outnumber all others in the six northeastern counties. Catholic visibility is somewhat diminished by the fact that they have only one-fourth as many churches. In Hawaii, Catholics have an overwhelming numerical presence but have far fewer churches than Conservative Protestants. The latter have 42 percent of all the congregations, giving them the greatest Christian visibility, especially on the islands of Maui and Hawaii. Eastern religions are second in adherence on the islands of Kauai and Honolulu, but their presence is not so visible given that they have far fewer congregations than even Catholics.

In California, Catholics are more concentrated (greater than 50 percent) along the coast and in a narrow sector of counties extending from San Francisco to the Nevada border. Holiness/Pentecostal members are concentrated in second position in many of the central and northern California counties, and especially in Trinity County. Baptists have a strong presence in the southern and central counties, and especially in Solano County. Conservative Protestants exceed 80 percent in the inland central and southern counties of Imperial, Kern, Mono, and San Bernadino. Mainline Protestants are strongest in the counties surrounding San Francisco. Jews are concentrated around San Francisco and Los Angeles. Muslims are clustered around San Francisco (and in Alameda, Santa Clara, and Sutter counties) and around Los Angeles (and in Orange, San Bernardino, and Riverside counties).

Looking at the state as a whole, over half of all congregations are Conservative Protestant—mostly Holiness and Pentecostal. In contrast, Catholics, who constitute a majority of the population, have only 7.8 percent of the congregations. By reading the list of Sunday worship services in the religion page of local newspapers, one would get the mistaken impression that California is largely Protestant.

Specific Religious Groups in the Region

Catholics

As is obvious by now, there are more Roman Catholics in the region (and in all three states) than any other single religious constituency. From 1971 to 2000, the Catholic population grew much faster in Nevada (260 percent) and California (155.8 percent) than in the country as a whole (38.3 percent), largely as a result of Latino in-migration. The Catholic population of Hawaii grew by 23.5 percent. According to the ARIS study, 58.1 percent of Catholics in the Pacific region are Latino, 32.2 percent are white, non-Latino; 9.7 percent belong to other minorities; and less than 1 percent are African American. Among the huge number of Latino Catholics, there is a wide range of nations represented—Mexico mainly, but also El Salvador, Guatemala, Nicaragua, and elsewhere in Central and South America. The nearly 10 percent who belong to other minorities are mainly Asian; the largest groups being Filipinos, Chinese, and Vietnamese.

Historically African-American Protestants

This religious sector includes a large number of denominational bodies: African Methodist Episcopal Zion Church, Christian Methodist Episcopal Church, Church of God in Christ, Fire Baptized Holiness Church, Black Baptists, and the African Methodist Episcopal Church. The largest single constituency in each of the three states is the Church of God in Christ, a Pentecostal church that accounts for 49.5 percent of the African-American memberships throughout the region. This church was organized in the early twentieth century, later than most of the historic Baptist and Methodist bodies, but grew rapidly during the latter half of the century. Black Baptists are second largest in this category, with 40 percent, but are represented only in California and Nevada.

Jews

As early as 1890 both Reform and Orthodox Jews were present in California's two major cities, San Francisco and Los Angeles; the Reform membership was somewhat larger. Not until the 1950s did Jews show up in significant numbers in Nevada, but their numbers grew rapidly in the second half of the twentieth century. In 1951, only one Jewish congregation was reported in Hawaii. Relative to other religious populations, Jews today have a stronger representation in Nevada (10 percent of all adherents) than in California (5.5 percent) or Hawaii (1.3 percent). Of the region's total Jewish population, 92.2 percent are in California, 7.2 percent in Nevada, and 0.6 percent in Hawaii. All major types of Jewish congregations are now found throughout the region. Jews have fashioned a style of Judaism somewhat distinct from that elsewhere and thrive in the region's multicultural mix.

Other Conservative Christians

The 20 different conservative bodies that make up this category vary considerably in size. Regionally, the largest memberships are those of the Seventh-day Adventist Church (18.5 percent of all adherents in this category), followed by Jehovah's Witnesses (16.3 percent), Calvary Chapel Fellowship Churches (13.5 percent), and Independent Non-Charismatic churches (13.2 percent).

Holiness/Wesleyan/Pentecostals

The Wesleyan tradition gave birth to many Holiness and Pentecostal bodies that took root in the Pacific region. Offshoots mainly from Methodism in this country, many of these bodies have grown rapidly as a result of aggressive evangelism and missionary zeal. Others are small splinter groups.

The largest Pentecostal group in the region (and the largest such movement worldwide) is the Assemblies of God, with 34.6 percent of the adherents in this category. Second is the Independent Charismatic group, making up 19.5 percent of this category, though charismatics are under-represented in Nevada. Third is the International Church of the Four Square Gospel, with 13.1 percent. Fourth is the Church of the Nazarene, with 9.2 percent. Together, these four bodies account for over 75 percent of all the members within this category. Except for the Church of the Nazarene, which originated after the Civil War with the rise of the Holiness movement, the other major bodies are Pentecostal and arose during the early decades of the twentieth century. The Four Square Church was founded by Aimee Semple McPherson in 1927 in Los Angeles.

Baptists

Twenty-eight different Baptist denominations have members in the Pacific region, as reported in the NARA. By far, the largest of these are the Southern Baptists, with 58.4 percent of all Baptists in the region. Next are the American Baptists, with 18.8 percent. The third largest is the Baptist General Conference, with 7.6 percent, followed by Conservative Baptists, with 6.1 percent. All the remaining Baptist bodies, mostly splinter groups, are quite small and doctrinally conservative. Historically, American Baptists (known earlier as National Baptists) reached the region first and for a long time outnumbered all other Baptists. But since the 1970s, Southern Baptists have grown very rapidly and now outnumber all other Baptists combined in the three states. Having overtaken the more moderate-minded American Baptists in membership, the Baptist presence in the region is now decidedly more conservative.

Eastern Religions

This category, of course, is made up of diverse traditions largely from China, Japan, India, and Iran. Among them, Buddhists are the most populous in the Pacific region—459,720 adherents, or 61.7 percent of Eastern Religion adherents. Among Buddhists themselves the great majority (85.4 percent) are in California (12.5 percent in Hawaii; 2.1 percent in Nevada), although as a proportion of the population they are a more visible public presence in Hawaii, a state where Eastern religions claim 13 percent of all religious adherents. The Japanese and Chinese were among the first immigrants into these states from the East, bringing Buddhism and Confucian teachings to the region. The next largest are Hindus with 205,963 adherents, most of whom have come to the region more recently. Of all Eastern religions, 93.6 percent of adherents live in California, 5.7 percent in Hawaii, and 0.7 percent in Nevada. Baha'is number 25,973—95.7 percent in California; the remaining 4.3 percent in Nevada. Surprisingly, there are no Baha'is reported for Hawaii to the NARA. Taoists number 24,472, all residing in California, as reported to the NARA. There are 20,316 Sikhs—93.8 percent of them in California, 4.7 percent in Nevada, and only 1.5 percent in Hawaii. There are also 4,557 Zoroastrians, all reported in California.

Latter-day Saints

The Church of Jesus Christ of Latter-day Saints (Mormon) continues to grow in the Pacific region. Although in the early years The Reorganized Church under the leadership of Joseph Smith III had a larger membership in California, this splinter group was soon overtaken by the growth of its parent body. The latter's membership increased significantly between 1971 and 2000, especially in Nevada (147.4 percent), exceeding the country's 98 percent increase, but also significantly in Hawaii (69.6 percent) and California (44.1 percent). Based in rural areas historically, its members now live mainly in cities and suburbs. A religion that arose on the American frontier, Latter-day Saints offers a distinctive theology with its own texts reinterpreting Jewish and Christian traditions. Because of its strict views on doctrinal matters and strong emphasis on the importance of the family, it shares many moral values with Conservative Christians.

Orthodox Christians

As we have seen, Orthodox Christians have long been present, though in small numbers, in the region. Today they are still disproportionately present in California (1.5 percent of all adherents), followed by 1.1 percent in Hawaii and 0.6 percent in Nevada. Their congregations tend to be organized along cultural and ethnic lines—mainly Russian, Greek, and Slavic, but also some indigenous Alaskans.

Muslims

The Muslim population has grown considerably since 1965, when immigration policy in the United States was liberalized. There is considerable debate over the size of the Muslim population in California, where 99 percent of Muslims in the Pacific region live, as reported by NARA. With respect to ethnic and national background, large numbers within the region are African American, Indo-Pakistani, Arab, African, and Iranian.

Confessional/Reformed/Non-UCCs

More than two dozen religious bodies are included in this category, most of them small ethnic groups with Lutheran, Presbyterian, Reformed, or Brethren names. The largest denomination in all three states is the Lutheran Church–Missouri Synod, which accounts for 55 percent of the total adherents in this category; it is heavily concentrated in California. The church has enjoyed considerable growth since 1971. Second largest is the Reformed Church in America, with 14.3 percent, represented only in California. Third largest is the Christian Reformed Church in North America, with 9.4 percent, concentrated in California. Fourth largest is the Wisconsin Evangelical Lutheran Synod, with 4.2 percent.

United Methodists

The Methodists have had a long and significant presence within the region, especially in California. Historically, most of their members belonged to the Methodist Episcopal Church, which traces its origins to the movement begun in England by the Anglican priest John Wesley (1703-1791). But sizable numbers of migrants from the southern states brought their memberships with them in the Methodist Episcopal Church, South, which broke away in 1845 largely over the issue of slavery. The two bodies were reunited in 1939, and then in 1968 this Methodist body merged with the Evangelical United Brethren, a group with similar polity and theology, becoming The United Methodist Church. Theologically, the church has sought to maintain a balance between religious experience and evangelicalism on one hand, and social action and justice on the other. Since 1971 the United Methodist membership has declined in California by 36.6 percent, faster than in the country (10.1 percent), and declined by 4.2 percent in Hawaii; it has actually grown by 37.8 percent in Nevada even though its numbers there are quite small.

Presbyterian USA

The Presbyterian Church USA is the largest Presbyterian body in the country today, formed by at least 10 denominational mergers over the last two and a half centuries. Historically there have been many doctrinal and regional schisms. Like other mainline Protestant bodies, Presbyterians faced serious controversies during the past several decades over ordination, gender, and lifestyle issues. Since 1971 Presbyterians in California have declined by 21.9 percent, more so than for the nation (11.4 percent); there have been slight gains in Nevada and Hawaii, but the number of Presbyterians in these states has always been, and continues to be, quite small.

Episcopalians

Never a large denomination in the Pacific region, the Episcopal Church in the USA is affiliated with the worldwide Anglican Communion with its three sources of religious authority: scripture, tradition, and reason. Because its members are generally more educated and wealthier than those of most other Protestant denominations, the civic and political influence of Episcopalians is greater than might be expected. In Nevada's early history, Episcopalians were influential as community leaders. The church has lost members since 1971 in all three states. Proportionately, Episcopalians have a stronger representation in Hawaii (2.2 percent of all adherents in the state) than in California (0.9 percent) or Nevada (0.7 percent).

Lutherans (ELCA)

The Evangelical Lutheran Church in America (ELCA) was organized in 1987, bringing together several Lutheran bodies. Historically, its constituent bodies were largely of German and Scandinavian background, all rooted in the teachings of Martin Luther. As early as 1890, there were small settlements of Lutherans in California, known then as Evangelical Lutherans, the Buffalo Synod, Norwegian Church in America, Danish Christians in America, and the Danish Association in America. From 1971 to the present, adherence to the denomination has remained proportionally about the same relative to other faith groups, and better than for most other mainline Protestant denominations. Today, the ELCA has a somewhat larger share of the religious market in Nevada (1.4 percent of all adherents in the state) than in California (0.9 percent) or Hawaii (0.5 percent). These figures do not include other, generally more conservative Lutheran bodies, which are included here in the Confessional/ Reformed/ non-UCC Congregational category.

United Church of Christ

This denomination emerged in 1957 when the Congregational Christian Churches united with the Evangelical and Reformed Church. This merger pulled together the religious heritages of English and German populations, all emphasizing congregational autonomy, the role of conscience in belief and practice, and a strong commitment to civic responsibility and social betterment. Of the three states within the Pacific region, the church had its strongest public influence historically in Hawaii. But since 1971 its numbers have declined, by 10 percent in Hawaii, 8.6 percent in Nevada, and 8 percent in California.

Christian (Disciples of Christ)

A frontier Protestant tradition, the Disciples is known for its lack of emphasis on doctrine and simple statement of belief in Jesus Christ. The church is characterized by informality and openness to diverse thinking. It is ecumenically minded and involved in many social programs, both nationally and globally. Though the Disciples organized churches early on in the westward movement, it never attracted a large membership in the Pacific region. Since 1971 the denomination has lost more members than any other tracked in this study; 70 percent of its members in Hawaii and 48.6 percent in California. In Nevada it has grown slightly, although its numerical base in 2000 was only 655.

Other Mainline Protestant/Liberal Christian

Included here are four churches or traditions—Community of Christ, Friends (Quakers), Universal Fellowship of Metropolitan Community Churches, and the Unitarian Universalist Association. In theology and social teachings, this is a very mixed group. The group now called the Community of Christ was once known as the Reorganized Church of Jesus Christ of Latter-day Saints and is more liberal than the major Latter-day Saints body. Unitarian Universalists are known for their disavowal of traditional Christian creeds; Metropolitan Community Churches for their inclusiveness and outreach to the gay community; and Friends for pacifism and liberal social consciousness. By far, Unitarian Universalists are the largest of the four within the region (44.1 percent of all in this category), in fact, the largest in each of the three states. Next are Friends (26.1 percent), the Community of Christ (21.1 percent), and Metropolitan Community Churches (8.7 percent).

Pietist/Anabaptist

This category consists of 10 groups within the region, almost all of them Brethren or Moravian. Both are "peace church" churches associated with the radical Protestant tradition that sought a complete break with the Roman Church and a return to New Testament Christianity. All 10 are found in California; however, only one—the small Mennonite Church, USA—is found in both California and Hawaii. None of the groups are found in Nevada, according to the NARA. By far the largest group is the Mennonite Brethren Churches (52.9 percent of adherents in this category), with all its adherents in the region residing in California.

Religion and Public Life

In a religious environment as fluid and mutable as the Pacific region, religion's public face is constantly changing. Lacking a dominant religious establishment, religion's presence and influence rest to a considerable extent upon convergences of opinion among the larger religious constituencies at any given time. Coalitions among religious bodies around specific issues help to shape its public face, and so do values and perspectives that some faith communities share with the large numbers of non-churched or "weakly churched" people within the region. This latter affinity is especially important, though itself ever shifting.

To begin with, we compare the region's cultural climate with that of the nation at large. **Figure 1.4** shows the percentage difference between scores for the region and the nation on 11 social indicators in the Akron/Pew data set. This makes clear that the region exceeds the nation by 4.7 percent on self-reported liberal ideology; 2.4 percent identifying as Democrat; 1.4 percent favoring help to minorities, 8 percent who are pro-choice on the abortion issue; 3.4 percent favoring gay rights; 3.4 percent who support national health insurance; and 0.8 percent in support of environmental protection. Likewise, the region scores less than the nation by a difference of 26.1 percent on conservative ideology; 1.3 percent less identifying as Republican; 1.1 percent less identifying as Independent; and 1.2 percent less favoring school vouchers.

Consistently, as we see with these items, the region is more liberal than the rest of the country, though in some instances the extent of the difference is not very large. The region stands out especially in its liberal views with respect to abortion, ideology, gay rights, and national health insurance; on ideology, for example, the region has the highest liberal score (35.6 percent) of any region.

Among religious groups, too, there are important differences. In making such comparisons, it is important to distinguish between economic and moral issues. Knowing about someone's economic conservatism tells us little, if anything, about that person's moral values and attitudes, and vice versa. People may be "liberal" on one but "conservative" on another; indeed, much survey evidence points to this cleavage in attitudes and behavior. **Figure 1.5** shows these differences by religious community. Note that the large faith constituencies are broken down by level of institutional commitment ("high" versus "low"), which adds an insightful dimension to our understanding of religion's role in public life.

Several observations follow:

First, on controversial moral issues like abortion and gay rights, there are big differences among the large white Christian communities. Evangelical Protestants score much lower than mainline Protestants in liberal views; Catholics also score lower than mainline Protestants, as would be expected. But on economic issues

Figure 1.4 Social and Political Indicators: Pacific Region in Comparison to the Nation (NSRP)

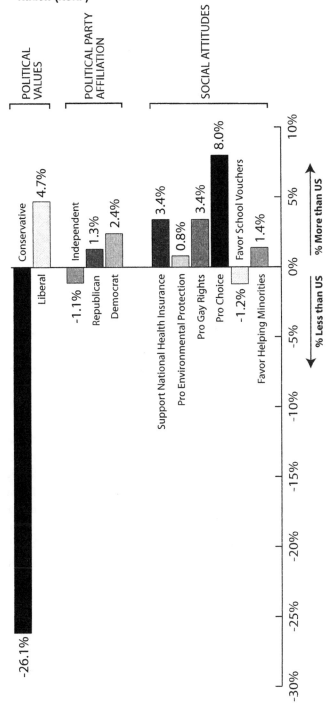

Figure 1.5 **Social Attitudes by Selected Religious Constituencies, by Percentages (NSRP)**

	Pro-Choice	Favor Gay Rights	Favor Helping Minorities	Favor More Welfare Funding
Nation	41.1	56.7	39.4	51.4
Pacific Region	49.1	60.1	40.8	52.9
Evangelical Protestant				
High Committed	16.6	31.8	31.6	46.8
Low Committed	45.2	48.7	28.7	46.8
Mainline Protestant				
High Committed	52.7	57.4	29.6	53.7
Low Committed	61.2	77.0	28.8	42.8
Catholic				
High Committed	22.0	49.5	37.9	57.9
Low Committed	67.2	75.2	36.7	53.5
Hispanic Catholic	36.5	62.2	56.7	61.7
Black Protestant	32.8	48.8	57.8	65.1
Other Christian	62.8	54.7	34.0	44.7
Non-Christian	60	60.9	49.5	61.8
Secular	64.5	71.4	71.4	51.3

such as helping minorities and welfare spending, differences among the large communities are not so huge. Moral and lifestyle issues are far more likely to divide them than economic interests.

Second, there are striking differences *within* the large white Christian communities between high-commitment and low-commitment adherents (high-commitment adherents are those who attend worship once a week or more). Among Catholics, for example, there is a 45-percent difference between the two in the views on abortion. In fact, low-commitment Catholics are the most pro-choice constituency of all the religious groups—even more so than secularists! In the case of gay rights, low-commitment mainline Protestants are the most liberal of all. This same constituency is highly favorable on environmental protection, second only to Non-Christians.

In every instance, high-commitment adherents within a religious group are *less* prone to the liberal position on abortion, gay rights, and environmental protection. But on economic issues, the spread between the two levels of institutional commitment is much smaller, and the pattern is reversed: those who are highly committed are *more* in favor of the progressive position, especially among mainline Protestants and Catholics. High-commitment evangelical Protestants, as well as their counterparts among Catholics and mainline Protestants, are more likely to oppose school vouchers and national health insurance than those who are less committed.

Third, patterns for Latino Catholics and African-American Protestants fit general expectations. On moral issues Latino Catholics score mid-way between high-commitment and low-commitment non-Latino Catholics. And African-American Protestants score mid-way between evangelical and mainline Protestants. But on economic issues, as would be expected, both are far more liberal than either the white Catholic or Protestant constituencies. Along with non-Christians, they are strong supporters of more welfare spending and national health insurance.

Fourth, three relatively small constituencies—other Christians, Non-Christians, and secularists—are all very liberal on moral issues; far more so than Latino Catholics or African-American Protestants, though not more so than the majority of low-commitment Catholics and mainline Protestants.

This latter observation leads to a plausible hypothesis: there is a close but shifting affinity between other Christians, non-Christians, and secularists, on one hand, and low-commitment Catholics and Protestants on the other. By mapping the ARIS scores for the religious groups in two-dimensional space, as shown in **Figure 1.6**, a better sense of this loose connection appears.

Pro-choice scores on abortion represent moral liberalism, plotted on the vertical dimension; and favorable scores on helping minorities represent economic liberalism, plotted on the horizontal dimension. As can be seen, two groups are low on both dimensions—high-commitment evangelical Protestants and high-commitment Catholics. At the opposite end of the ideological spectrum are non-Christians, high on both dimensions.

Latino Catholics and African-American Protestants are mixed, economically liberal but generally conservative on moral issues. These three groups lead the way in support of progressive political and economic change. Along with secularists, other Christians, and the large sector of low-commitment Catholics (but not high-commitment Catholics) vote Democratic.

Two groups then—low-commitment mainline Protestants and low-commitment Catholics—occupy crucial positions ideologically. With regard to moral liberalism, the two are very similar in outlook with other Christians, secularists, and non-Christians. This amounts to a sizable ideologically liberal constituency—over 50 percent of the region's population. Because it consists of a majority of all Catholics and mainline Protestants, this sector amounts to a crucial swing vote—leaning in a liberal direction on lifestyle and cultural issues, favoring a high level of personal freedom and choice, but on occasion allying with their more conservative (and more religiously committed) Catholic and Protestant

Figure 1.6 Religious Groups by Moral and Economic Liberalism (NSRP)

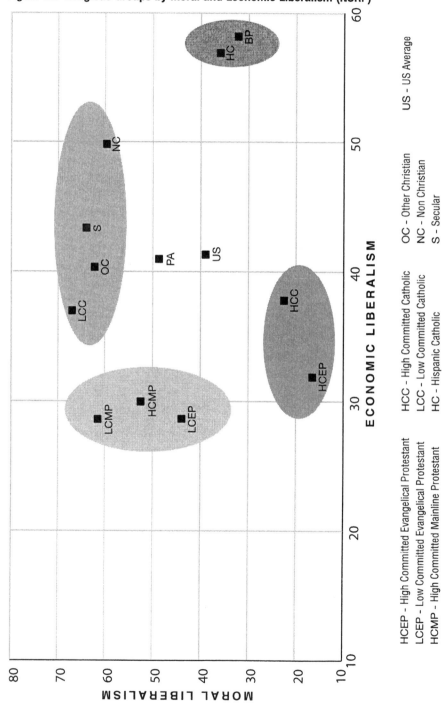

friends on bread-and-butter issues. Larger than their counterparts for the country as a whole (44.6 percent), this majority yields a disproportionate influence on public life within the region. It sets the moral and political tone. It also greatly contributes to the fluid, ever-shifting public role for religion.

Endnotes

1. Las Vegas as a Standard Metropolitan Area is constituted by Clark County.
2. In 2000, the Census Bureau asked people to identify themselves racially, hence some people identify with more than one racial and/or ethnic category. Thus totals for all racial categories may exceed 100 percent.
3. For Honolulu, the boundaries of the Standard Metropolitan Area are defined by Honolulu County.
4. Here we refer to the Standard Metropolitan Area known as Los Angeles-Long Beach-Santa Ana, which is constituted by Los Angeles and Orange counties.
5. The actual name of this Standard Metropolitan Area is San Francisco-Oakland-Fremont, consisting of the counties of Alameda, Contra Costa, Marin, San Francisco, and San Mateo.
6. San Diego County constitutes the boundaries for the Standard Metropolitan Area of San Diego.
7. Eldon G. Ernst, "Religion in California," *Pacific Theological Review* (Winter, 1986): 46. Here he is making reference to California.
8. Data are taken from H.K. Carroll, *The Religious Forces of the United States* (New York: The Christian Literature Company, 1893); *Religious Bodies: 1906* (Washington: Government Printing Office, 1910); *Religious Bodies: 1926* (Washington: Government Printing Office, 1930); *Religious Bodies: 1936, Selected Statistics for the United States by Denomination and Geographical Divisions* (Washington: Government Printing Office, 1941), Table 4.
9. Richard V. Francaviglia, *Believing in Place: A Spiritual Geography of the Great Basin* (Reno: University of Nevada, 2003), xxi. Also see Kenric F. Ward, *Saints in Babylon: Mormons and Los Vegas* (Bloomington, IN: 1st Books Library, 2002).

10. Paul Spickard, "Hawaiian Religions," in Wade Clark Roof, ed., *Contemporary American Religion*, Vol. 1 (New York: Macmillan Reference USA, 2000), 291. Elsewhere, John F. Mulholland writes, "When dedicating a new building, a Chinese merchant (member of a Christian church) will follow the Chinese practice of using gongs and exploding firecrackers, but he will also have a Hawaii ritual with salt water and maile leaves. No attempt is made to give intellectual explanation, but psychologically the mixture of religions is satisfying." (*Hawaii's Religions* (Rutland, Vermont: Charles T. Tuttle Company, 1970), 21).

11. Richard C. Schmidt, "Religious Statistics in Hawaii, 1825-1972," *Hawaiian Journal of History* 7 (1973): 41-47. Also see the special issue on "Sociology of Religion in Hawaii" in *Social Process in Hawaii*, 16 (1952).

12. These data are taken from H.K. Carroll, *The Religious Forces of the United States* (New York: The Christian Literature Company, 1893).

13. William M. Ferrier, "The Origin and Growth of the Protestant Church on the Pacific Coast," in C.S. Nash and W.B. Hohn, eds., *Religious Progress on the Pacific Slope* (Freeport, NY: Books for Libraries Press, 1968), 61.

14. Elden G. Ernst (with Douglas Firth Anderson), *Pilgrim Progression* (Santa Barbara, CA: Fithian Press, 1993), 53.

15. Edward J. Soja, *Postmodern Geographies: The Reassertion of Space in Critical Social Theory* (New York: Verso, 1989), 223.

CHAPTER TWO

TOWARD AN ESTABLISHED MYSTICISM: JUDEO-CHRISTIAN TRADITIONS IN POST-WORLD WAR II CALIFORNIA AND NEVADA

Douglas Firth Anderson

Judeo-Christian traditions historically have influenced the public life of California and Nevada, and they continue to do so today. For this chapter, these "familiar players" in the public arena include Judaism, Roman Catholicism, Orthodox Christianity, Protestantism, and Mormonism (the Church of Jesus Christ of Latter-day Saints).

The living presence of such traditions, however, does not undergird any coherent religious quasi-establishment. The persistent fluidity of society and culture in post-1846 California—a fluidity that eventually engulfed Nevada—has made the power of any religious group in the region's public life evanescent and ambiguous. For the Judeo-Christian traditions in particular, the regional history has been a generally disconcerting one, tending early on toward a de-privileging of those accustomed to social and cultural "insidership" elsewhere.

The American era of California and Nevada, then, provides a regional case of the more general history of religious disestablishment in the United States. Yet, the region is not so much representative as it is a leading indicator of future directions. Wallace Stegner, a twentieth-century essayist and novelist, wrote in the *Saturday Review* in 1959 that the West Coast was "pretty much like the rest of the United States, only more so."[1] The peculiarity of the region's religious history lies in the area's sociocultural fluidity—a fluidity that the sociologist Zygmunt Bauman calls "liquid modernity"—relative to the rest of the nation.[2]

Certainly California and Nevada have had distinct histories, and their respective natural, social, and cultural landscapes are not synonymous. Nevertheless, their modernization has made for a region that is fluid like America, "only more so." It is this "more so" modernity of California and Nevada that makes the region a borderland, a sociocultural place of complex and dynamic encounters and transformations. The Judeo-Christian traditions have had to accommodate themselves to historical trends in the area; this has made for a loose cultural establishment of mystical religious sensibilities.

Such accommodation has been in some ways difficult. Cultural custodianship and prophetic criticism of society are each deeply rooted in the sacred texts of the Judeo-Christian traditions predominant in California and Nevada. Yet, paradoxically, accommodation has also been increasingly easy.

California and Nevada have participated like the rest of the nation in religious developments linked with the developing liquidity of marketplace and American dreaming—only more so. The Gold Rush focused the eyes of the world on California. It also launched at least two things—one social, the other cultural— that have liquefied, so to speak, the state's religious development to the present (and in a more delayed and indirect manner, Nevada's as well).

First, the Gold Rush marked the beginning of a relentless stream of immigration to the state from the mid-nineteenth century to the present. "[W]ith its population almost doubling every twenty years for a dozen decades," the historian Moses Rischin observed several decades ago, "California has never had a respite to consolidate its institutions or to firm up its identity, to assert the authority of tradition or reputation."[3] Persistent, sizable immigration, in other words, is the social waterfall feeding the area's distinctive and historic fluidity.

Second, the Gold Rush made indelible a widespread mystique associated with California: at the western edge of the continent, the possibilities—material and otherwise—were limited only by human will and imagination. This mystique provided an additional geographic focus for the American Dream. The California mystique, in other words, is the cultural well of the region's identification (from within and outside itself) as a place for fulfilling the American Dream.

Immigration and mystique as post-1848 traditions in California are fundamental sources of the larger area's liquid modernity in religion, as well as much else. A further important element affecting California's and also Nevada's religious milieu is historical timing. In the mid-nineteenth century, mining rushes brought an "instant" industrial-urban society that dominated the life of both states (the 1850s for San Francisco, the 1860s for Virginia City). This means that the region was decisively reshaped at the time when the American marketplace was becoming national rather than local and industrial rather than pre-industrial. In effect, California and its quasi-colony of Nevada were on a fast-track of modernization even before 1900—like America, only more so.

Two final introductory things. First, in the analytical narrative that follows, religious places (congregations, seminaries, community houses, monuments, institutional offices, ecclesiastical districts, etc.) provide illustrative specificity. People of course visit or inhabit such places; indeed, places are human constructs in and on the natural landscape. Thus, the places in what follows are intended to humanize as well as geographically ground the account.

Second, what follows is, by necessity, an interpretive sketch. Judeo-Christian traditions are "familiar players," but that is because of their power and precedence in regions to the east, south, and north of California-Nevada. Yet perhaps because the culturally exotic is more intriguing than the culturally familiar, Judeo-Christian traditions in the West in general, and certainly in California and Nevada in particular, have at best received only fitful critical attention.

Judeo-Christian Traditions In California

Next to native peoples' traditions, Catholicism is the oldest continuing religious tradition in California. In 1769, Fr. Junípero Serra founded the first of 20 California missions under Spanish rule. Yet even before the U.S. conquest of California in 1846, Russian, French, British, and U.S. ships stopped at California ports, bringing Orthodox and Protestant Christians as well as more Catholics to settle with those already there. Religious diversity was extended further through 1850 with the arrival of adherents to Mormonism and Judaism. A century later, Judeo-Christian traditions were still not at ease with the region's liquid public realm.

Catholicism

By 1940, Roman Catholicism was the largest religious group in California, dwarfing Protestant and Orthodox Christianity, Judaism, and Mormonism. While Protestants nationally tended to consider themselves privileged culturally and socially, in California they had always to recognize the historical precedence of Catholicism. While a Protestant flavor lingered in southern California's public realm, Catholicism's public power was long standing in San Francisco-dominated northern California.

The Archdiocese of San Francisco and Los Angeles, 1940-1960

California Catholicism in the 1940s and 1950s was split by ecclesiastical boundaries. The Archdiocese of San Francisco, created in 1853, dominated northern California, while the Archdiocese of Los Angeles, created in 1936, dominated southern California. Through the 1940s and 1950s the Archbishop of San Francisco, John J. Mitty, tried to assert leadership over Catholicism in the entire state, but southern California, led by Archbishop John Cantwell of Los Angeles, resisted.

Differences between the San Francisco and Los Angeles archdioceses included approaches to administration. San Francisco's Archbishop Mitty was highly regarded for his managerial—particularly financial—skills. During his episcopate, the archdiocesan Catholic population nearly tripled, from 405,000 in 1935 to 1,125,000 in 1961, which led to more than 560 major building projects. But he also made the Church a major player in San Francisco's wartime-postwar power coalition. In the view of two historians, Mitty's leadership was a major factor in creating a Cold War labor, business, and government "coalition of the center" in San Francisco.

Moreover, by the 1950s Mitty and Sacramento Bishop Joseph T. McGucken saw that Mexican and Mexican-American migrant laborers constituted a burgeoning group with special needs. This led to Mitty's formation of the Spanish Mission Band (SMB), a small group of priests who provided not only spiritual services to the migrant laborers but also initiated credit unions, cooperative housing, and job referral services. In time the SMB priests adopted Cursillo, a Spanish-born movement, in order to foster personal commitment to Christ and his Church. A young César Chávez was decisively shaped by the SMB's work.

In the orbit of the Archdiocese of Los Angeles, however, the Cold War era made for a theological and social conservatism that resonated with that region's Protestant tendencies. James F. McIntyre became Archbishop in 1948, and in 1953 he became the first Cardinal on the West Coast. A native New Yorker, he was a contemporary and protégé of New York's Cardinal Spellman. McIntyre was an effective administrator; he was also committed to ecclesiastical and social hierarchy and deeply suspicious of theological or social "novelties."

The 1960s and an Increasingly Fluid California Scene

In California, Catholic leadership was more openly contested in the public realm in the 1960s and 1970s than it ever had been in the twentieth century. In many respects, this was due to forces larger than, and exterior to, Catholicism, such as economic trends and political policies. In other respects, though, the turmoil was internally driven. Baby boomers and Latinos were fueling Catholicism's demographics in California and Nevada—American Catholic dynamics, only more so. Moreover, the Second Vatican Council augmented turmoil within the Church by providing theological rationale for, and expectations of, a reformed Catholicism.

In San Francisco, Joseph T. McGucken succeeded John J. Mitty as Archbishop in 1962, the same year the Second Vatican Council began. He was generally in favor of its reforms, but cautious about implementing them and worried about how "our people here at home" would understand them.[4]

An accidental fire in St. Mary's Cathedral made the building of a new St. Mary's central to McGucken's episcopate in the 1960s. Widely visible atop Cathedral Hill, the new St. Mary's—costing over $9 million and completed in 1970—was described as "the first Cathedral truly of our time and in harmony with the liturgical reforms of the Council."[5] Yet the Vatican Council also provided local critics grounds for complaint: the cathedral was too costly in light of the imperatives of social justice.

McGucken had other public controversies to contend with before the new St. Mary's was dedicated in 1971. The archdiocesan seminary underwent a major revision in curriculum and also community life. As part of this reform, Father Eugene Boyle began teaching a social concerns seminar at the seminary in 1967. A report done by seminarians in the course drew front-page newspaper coverage in 1968 for its conclusion that San Francisco was ripe for a race riot. The following year, when there was some public outrage over the Black Panther Party's use of Fr. Boyle's parish hall for a breakfast program for children, McGucken cancelled Boyle's seminary course. Protests over the cancellation were swift and widespread, and on one occasion the Archbishop was heckled on the steps of his chancery.

The 1971 dedication of the new St. Mary's was thus charged with tension. Police sealed off the cathedral the day before its dedication in order to forestall a bomb scare. The following day, one group picketing the dedication was the Chicano Priests' Organization. Its handouts quoted the Catholic labor leader César Chávez: "We don't ask for more Cathedrals, we don't ask for bigger Churches or fine gifts. We ask for the Church's presence among us. We ask for the Church to sacrifice with the people for social change, for justice, and for love of brother."[6]

César Chávez represented a new development not only for Catholicism in the 1960s, but also for California's public realm: a self-conscious Latino activism. In the wake of the disbanding of the SMB, Chávez moved to Delano in California's Central Valley in 1962. There, he led in the formation of a union that eventually became known as the United Farm Workers of America (UFW).

If the new St. Mary's became the symbolic center of the Archdiocese of San Francisco by 1970, Delano became the center of Chávez's movement. In 1967, UFW headquarters moved to alkali land near the city dump that became known as "The Forty Acres." It was from Delano that the UFW announced its national grape boycott in 1965, intended to pressure growers into signing contracts with the union. It was also from Delano that a "penitential" march to Sacramento started in Lent in 1966; the march was meant to dramatize the strike and to garner the support of Governor Pat Brown, a Democrat and a Catholic. Finally, it was at the Forty Acres that Chávez stayed for his 25-day fast in 1968. Nationally, the Chicano and other social movements were questioning or even rejecting nonviolence. Chávez wanted to refocus the UFW's strike on nonviolence. In a storage room of the co-op service station, he set up a monastic cell; there he received visitors and from there he attended daily mass. It was also there that the aspiring presidential candidate and fellow Catholic Robert Kennedy joined him when he ended his fast.

Perhaps the most dramatic moments in the 1960s dilution of Catholic solidity in the public realm came not in Delano or San Francisco, but rather in Los Angeles. For Cardinal McIntyre of the Archdiocese of Los Angeles, Catholicism and the American Dream were best served by elites in Church, business, and government working together against the threat of godless Communism. This elitist conservatism led to McIntyre's involvement in three controversies between 1964 and 1969 that were tied to Catholicism's voice in the region's public realm.

The first controversy came in 1964, in connection with challenges to racial segregation in residential districts. A fair housing measure (the Rumford Act) was enacted by the California legislature in 1963. In 1964, Proposition 14, an amendment to the state constitution, was placed before voters. It was sponsored by the California Real Estate Association, which claimed that the Rumford Act was "forced housing," not fair housing, and thus should be repealed, in effect, by passing the proposition. In the north, Archbishop McGucken established an Archdiocesan Social Justice Commission. The commission freely spoke out against Proposition 14, and two weeks before the election, McGucken denounced the proposition in a pastoral letter. In the south, McIntyre proclaimed that the Church was neutral on the proposition; in a letter to the apostolic delegate, however, he went so far as to claim that the Rumford Act was "excessive" and that Los Angeles was a "well integrated city." Fr. William DuBay, a young priest in a predominantly African-American parish, called for the Pope to remove McIntyre because he had shut down any clerical discussion of civil rights. DuBay was suspended. The proposition passed, but it was overturned by the U.S. Supreme Court in 1967.[7]

The second controversy came in 1967, in connection with feminism. By the 1960s, the California Sisters of the Immaculate Heart of Mary (IHM) had been in the state for almost a century. The order had become integral to Los Angeles' parochial school system. The IHM had Americanized from its Spanish origins, and its motherhouse was clustered with Immaculate Heart High School and College in the Hollywood hills. The Second Vatican Council's reforms were eagerly embraced by the IHM. A program of experimentation was adopted in 1967. Among other things allowed, birth names could be reassumed (e.g., Mother General Mary Humiliata became Sister Anita Caspary) and religious habits could be exchanged for secular clothing. Such reforms were, however, unacceptable to Cardinal McIntyre. The IHM refused to rescind its reforms, and McIntyre in effect fired the IHM from archdiocesan schools in 1968. The IHM's renewal became a cause célèbre, not only in Los Angeles but throughout the U.S. Catholic Church. At issue were not just the Vatican II reforms and hierarchical authority, but also women in the church. From Sister Anita's perspective, and that of many others, "At the heart of controversy, the real protagonist may have been the unchanging (and unchangeable?) male hierarchical system, and the antagonist, the female agents of change, viewed as inevitably destructive of that system."[8]

The third and final controversy came in 1969, in connection with the Chicano movement. That year, McIntyre opened a new proto-cathedral, St. Basil's Church. Constructed for $4 million on Wilshire Boulevard, the church harkened to the 1920s' opulence of the district. Also that year, the work of César Chávez inspired the organization of Católicos por La Raza. Seeking an equal voice for Chicanos in the archdiocese, the new organization also sought a public disclosure of archdiocesan finances. As the Cardinal was celebrating Christmas Eve Mass at St. Basil's, some 100 supporters of Católicos por La Raza marched from Lafayette Park to the new church. Before the night was over, a riot squad of police had been called in, punches and kicks had been exchanged, and the shouting of the protesters had at one point been counterposed to the singing of "O Come, All Ye Faithful" by the worshippers. Protestors reappeared in a picket line on Christmas Day. McIntyre reportedly compared the demonstrators to "the rabble at Christ's crucifixion."[9]

In January 1970, Cardinal McIntyre was forced by the Vatican to retire. His successor made clear that the archdiocese was centered at the old cathedral, St. Vibiana's, not at the new St. Basil's.

The Cathedral of Our Lady of the Angels and Post-1970 Catholicism in California

By 1972, California's bishops had founded the California Catholic Conference (CCC), "the official voice of the Catholic community in California's public policy arena."[10] However, any sense that the CCC could speak for all the state's Catholics was very difficult to sustain. "Official voice" seemed to mean less the bishops speaking on behalf of the faithful than the bishops speaking on their own behalf what they hoped to persuade the faithful about in a fluid society. The major places of post-1940 California Catholicism considered thus far reinforce this point. The turmoil around the new St. Mary's Cathedral in San Francisco, let alone St. Basil's in Los Angeles, suggested that ecclesiastical authority was subject to increasing public questioning. The UFW's Forty Acres signaled that both Latinos and the Central Valley needed more culturally sensitive attention. Finally, the politicized controversies in the San Francisco and Los Angeles archdioceses in the 1960s highlighted that adherents were anything but united about what it meant to be a modern Catholic.

More recently, other issues, most notably concerns over clerical sexual abuse of children and young people, have continued to dilute Catholic solidity in the region's civil society. Some of the ongoing tensions in the Catholic Church's public presence are suggested by yet another place: the new Cathedral of Our Lady of the Angels.

The Cathedral of Our Lady of the Angels "sinks its foundations in the very heart of the City of Los Angeles," claimed Cardinal Roger M. Mahony. Cardinal

Mahony, Archbishop of Los Angeles, sought to set parameters for the meaning of the $189.5 million cathedral in his homily at its dedication on September 2, 2002. At the heart of Los Angeles, the Cardinal continued, the cathedral sits "astride today's El Camino Real—today's less colorfully named Hollywood Freeway— where it will stand and soar for many centuries as a sign of God's enduring presence in our lives and community."[11]

Mahony's evocation of the region's Mexican and Spanish past was historically appropriate and pastorally prudent. The old cathedral of Saint Vibiana's, opened in 1876, had been damaged in the 1994 Northridge earthquake. The bishop in 1876, Tadeo Amat, Spanish-born but imbued with Romanizing zeal, had substituted St. Vibiana, a Roman martyr, in place of Our Lady of Refuge, a Mexican Madonna, as the patron saint of the diocese. In the estimation of the historian Michael Engh, the Cathedral of St. Vibiana, opened in 1876, "split local Catholicism along socioeconomic lines" by relegating the poor Mexicans to the Plaza church, named Our Lady of the Angels.[12] The new cathedral of 2002 joined together the name of the Plaza parish, the design of a Spanish architect (Jose Rafael Moneo), and elements of old St. Vibiana's in the cathedral's mausoleum. Cardinal Mahony, the orchestrator of this conjoining, is ethnically Irish-American, a native of the archdiocese, and fluent in Spanish.

Bridging divides between workers and employers, and between Latinos and whites, among the Catholics of the Los Angeles archdiocese was important in the process leading to the new cathedral. Such boundaries have been longstanding, and they have been publicly contested. By the time Mahony became archbishop in 1985, Los Angeles was well on its way to encompassing a larger number of Catholics than any other U.S. archdiocese. As 2002 ended, Los Angeles had 287 parishes and an estimated 5 million Catholics speaking over 50 languages and representing even more cultures.

While the new cathedral seeks to solidify a religious center (administratively, theologically, culturally, and architecturally) in metropolitan Los Angeles, its material presence does not assure its centralizing and reconciling efficacy. Moreover, its solidity (material and ideal) is in tension with the region's fluid society and multicentered urban landscape. In his dedication homily, Mahony explicitly linked the cathedral's freeway location with the locale's historic royal road. Rather than walling off the new cathedral from the Hollywood Freeway, the architect placed an observation window in the plaza wall overlooking the interstate. Nevertheless, Our Lady of the Angels is an ecclesiastical oasis, removed from residential life and difficult to reach even by car. The surrounding government buildings are empty on Sundays, and there is no proximate restaurant, bar, or café. The new cathedral does not function as a node in a living city center; rather, in the view of *Los Angeles Times* architectural critic Nicolai Ouroussoff, its "indifference to context" is "quintessentially Los Angeles." It is a public space "in a suburban landscape without a true sense of center" and "whose communal tissue remains, to a large degree, its freeways and shopping malls."[13]

The contemporary public visibility yet ambiguous influence of Catholicism extends further in the archdiocese than Our Lady of the Angels. The archdiocese had one of its own as Mayor of Los Angeles when Richard J. Riordan served two terms (1993-2001). Prior to his election, Riordan—a lawyer and financial advisor—had worked closely with Cardinal Mahony on many archdiocesan matters. Riordan's time in public office was marked by a creative conservatism that included some strengthening of the power of the mayor, significant expansion of the police force in the aftermath of the 1992 South Central Los Angeles uprising, and the encouraging of flexibility in the delivery of city services and the promotion of business growth. Ironically, his decision to remarry in 1998 led to open rebuke from Cardinal Mahony. Twice divorced (the first but not the second marriage was officially annulled), Riordan flouted Catholic canon law when he announced his third marriage. Mahony issued a statement that the civil wedding would mean the Riordans could no longer receive their Church's sacraments. If Los Angeles' leading Catholic office-holder in 1998 was not overtly Catholic in his administration and also made a private choice that went against Catholic legal and moral authority, then Catholic power is far less monolithic and far more privatized than demographics suggest.

Moreover, almost immediately after the dedication of the new cathedral in early September 2002, the archdiocese announced that it was cutting at least 60 jobs and eliminating or reducing several programs. Funds for the cathedral had been raised independently of other archdiocesan programs, so the archdiocese has denied that the costs of Our Lady of the Angels led to the cuts. In dioceses and archdioceses across the United States, income from investments has declined in tandem with the stock market. Yet it is clear that the post-World War II numerical growth of Catholicism in Los Angeles has not translated into recession-proof financial growth.

The building and dedication of the Cathedral of Our Lady of the Angels serves as a prism, refracting various historical and contemporary religious and non-religious hues for the region. These include Catholicism's historical precedence as a Judeo-Christian tradition; the contentiousness of culture and class inside and outside religious structures; the difficulties of religious traditions—even ones with demographic advantages—positioning themselves in a fluid, religiously privatized public realm. The new cathedral gives geographic and material location for things that are often elusive. But it represents less a new situation for Judeo-Christian traditions in the region than a new marker amidst a sociocultural tide.

Protestantism

Consistent with its tradition, Protestantism in California has been marked by institutional multiplicity rather than unity. Such diversity, though, makes understanding Protestantism in relation to the state's public realm complicated. In this section, various California places—especially a monument, a seminary, four congregations, and a research/advocacy organization—will provide an archipelago of sorts from which to consider the streams and eddies of the Protestant tradition since World War II.

Mainline Protestantism

Although they never held the establishment or quasi-establishment status here that they did in the rest of the country, the mainline Protestant denominations had deep roots in the San Francisco region. The Congregationalist, Presbyterian, Methodist, Episcopal, and Baptist home missionaries and other adherents who came during and soon after the Gold Rush were by and large "evangelical." That is, they assumed that the foundations of Christian belief should be bibliocentric; that Christian experience should be Christocentric, personalistic, and conversionist; and that Christian life should be moralistic and activist. They also readily blurred the lines among religion, culture, and politics because, in their view, God was patently leading the world toward the millennium, in part through the growth of a "Christian America." They planted Protestant institutions, most notably theological seminaries and religious weeklies, in the Bay area, making it their West Coast organizational and intellectual center.

In the years following World War I, native-born, middle-class Protestants in northern California became largely resigned to their long-standing minority status in numbers and cultural power. In metropolitan San Francisco, an urban-dominated political culture that aspired to social tolerance and progressive reform—and dominated, in the eyes of local Protestants, by Catholics—was one with which most Bay-area Protestant adherents had learned to live and to which a few were even enthusiastic contributors.

One site has been a notable mirror of the diffuse and shifting public presence of mainline Protestants: the cross atop Mt. Davidson, San Francisco. Nondenominational Easter sunrise services began at the site in 1923, when the land was privately owned. At first, a wooden Easter cross was erected; fire, wind, and/or vandals destroyed several successive crosses until a steel-reinforced concrete one, 103 feet high, was put in place in 1933. By then, the city and county of San Francisco had purchased the top of Mt. Davidson as a city park. The 1933 cross was funded by the local government. The city attorney opined at the time that "The holding of religious services on public property is no violation of any constitutional provision. The erection of a cross is not a grant of aid to any religious sect. The cross is merely a monument erected in a public place, nor is it erected for any sectarian purpose."[14]

The Easter services and the cross were Protestant in origin and ecumenically Christian in concept. James Decatur—an Episcopal layperson, a YMCA director, a Salvation Army volunteer, and an employee of Western Union—was the single most vociferous and persistent promoter of the services and the cross. For him, they were public reminders of Christian teachings in a park-like setting—Christianity and nature as partners in a morally needy urban environment. The public support, though, was undoubtedly less Protestant tinged, given the weakness of Protestant numbers in the area and the contrasting strength of Catholic and Jewish numbers. The site became as much an expression of civic Christianity as it was a specifically Protestant place. At the March 1934 cross dedication ceremonies, Protestant leaders were prominent, yet so was Mayor Rossi, a Catholic. Easter sunrise services at the Mt. Davidson cross were often broadcast by CBS in the late 1930s and early 1940s. In 1941, an estimated 75,000 people attended the service as the public fretted about possible war.

The Mt. Davidson cross represented the mainline Protestantism that predominated in northern California in the 1930s and 1940s. In the second half of the twentieth century, the same liquid modernity that worked to dilute the apparent public strength of Catholicism in California made for the even greater marginalization of mainline Protestantism. Consideration of Mendocino First Presbyterian Church, Glide Memorial United Methodist Church, and the Mt. Davidson cross after World War II serve to illustrate some larger trends.

Mendocino Presbyterian Church, with its 1869 whitewashed wood sanctuary, has helped enhance the picturesqueness of its town, situated on the coast north of San Francisco. Up until the 1960s, Mendocino Presbyterian reflected the affluence and conventionality of much of white, middle-class mainline Protestantism. Between 1962 and 1972, though, two successive pastors attempted to galvanize the congregation into involvement in social-justice issues from a liberal perspective. By 1972, the church was fractured over the cultural and political issues, and attendance declined. However, one member of the congregation, an evangelical, had begun a ministry to the local counterculture in 1969. In 1971-1972, a nearby hippie commune was swept by a revival, and the commune and countercultural ministry merged and became a base within Mendocino Presbyterian. Thus, evangelicals were strong enough to dominate the search for a new pastor in 1972. The new pastor was a graduate of Fuller Theological Seminary (nondenominational and evangelical). The previous two "liberal" pastors were graduates of San Francisco Theological Seminary (Presbyterian and mainline).

The congregation's social and theological shifts from the 1950s to the 1980s illustrate some of the major postwar tensions within California mainline Protestant denominations. Further, the sociologist R. Stephen Warner argues for a greater significance: "In its close fit with historical trends, the Mendocino church is atypical as a congregation yet a microcosm of the United States."[15] Put another way, Mendocino Presbyterian is an American mainline Protestant church, only more so, since it is in California.

To the south of Mendocino, San Francisco's Glide Memorial United Methodist Church developed in a notably different direction. Glide Memorial Church had been planted in the Tenderloin district of San Francisco by Lizzie Glide, a Methodist philanthropist who had purchased the land, paid for the church building (1931), and left it with an endowment.

In 1963, the Rev. Cecil Williams, a young African-American clergyman from Texas, arrived to be the director of community involvement; three years later, he was the pastor. In 1967, he had the cross removed from the sanctuary, reminding the congregation, "We must all be the cross."[16] Under Williams, Glide Memorial regularly came to have a full sanctuary for "celebration" services of personal testimonies, poetry, dance, and contemporary music, the latter often drawing on black traditions. Glide also became known for leadership in demonstrations advocating black studies and affirmative action, for its meal program, for opening its facilities to use by groups ranging from the Hookers Convention to the American Indian Movement, for opposition to the Vietnam War, and for ministry to bring recovery to city dwellers contending with drug, alcohol, and other dependencies.

Williams also organized the Council on Religion and Homosexuality in 1964. San Francisco had long been a center of relative toleration for gays and lesbians, and Glide Memorial's congregation embraced people of all sexual orientations as well as all races and classes. Social tolerance of and civil rights for gays and lesbians were especially contested, locally and statewide, in 1978. That year, the gay activist Harvey Milk, who had been elected a San Francisco supervisor the year before, was murdered along with San Francisco Mayor George Moscone. The double murder came immediately after a hard-fought battle in the state that ended in the defeat of Proposition 6 (the Briggs initiative), which would have barred anyone engaging in "public homosexual conduct" from employment in the public schools.[17] Glide Memorial became a major site for grieving, comfort, and the defusing of potential civic disturbances.

While mainline Protestant civic tolerance in the fluid society of California was at its most controversial at Glide Memorial, at the Mt. Davidson cross in 1979, similar Protestant religious sensibilities aspired to embrace a metropolis, but without the stridency. That year, the Easter sunrise services at Mt. Davidson had as a theme "Reconciliation After a Year of Tragedy," recalling not only the Milk-Moscone murders, but also the People's Temple mass murders and suicides in Guyana. The services were broadcast on CBS News; as was explained on the broadcast, "if ever a city needed a service of resurrection, it is San Francisco."[18] Mainline Protestantism in California, however, whether in its more prophetic form as at Glide Memorial or in its more priestly form as at the Mt. Davidson Easter sunrise services, remained in the late-twentieth century what it had been since its arrival in the area in the mid-nineteenth century: a vocal player, but with far larger aspirations than actual heft—either symbolic, economic, administrative, or electoral—in the public square of the Bay area or California.

Indeed, in the 1990s the Mt. Davidson cross came to symbolize disconcerting changes in the mainline Protestant situation in an increasingly fluid society. The cross, first built under mainline Protestant auspices, received significant ongoing Protestant support (e.g., for organizing the Easter sunrise services and for nighttime lighting) into the 1980s. By 1990, though, the historian Marie Bolton notes, the Mt. Davidson cross had "become a divisive symbol." The city of San Francisco became a defendant that year in a lawsuit filed by Americans United for the Separation of Church and State, the American Jewish Congress, and the American Civil Liberties Union. The city was asked to either divest itself of the cross or the land under the cross. Pluralism, observed Bolton, was in conflict with "respect for the symbols of various groups," particularly "symbols from the past" whose public meanings became "an uncomfortable memory."[19] In 1997, the San Francisco Board of Supervisors and the voters of San Francisco approved the sale of the Mt. Davidson cross and the parcel of land on which it sits.

The group that now owns the cross is the Council of Armenian American Organizations of Northern California, a nonprofit group representing 24 agencies. The cross is maintained as a memorial to the genocide experienced by Armenians in their homeland in the early twentieth century. What had been erected at the instigation of mainline Protestantism and approved by a Catholic-dominated city government in the 1920s and 1930s was sustained at the turn of a new century by an ethnic group whose identity is intertwined with Christianity (Non-Chalcedonian Orthodox and Protestant) and the experience of persecution.

Mainline Protestantism seems to have largely dispersed into the sea of tolerant, personalized California dreaming. Insofar as it is a public presence, it has become bifurcated. It tends to be either something like the Mt. Davidson cross—a public symbol that draws minimal attention and commitment once it is clearly privatized— or something like Glide Memorial United Methodist Church—controversial yet largely marginal in its impact in regional civil society.

Evangelical Protestantism

Protestantism in southern California arrived in force later than in the north. Southern California's population did not begin to explode until the last two decades of the nineteenth century. By then, mainline Protestant institutional centers were already established in northern California. But also by then, the mainstream of Protestantism was beginning to develop multiple channels and even offshoots. The majority of Protestant adherents who moved to southern California in the late nineteenth and early twentieth centuries seemed more troubled with the liquid modernity that accompanied the pursuit of the American Dream in California than did the majority of Protestants in the north. Southern California, then, became the place where evangelicalism became most solidly centered in the region's fluid society.

Considered historically, evangelicalism of the twentieth and twenty-first centuries is closely related to that which formed the core of mainline Protestantism in the nineteenth and early twentieth centuries. American evangelicalism—a religious mass movement—has always been tied to particular religious organizations, whether denominational, interdenominational, or nondenominational, yet it has always cut through many religious institutions as well. The movement's "great" tradition, the wellspring of its identity, is an unambiguous emphasis on commitments that, in the paradoxical manner of Protestantism, have been worked out in a multiplicity of ways: biblical authority (supernaturalist theological norms), conversion to Christ as Savior (personalized religious experience), practicing disciplines of discipleship (a moralistic set of religious sensibilities), and mission to others (faith-based activism).

The key divide between contemporary evangelicalism and its nineteenth- and early-twentieth-century form is a cluster of trends that transformed the United States. Between roughly 1900 and 1950, the country changed from being a society that privileged ideals such as hard work, production, and the farm to being a society that privileged ideals such as expertise, consumption, and the corporation.

Evangelicalism in the nineteenth century saw itself (and was seen by many others) as roughly synonymous with the Protestant and American mainstream of culture. But after the turn of the century, the fluidity of American society made evangelicalism less willing to uncritically identify with either mainline Protestantism or American social and cultural modernity. Consideration of four organizations rooted in southern California helps illuminate important aspects of the rise of evangelical Protestantism both before and since World War II.

First, Fuller Theological Seminary embodies much of the history of fundamentalism and allied conservative Protestantism in the state. Founded in 1947 in Pasadena, the institution was self-consciously "new evangelical," looking to "reform fundamentalism," as incisively explained by the historian George Marsden.[20] This "new evangelicalism" represented by the Pasadena seminary had strong local sources feeding into a nationwide movement.

The holiness movement, for example, had local sources through the work

of the Los Angeles pastor Phineas F. Bresee, a founder of the Church of the
Nazarene in 1895. Pentecostalism, which stressed the supernatural gifts of the
Spirit, became a worldwide multiracial movement through the Los Angeles
preaching of the black evangelist William J. Seymour at the Azusa Street Mission
in 1906. In 1923, "Sister" Aimee Semple McPherson deepened the local base
of Pentecostalism when she opened her 5,000-seat Angelus Temple and a few
years later incorporated a new denomination, the International Church of the
Foursquare Gospel. Fundamentalism—characterized by Marsden as "the response
of traditionalist evangelicals who declared war on . . . modernizing trends"—
found important local support in Immanuel Presbyterian Church, Los Angeles.[21]
There, Lyman and Milton Stewart had the money (from Union Oil Co.) and the
theological inclinations to fund foreign missionaries, pay for the publication and
distribution of the pamphlet series *The Fundamentals* (1910-1915), and help
found the Bible Institute of Los Angeles (Biola).

A fundamentalist convert who graduated from Biola in 1921 was the Los
Angeles native Charles E. Fuller. Well-off from his family's involvement in the
citrus industry, Fuller became imbued with the missionizing ethos of Biola. In
1930, a Bible class that he had begun had grown into an independent congregation
that broadcast an evangelistic service on a local radio station. In taking to the
radio, Fuller was following the lead of other Los Angeles conservative Protestants
such as Sister Aimee, who had founded her own radio station in 1924, and the
Rev. Robert P. "Fighting Bob" Shuler, the fundamentalist pastor of Trinity
Southern Methodist Church. Fuller's earnest and irenic "Old Fashioned Revival
Hour" debuted nationwide in 1937 via the Mutual Broadcast System. By 1944,
during World War II, extensive correspondence bolstered estimates that "Revival
Hour" listeners numbered some 20 million. With his program on 575 stations
and short-wave bands, the southern-California native was the unquestioned leader
in religious radio broadcasting. Also, in the assessment of the historian Philip
Goff, "by combining war concerns, domestic revivalism, and foreign missions,"
Fuller and his broadcasting were central to the jelling of "a united, popular
evangelicalism" in postwar America.[22]

The success of his congregation and radio ministry enabled Charles Fuller
to launch Fuller Theological Seminary. Following Fuller himself, the seminary
deliberately moved away from such fundamentalist distinctives as separatism,
anti-intellectualism, and anti-modernist militancy. These moves, though, were
not uncontested. By the 1980s, the school had weathered conflicts from inside as
well as outside the institution. Even so, the seminary has thrived. In the 1960s,
Schools of Psychology and World Mission were added to the seminary proper.
The unchallenged leader of what is called "progressive evangelicalism," Fuller is
now the largest Protestant nondenominational seminary in the United States.

The pre-history and history of Fuller Theological Seminary suggests southern California's notable hospitality to evangelicalism. Another example, but at a different point on what could be called the coral reef of regional evangelicalism, is the Crystal Cathedral.

The Cathedral began in 1955 as the Garden Grove Community Church. It was founded by the Rev. Robert H. Schuller, an Iowan sent to start a congregation for the Reformed Church in America in the suburbs of Orange County. Southern California was a particular beneficiary of defense-related spending during the Cold War. The historian Lisa McGirr has described the Orange County milieu of the 1950s-1960s as one of "middle-class men and women who . . . found meaning in a set of politics that affirmed the grounding of their lives in individual success and yet critiqued the social consequences of the market by calling for a return to 'traditional' values, local control, strict morality, and strong authority."[23] It was not an accident that the year Schuller arrived to organize a congregation was also the year Disneyland opened in Anaheim. Walt Disney's theme park fit Orange County, "with its mixture of nostalgia for a simple American past and its bright optimism about the future."[24] In other words, the California mystique took a decidedly neo-conservative turn in postwar Orange County.

Rev. Schuller believed new forms of American life called for new forms for worship and church life. The Reformed Church was a mainline denomination with little to no cachet in the region. Further, southern California's built landscape was designed for the automobile. To reach the unchurched, Schuller took three innovative steps that led to the congregation becoming a mega-church of some 10,000 members by 1980.

- First, he decided to mute (but not sever) denominational ties. The congregation was named Garden Grove Community Church rather than Garden Grove Reformed Church.
- Second, he built big for a mobile, dispersed congregation, and in a way that made the congregation analogous, in some respects, to Disneyland. At its start, Garden Grove Church rented a drive-in theater. By 1980, when the $20 million Crystal Cathedral was opened, worshipers could participate in services in one of three modes: indoors, outside in their vehicles, or via the televised "Hour of Power" program (started in 1970).
- Third, Schuller innovated by combining two disparate streams of Protestant thought into what he terms "possibility thinking." Possibility thinking combines evangelicalism with self-help through mind-conditioning—a therapeutic gospel suited for the American Dream. "It's obvious that we are not trying to impress Christians," Schuller has said about his religious site. "We're trying to make a big, beautiful impression upon the affluent non-religious American who is riding by on this busy freeway."[25]

Fuller Seminary and the Crystal Cathedral both suggest that the booming postwar California suburbs provided a distinctive social and cultural fluidity, not only for the flourishing of Protestant evangelicalism but also for "postdenominationalism." Fuller Seminary is evangelical and nondenominational. The Crystal Cathedral is evangelical and denominational—but evangelicalism receives the emphasis over ties to the Reformed Church. Traditional mainline denominational structures are becoming less important in comparison to more fluid forms and connections. The historian Russell E. Richey has noted that congregations "increasingly chart their own course" because mainline denominational "regulating, granting, consulting, franchising, marketing, [and] training" are not functions that "energize . . . the denominations in the way that the grand cause of a Christian America once did."[26]

Calvary Chapel of Costa Mesa illustrates the more flexible forms that are developing alongside of, as well as within, more traditional Protestant denominations. Calvary Chapel is also an exemplary site from which to consider yet another current in postwar evangelicalism, one that is more overtly supernaturalist and critical of modernity than that represented by Fuller Seminary or Crystal Cathedral. Calvary Chapel is, in the estimation of the sociologist Donald E. Miller, a significant example of an emerging set of "new paradigm churches" centered in southern California. Such churches challenge "not doctrine but the medium through which the message of Christianity is articulated."[27]

In 1965, the Rev. Charles "Chuck" Smith accepted a call to Calvary Chapel, a struggling congregation in Orange County's Costa Mesa. Although he began his pastoral work within the International Church of the Foursquare Gospel (founded by Aimee Semple McPherson), Smith had left the evangelical denomination by the time he moved to Calvary Chapel. "The more spiritual a man is, the less denominational he becomes," he declared.[28]

Whereas Robert Schuller targeted for evangelization the unchurched middle-class families of Orange County, Chuck Smith targeted the young people drawn to the nearby beach during the 1960s and 1970s. Smith did not object to the young people's clothing styles, and he welcomed adapting their music for worship services, but he insisted on personal conversion to Jesus Christ as Savior and regular Bible study in order to ground individuals in a lifestyle of responsible love to others. Smith soon had what became, in effect, a new denomination that updated informal forms of pentecostal traditions. In 1974, Calvary Chapel built a new sanctuary that seated 2,300 people. Smith emphasized the gifts and leading of the Holy Spirit over institutional or professional order. Costa Mesa was the mother church of a host of Calvary Chapels, and Smith the father figure, but each Calvary Chapel founded by Smith's direct or indirect protégés was (and is) separately incorporated, and there was little reporting back to Smith or Costa

Mesa. Moreover, another "new paradigm" neo-denomination, the Vineyard Christian Fellowship, arose from Calvary Chapel after 1974. Calvary Chapel's flexible order and baby-boomer-friendly ethos has distinctively reflected important aspects of late-twentieth-century California metropolitan society.

Calvary Chapel is an important example of postwar evangelicalism's ready growth through adaptation to California's liquid modernity. It is also a component in the conservative political bent of Orange County in particular and southern California more generally. The Calvary movement refrains from taking overt positions on contested issues in the public realm. Nevertheless, the movement's premillennial eschatology and emphasis on traditional patriarchal family values reinforce rather than challenge conservative politics in the region.

California has been a major region for postwar evangelical Protestant institutions other than churches and seminaries. The Institute of Creation Research (ICR) illustrates one issue that has served to spur many evangelicals into directly influencing public policy. Examining the ICR also affords a glimpse of the southern California gestation of major elements of what has come to be termed the New Religious Right.

Modern creationism (or creation science) took shape in the wake of the Scopes Trial (1925) as a religious movement that found an intellectual home among conservative Protestants concerned to defend the Bible's inerrancy. It combined pressure-group political techniques with scientific evidence and logical argumentation for a "young" earth and against "evolution." The ICR, founded under a different name in 1970 in the San Diego area and reorganized two years later, has become the movement's national intellectual center.

The founder of the ICS was Henry Morris, Ph.D (civil engineering). In 1961, he and John Whitcomb published *The Genesis Flood*, the "bible" of modern creationism. Now retired, Morris has passed the presidency of ICR to his son, John D. Morris (also a civil engineer with a Ph.D). Through the ICR, the Morrises and others have had countless speaking engagements. More significant for the vitality of the movement, though, the ICR has produced a steady stream of resources in various media for use in education. Further, in 1981 it launched a graduate school. Southern California, not merely populous but also a center for the country's military-industrial complex, provides or draws to the school sufficient numbers of scientifically credentialed faculty. While the graduate school's approval/accreditation has been contested, the ICR currently offers master's degrees in astro/geophysics, biology, geology, and science education.

Moreover, the Morrises and ICR represent only a few of the many other personalities and institutions that have inhabited the most conservative end of the coral reef of evangelical Protestantism in postwar California. Perhaps the most significant of ICR's connections is the Rev. Tim LaHaye. Of late, LaHaye has been on bestseller lists, talk shows, and periodical covers for his (and co-author Jerry Jenkins') *Left Behind* series of premillennialist apocalyptic novels. In the mid- and late-1980s, LaHaye was active as a Washington-based leader of the Religious Right. From the 1960s into the mid-1980s, however, the young LaHaye worked primarily in California. He arrived in metropolitan San Diego in the 1960s and became pastor to a church that eventually grew to three. He also built a local system of Christian schools, the capstone of which is Christian Heritage College; the college's research division became the ICR.

Rev. LaHaye, like Robert Schuller and other evangelical clergy immigrants to the area, found the society in Cold War southern California fluid enough to provide opportunity for religious entrepreneurship. Unlike Schuller, LaHaye is a fundamentalist. He was—and remains—relentless in his concern for the salvation of individuals and also with what the political scientist Michael Lienesch has termed the "redeeming of America" through a "politics of moralism."[29] The urgency, for LaHaye as well as many of his supporters, is based on their dispensational premillennialism: the eschatological clock outlined in the biblical books of Daniel and Revelation is ticking; God is on the move in our times as seen in the rise of the state of Israel; and the Second Coming of Christ, prior to a period of apocalyptic tribulation on the earth, could come at any moment.

Beverly LaHaye, LaHaye's wife, meanwhile led the founding in 1978 of Concerned Women for America (CWA). Around the same time, James Dobson, a psychologist and a devout Church of the Nazarene layman, resigned his staff position at the Children's Hospital in Los Angeles in order to devote his time to a ministry of teaching, writing, and broadcasting. His organization was called Focus on the Family (FOF). The LaHayes and Dobson brought a significant southern-California base to the table when the Religious Right jelled around the 1980 presidential elections.

Evangelicalism, although more of a public presence than mainline Protestantism, is anything but monolithic. Privatization is as strong and deep a current among evangelicals as among mainline Protestants. Nevertheless, important elements of California evangelicalism have contributed to the shaping of a resurgent political conservatism. Such elements also led to a conservative religious dominance of the California Republican Party for much of the 1980s and 1990s.

Yet, the 2003 recall of Democratic Governor Gray Davis in favor of Republican Arnold Schwartzenegger—both pro-choice Catholics—suggests that the moralism of the Religious Right has its limits in the public arena. In a fluid, diverse regional society, faith-based values can elicit widespread support, but always in a context of a political culture of tolerant pluralism.

Orthodox Christianity and Judaism

Orthodox Christianity and Judaism were planted in California in the nineteenth century. As a proportion of the state's religious adherents, they have always been small. Yet they have been well placed for image-making in the public realm. The California mystique has always been tied to image-making. With the rise of film and television in the twentieth century, Orthodox Christianity for a moment, and Judaism much more substantially, have had opportunities to noticeably emplace themselves in the region after World War II.

Orthodox Christianity

Orthodox Christianity entered the continental United States through Russian Alaska and then California in the nineteenth century. In 1872, the see of the Russian Orthodox Church in America moved from Sitka to San Francisco, where it remained until moving to New York City in 1905.

Small numbers of Russian and Greek immigrants before the 1960s limited Orthodox Christianity's public presence in California. One figure, however, merits notice. Charles P. Skouras moved to Los Angeles in 1932. By the late 1940s, Skouras and his brothers controlled Twentieth Century Fox and a majority of the then-existing movie theater chains. Pursuit of the American Dream had dominated Skouras' life—and marginalized any adult commitment to the faith tradition in which he was raised. But near the end of this life, reclaiming Greek religious tradition became important to him. His parents had built churches in Greece, so Skouras determined "to build a monument to Orthodoxy in the New World to commemorate the monument of [Roman Emperor] Justinian on the banks of the Bosphorus [i.e., Hagia Sophia]."[30] In 1948, ground was broken for Saint Sophia Cathedral. The church's site in Los Angeles was near Skouras' penthouse. He took care of the design and the fundraising for the cathedral. He also had his mausoleum built next to the church.

Saint Sophia opened in 1952. It was less a New World Hagia Sophia than an ecclesiastical version of a Fox Theater. The dedication was, literally, a Fox production. The Governor, the Mayor, and the Roman Catholic Archbishop joined Orthodox dignitaries in the ceremony and opening service, which was televised live on local Fox Channel 11. Two years later, Skouras was dead and the family's movie oligarchy had been disbanded by an anti-trust court order. Skouras' death drained what little public weight there had been behind the new Orthodox Christian public symbol.

Judaism

Far more substantive than Orthodox Christianity were the places, the numbers, and the economic power connected with a second religious tradition, Judaism. The

Gold Rush lured many Jews—largely from Germany and Poland—to the Golden State. San Francisco's Jewish population in the 1870s (some 16,000) was second in the country only to New York City's. Religiously reformist in its tendencies, this Bay-area Jewish community was thriving as late as 1906. Metropolitan San Francisco, in the words of one historian, was a locale in which Jews of the late nineteenth and early twentieth centuries, religious or not, felt "the freedom to pursue varied opportunities and . . . to assimilate the best of modern America and the modern world, and to satisfy their special needs as Jews, which they could not readily do in small towns."[31] The heavy immigration of Eastern European Jews to New York and the Greater Northeast in the early twentieth century, together with the destruction caused by the San Francisco earthquake and fire of 1906, eclipsed the size and undercut the vibrancy of Bay-area Judaism.

As San Francisco and its Jewish community recovered after 1906, the Los Angeles region overtook the Bay region in population. The inrush to southern California of 1900-1940 included, as we have seen, Charles Skouras. His eventual eminence in the world of Hollywood, however, was preceded by that of Jewish theater owners who had established movie production studios. Indeed, one historian notes that Jewish business associates of Skouras "together gave more money [to Saint Sophia] than did the Greek people in all of Southern California."[32] And by the time Skouras was buried next to Saint Sophia's, Los Angeles was well on it its way to being the third largest Jewish city in the world, behind New York and Tel Aviv.

Before World War II, Los Angeles' Jewish population was 130,000. Jewish leadership in the film industry and growing numbers of Jewish clerical and garment workers provided the base for the flourishing of Jewish religious life in southern California after 1920. The elite side of this Jewish religious life was exemplified in Wilshire Boulevard Temple. Built in 1929 under the leadership of San Francisco-born Rabbi Edgar Magnin, architecturally it was modeled after Rome's Pantheon. The temple was a material place symbolizing the wealth and influence of its congregants, such as Carl Laemmle (Universal Pictures), Harry and Jack Warner (Warner Brothers), Louis B. Mayer (Metro-Goldwyn-Mayer), and William Fox (Fox Film Co.).

By 1951, World War II and its aftermath had attracted a new wave of Jewish migrants to Los Angeles. As one migrant recalled, "Here I was in California where oranges were growing on trees and the sun was pouring down like melted butter. . . . I didn't know, I thought I was going to heaven."[33] Hollywood's Temple Israel, particularly under the leadership of Rabbi Max Nussbaum, helped focus locally a post-war Jewish political impulse that was Zionist and activist for civil rights for all.

In 1953, Rosalind Wiener was elected to the Los Angeles City Council. The "nice Jewish girl" deliberately cultivated the support of the growing Jewish population concentrated in the Beverly-Fairfax district. In her 12 years on the council, she sponsored Jewish-specific legislation, such as a resolution for support of Israel and another measure to allow Jewish city employees to take Rosh Hashanah and Yom Kippur as holidays.

Meanwhile, the House Un-American Activities Committee's investigation of Communism in the film industry and the ensuing blacklisting of the Hollywood Ten (1947) divided the local Jewish community over issues of Americanism and social justice and made many Jews connected to Hollywood uneasy about their associations, religious and political. Despite such fears, the financial and critical success in 1960-61 of the pro-modern-Israel film *Exodus* indicated that Zionism had become a well-entrenched marker of post-World War II Judaism, in the region and beyond.

During the 1960s-1970s, though, the liquidity of Los Angeles was fostering further redefinitions of being Jewish and being American. Los Angeles Jews, in the words of the historian Deborah Dash Moore, "made their choices surrounded by affluence and captivated by self-fulfillment."[34] One choice many made was to disperse outward from ethnic neighborhoods like Boyle Heights and Fairfax. Other choices involved political and religious affiliations. There was still what one sociologist called a "civil Judaism," expressed through an emphasis on "the mutual responsibility of Jews, the centrality of Israel . . . , and the need to challenge both the internal and external threats to Jewish survival through political activities."[35]

Many Jews were choosing to be unaffiliated with any distinctively Jewish organization. Many others were choosing to redefine Jewish religion as voluntary participation and commitment rather than communal tradition and expectations. The regional direction of an individualized Jewish religiosity can be seen in the Stephen S. Wise Temple. Isaiah Zeldin established the new synagogue in 1964. By the mid-1970s, the temple had over 1,200 members. Under Zeldin's leadership, the temple developed a wide range of educational programs for all ages, including summer camping, a holiday workshop series, a parenting center for infants and mothers, day school, programming for teenagers, and family-life programs for single, adoptive, remarried, and intermarried parents. "We take you from the sperm to the worm," quipped one temple official.[36]

Judeo-Christian Traditions in Nevada

Judeo-Christian traditions were not new transplants to Nevada in the post-World War II era. However, whereas Catholicism had historical precedence in California, in Nevada Mormonism was the first to gain a footing. Most of what is now the state of Nevada was initially part of the Territory of Utah. Genoa and Las

Vegas, for example, were Mormon settlements in the 1850s. Mormon strength in Nevada's public realm, though, was primarily in rural and small town locales until the mid-twentieth century growth of Las Vegas and Clark County. And as the population grew, other Judeo-Christian traditions settled in.

What growth there was occurred largely in the northern part of the state; there the Comstock silver rush created Virginia City by 1860, and the Central Pacific Railroad, built across the new state (created in 1864) in order to complete a transcontinental railroad, brought settlers to the area. Mines and railroads were controlled by San Francisco-based investors, so post-1860 Nevada became an economic and cultural colony of California. The state's colonial status was reflected in the population's racial and ethnic diversity, but also in its small and unstable religious institutions. The Catholic Church, for example, did not establish a Nevada-based diocese until 1931; until then, Sagebrush State parishes and missions were under various California dioceses.

Nevada began to boom in unprecedented ways after 1930. First, by the 1930s gambling and easy divorce and marriage laws were permanently in place. Then, the construction of Hoover Dam (1931-1936) and the wartime and Cold War defense needs of the nation made southern Nevada, in particular, a recipient of federal money and a place of prolonged population growth.

Nevada's social developments were received with some ambivalence by the state's Judeo-Christian traditions. Religious leaders did not support easy divorce or marriage laws; but once in place the laws proved economically promising, if only temporarily. In Reno, First Methodist, First Congregational, and First Baptist churches, for example, experienced a rising demand in the 1930s and 1940s for clerical officiation at weddings. However, the rising income to churches and their clergy eroded in the 1950s as independent wedding chapels with their own clergy began to grow in numbers and appeal.

As for gambling, the moral and institutional ambiguities for Jews and Christians in Nevada were even more tangled. On one hand, for example, the Catholic bishop in Nevada refused to build a church on Las Vegas's Strip in the 1950s. On the other hand, one Mormon casino worker, looking back to her arrival in Las Vegas around 1960, observed, "There's no church edict against casino work. I'm working to make a living. Just because I'm serving liquor doesn't mean I'm drinking it. Because I'm working in a casino doesn't mean I'm gambling."[37] Her view no doubt articulates views similar to those of other religious adherents who began to move to Nevada's cities during and after World War II.

Gaming and the military-industrial complex, then, are at the center of a complex of related developments that have made Nevada at least a younger sibling of, if not quite an equal to, California in social and economic heft. The Judeo-Christian traditions have manifested themselves in Nevada's side of a regional society in ways that are particular to the state, yet of a piece with California's fluidity. Whereas Catholicism, Protestantism, and Judaism are the most notable of the "familiar players" in recent California, in Nevada they are Mormonism, Catholicism, and Judaism.

Judaism, Catholicism, and the Latter-day Saints

As the rise of Hollywood afforded opportunity for a vital Jewish community in Los Angeles, so the rise of gaming afforded opportunity for a dynamic Jewish community in Las Vegas. Ethnic Jews led organized crime's control of the city's gaming in the 1950s and 1960s. Benjamin "Bugsy" Siegel's murder in 1947, a year after he opened the Flamingo Hotel and Casino on the Strip, only made him the most (in)famous of Jewish casino entrepreneurs that also included Meyer Lansky, Davie Berman, Gus Greenbaum, and Morris B. "Moe" Dalitz. Temple Beth Sholom opened in Las Vegas in 1958. The Conservative synagogue never lacked for money. The synagogue's presidents included men such as Jack Entratter of the Sands Hotel and Casino and Mel Exber of the Las Vegas Club. "I call it a Jewish con man culture," recalled one synagogue participant; "at the end of the year the three angels [moneyed synagogue members] looked at each other, decided whose turn it was, and that guy ponied up his check for the balance" of the synagogue's budget.[38]

Guardian Angel Cathedral on the Las Vegas Strip indicates that in Nevada, the Catholic Church has had to accept gaming as central to the local economy. Bishop Robert Dwyer initially resisted building a church near the Strip. Catholic laity, clergy, and gaming interests changed Dwyer's mind in the early 1960s. Guardian Angel was opened in 1963, more for Catholic employees in Strip hotels than for tourists. Not only did the workers attend, but so did entertainers and tourists. At the shrine at the entrance of the church is inscribed an invocation inclusive of residents and tourists: "May the Holy Family bless our visitors and protect them on their journey homeward." Celebrities who have attended mass at Guardian Angel include Bob Newhart, Perry Como, Danny Thomas, and Frank Sinatra. Moreover, the church was elevated to co-cathedral status in a re-designated Diocese of Reno-Las Vegas in 1976-1977. Southern Nevada was being taken with increasing seriousness by the Church hierarchy. The area's continued growth, including the rise of a Latino workforce, led to the establishment of the Diocese of Las Vegas in 1995.

Meanwhile, Mormons were emerging as a major sector of postwar Las Vegas, and not only of Nevada's hinterlands. Mormons provided much of the labor the booming city needed in the 1940s and 1950s. Further, they had electoral and policy-making strength.

Some Mormons became important players in shaping the economic development of Clark County. "I work for the Mormons until noon, and from noon on for my Jewish friends," quipped the local financier E. Parry Thomas.[39] Thomas was a non-practicing Mormon, sent to Las Vegas in 1954 by a Salt Lake City bank to open the Bank of Las Vegas. Over the next few decades, Thomas became the leading local agent for development. His partner, Jerry Mack, was Jewish. Thomas also did a lot of business with the alleged mobster Moe Dalitz, who not only gave to Jewish causes but who also donated the land for Guardian Angel Catholic Church.

Through the 1970s, Mormons who worked in the casinos were not eligible for temple recommends (i.e., the recommendation of the local Mormon officials that one was a Saint-in-good-standing and thus able to use a temple). Nevertheless, Mormons in good standing were key advisors to Howard Hughes. Hughes, the eccentric heir to the Hughes Tool Co. fortune, began heavily investing in Las Vegas casinos between 1966 and 1970. He relied on Mormon financial advisors for this investing because, in his view, their religious commitments made them more trustworthy. Mormon-in-good-standing Harry Reid, a Democrat (and, as of January 2005 the Minority Leader of the United States Senate), became head of the Gaming Control Board in 1977. He led in a pivotal crackdown on organized crime in Nevada gaming.

By the mid-1980s, employment by a casino was no longer a bar for a temple recommend for a Mormon otherwise in good standing. Moreover, by the end of 1989, Las Vegas had its own Mormon Temple. Built on Sunrise Mountain overlooking the east side of Las Vegas Valley, the temple is easily discernable by its six white spires. Only two Mormon leaders from Salt Lake City attended the dedication, suggesting a certain hesitance about the Church's entanglement in Las Vegas' society. Nonetheless, as the journalist Kenric F. Ward has noted, the temple's opening indicated that "on the cusp of the twenty-first century, the Mormons of Las Vegas proved they could be players in both venues"—that of the world "below" and that of the spirit represented by "the high ground of Sunrise Mountain."[40]

As Mormonism matured institutionally in metropolitan Nevada, so did Judaism. Midbar Kodesh ("Holy Desert") was organized in 1994 as a new synagogue in Green Valley/Henderson. Young professionals had become an important group among migrants to southern Nevada in the 1980s and 1990s. Midbar Kodesh was born out of the desires of some of these for Jewish religious community in the residential districts to the south of the Strip. Hal Rothman, a historian and member of Midbar Kodesh, interprets the synagogue's vitality as a sign of permanence in "this transient community."[41]

The Nevada Test Site

Alongside gaming and entertainment as engines of growth for postwar Nevada are various manifestations of the military-industrial complex. One place in particular came to have religious associations: the Nevada Test Site. The test site is situated in a bleak basin-and-range desert sector northwest of Las Vegas. The Atomic Energy Commission opened the facility in 1951 for atomic bomb testing. There were 126 atomic tests at the test site between 1951 and 1963, above ground or only partially enclosed.

The first major religiously based protest of such testing came in 1957. On August 6, 25 activists, mostly Quakers and Catholic Workers from outside Nevada, demonstrated at the test site's gates; 11 breached the designated perimeters and were arrested. In 1982, the test site became a place of annual religious pilgrimage. That year, Franciscan religious, lay Catholics, Quakers, and others, mostly from Las Vegas and California, observed the first Lenten Desert Experience in connection with the 800th birthday of St. Francis of Assisi. In 1984, the annual 40-day vigil of contemplative prayer and nonviolent action for peace and against nuclear weapons testing was combined with an annual August commemoration of the destruction of Hiroshima and Nagasaki; it became the Nevada Desert Experience. During the 1980s, thousands of people made pilgrimage to the test site in connection with the desert experience. Since 1992, though, the numbers have declined, as the wake of the Cold War's end led to a moratorium on nuclear testing.

The Cold War's end also meant that the military-industrial complex that had driven the economy of Nevada—and California as well—for several decades began to retrench. By the 1980s and 1990s, however, Las Vegas's entertainment-tourist industry had gained a dynamism that expansively fueled southern Nevada's growth despite defense cutbacks.

Thus, the end of the Cold War has not brought decline to Las Vegas. Today, Nevada is positioned for the twenty-first century in a way that is American only more so. "In a time when nearly everyone wants to be a consumer," observes Hal Rothman, "when entertainment is culture and the cult of the self dominates, Las Vegas has preeminence."[42] Judeo-Christian traditions are more often prepared to accommodate than contest such consumption and to baptize rather than discipline the cult of the self.

Toward an Established Mysticism

The West in general, and California and Nevada in particular, have become "irrecoverably metropolitan" in a distinctively dispersed and multicultural way.[43] That is, gaining predominance over all locales in twenty-first-century California and Nevada is a society characterized by diversity (of individual and group identity), consumption (of services, goods, and resources), mobility (of people, goods, and information), and corporate order (for state, public, and private institutions). Parallel to this social structure is a metropolitan or post-urban culture. Carl Abbott, historian of the urban West, suggests that "in the tradition of urban specialization," greater Los Angeles has come to represent "the opportunities of consumption," while the Bay area has come to represent "freedom in the choice of individual behavior."[44] Meanwhile, Las Vegas has repositioned itself to be the next stage on from Disneyland—a theme park for all ages and tastes. But as the baby boomers age, their numbers and the number of their children have given heft to widespread tensions about what the American Dream means, who is included, and how it could and should be pursued. These tensions often play themselves out in battles over state and local propositions.

Since 1980, Judeo-Christian traditions have certainly remained visibly emplaced, in all sorts of ways, in the public realm of California and Nevada. There are many examples, only a few of which can be considered in this space. Yet any Judeo-Christian alliance that might have seemed to exist in World War II or the early Cold War years has long since dissolved.

Even during those years, Jewish and Christian structures and groups had little power in determining the shape of the region's social and cultural dynamics, though some religious groups and/or structures still exercised authority among the faithful. In the public realm, some regional religious groups or leadership were important balances or bridges between otherwise conflicting groups, and there was some deference to moral arguments presented in support of or in opposition to selected public issues. Since then, however, whatever public influence regional Judeo-Christian traditions might otherwise have is largely diluted by a liquid modernity. This social and cultural fluidity, in Zygmunt Bauman's view, fosters privatization by placing "the burden of pattern-weaving and the responsibility for failure . . . primarily on the individual's shoulders" while masking the power of globalizing structures.[45]

The distinctive liquid modernity of California and Nevada society in relation to religion has been termed "Californization" by Catherine L. Albanese. By this she means that the "digestive power" and "wild ferment" of religion and ethnicity that has long typified California are fostering a "mysticism" of "inwardness, direct experience, and metaphysical empowerment in material life" that will most likely become "a key distinguishing characteristic of the emerging American ethnos."[46] For Albanese, California and its environs are America, only more so, especially in the realm of religion.

Albanese's and Bauman's insights together suggest a perspective with which to understand contemporary Judeo-Christian traditions in relation to the public realm of California and Nevada. Insofar as there is anything becoming established, it is the privileging electorally of what is already the case legally, economically, and in media: a tolerant, privatized religiosity. That is, regional religion is more about an immanent divine satisfying the desires of the self than about a transcendent divine questioning ambitions, whether personal or social.

Nevada in general and Las Vegas in particular continue to be places with a libertarian political tradition, and no religious group seriously contemplates assaulting the gaming industry. Yet Mormons, for example, are strong enough to have, in company with other religious conservatives, followed the lead of California voters and led the 2000 campaign for Question 2. The initiative, which states, "Only a marriage between a male and female person shall be recognized and given effect in this state," passed with the organized support of the Latter-day Saints.

Compared to that of Nevada, California's society has had more complex developments in the last two decades. Also, the Golden State remains immense in its dynamic demographics and diversified economy compared to the Sagebrush State. But the same liquid modernity dominates the more populous as well as the smaller state.

The role of Christian and Jewish groups of color or recent foreign immigration in the public life of California and Nevada is growing, but little else is sure.

Perhaps the most telling regional developments have to do not with Judeo-Christian traditions and political movements but with Judeo-Christian traditions in relation to entertainment and tourism. Liquid modernity makes for political disengagement and for the privileging of structures that support consumption and personalized experience. The pursuit of the American Dream has an obvious resonance with this. The California-Nevada version of American dreaming makes for a quasi-establishment of mysticism—that is, a public prevalence of privatized religious experience. As regional politics keeps circling back to personality and single-issue politics, despite the efforts of ideologues, so regional religion tends toward mysticism, despite the efforts of dogmatists and religious activists. The personal and the experiential trump all other things placed on the public table.

In such a sociocultural landscape, where all experiences are subject to marketing and consumption, the lines among religious experience, entertainment, and tourism seem even less distinct than in earlier eras.

Being Jewish in Los Angeles and Las Vegas, for example, has been more about choosing what experiences, values, and activities give one meaning than assuming that being Jewish is "a matter of birth and inheritance, of family constraints and collective guilt."[47] The Crystal Cathedral, which began in a rented drive-in theater, is a place for religious experience—but it is also a place that draws the curious tourist, who may or may not be seeking a specifically religious experience. It is also a virtual place to millions via television. Similarly, the new Our Lady of the

Angels Cathedral in Los Angeles is a place of traditional religious pilgrimage, but it will no doubt also draw the tourist, who often is the same person as the pilgrim.

These two cathedrals, however—one Protestant and the other Catholic—are not likely to become like the California Franciscan missions. There, in the view of Thomas S. Bremer, tourism obscures religion; the old missions are "hybrid places" which purport to offer "authentic" religious and historical experience.[48] A similar commodification of experience also seems underway at the Nevada Test Site. Symbolically central to the Cold War military-industrial complex in the region and, as we have seen, once a site of faith-based protest pilgrimage, the test site is now making a bid for tourists. As of 1997, the U.S. Department of Energy takes some 9,000 people a year on tours of the test site by bus from Las Vegas.

In a sociocultural landscape of liquid modernity, all sorts of boundaries are subject to change. Adherents of Judeo-Christian traditions, given their region and their scriptures, might do well to ponder some of the words of Koheleth, the Preacher: "With many dreams come vanities and a multitude of words; but fear God" (Ecclesiastes 5:7, NRSV).

Endnotes

1. Wallace Stegner, "The West Coast: Region with a View," *Saturday Review* (May 2, 1959): 41. Later on, he honed his wording to "America only more so" and applied it to California and the West. See Wallace Stegner, "California Rising" in Jonathan Eisen and David Fine with Kim Eisen, eds., *Unknown California* (New York: Macmillan, 1985), 8; and "Variations on a Theme by Crevecoeur" in Wallace Stegner, *Where the Bluebird Sings to the Lemonade Springs: Living and Writing in the West* (New York: Random House, 1992), 103. I am claiming the resonance of the phrasing and its meaning for the more tightly defined region of California and Nevada.

2. "[L]iquids, unlike solids, cannot easily hold their shape. Fluids, so to speak, neither fix space nor bind time." Zygmunt Bauman, *Liquid Modernity* (Malden, MA: Blackwell Publishers/Polity Press, 2000), 2.

3. Moses Rischin, "Immigration, Migration, and Minorities in California: A Reassessment," *Pacific Historical Review* 41 (1972): 76.

4. Jeffrey M. Burns, "Postconciliar Church as Unfamiliar Sky: The Episcopal Styles of Cardinal James F. McIntyre and Archbishop Joseph T. McGucken," *U.S. Catholic Historian* 17 (Fall 1999): 74.

5. The description is by Pier Luigi Nervi, who was a member of the cathedral's architectural team. Quote in James P. Gaffey, "The Anatomy of Transition: Cathedral-Building and Social Justice in San Francisco, 1962-1971," *Catholic Historical Review* 70 (1984): 60.

6. Ibid., 72.

7. Quotations are from Jeffrey M. Burns, "Eugene Boyle, the Black Panther Party and the New Clerical Activism," *U.S. Catholic Historian* 13 (Summer 1995): 143, 144.

8. Anita M. Caspary, *Witness to Integrity: The Crisis of the Immaculate Heart Community of California* (Collegeville, MN: Liturgical Press, 2003), 5.

9. The incident is recounted in Mike Davis, *City of Quartz: Excavating the Future in Los Angeles* (New York: Vintage Books, 1992), 335.

10. California Catholic Conference, "About the Conference," www.cacatholic. org (2 May 2003).

11. Larry B. Stammer, "L.A. Cathedral is Dedicated," *Los Angeles Times*, http://www.latimes.com/news/local/la-me-cathedral3sep03.story (3 September 2002).

12. Michael E. Engh, *Frontier Faiths: Church, Temple, and Synagogue in Los Angeles, 1846-1888* (Albuquerque: University of New Mexico Press, 1992), 179.

13. Nicolai Ouroussoff, "Cathedral Embodies Spiritual Journey," *Los Angeles Times*, http://www.latimes.com/news/local/cl-et-ouroussoff2sep02.story (2 September 2002).

14. Quote in Marie Bolton, "Sacred or Profane? The Cross at Mount Davidson Park, San Francisco," *Pacific Historical Review* 67 (1998): 559.

15. R. Stephen Warner, *New Wine in Old Wineskins: Evangelicals and Liberals in a Small-Town Church* (Berkeley: University of California Press, 1988), xii.

16. Glide Memorial United Methodist Church, "History of Glide," www.glide. org (7 May 2003).

17. Quoted in Laura A. Belmonte, "Harvey Milk: San Francisco and the Gay Migration," in Benson Tong and Regan A. Lutz, eds., *The Human Tradition in the American West* (Wilmington, DE: Scholarly Resources, 2002), 219.

18. Quoted in Bolton, "Sacred or Profane?" 563.

19. Ibid., 569.

20. George M. Marsden, *Reforming Fundamentalism: Fuller Seminary and the New Evangelicalism* (Grand Rapids, MI: William B. Eerdmans Publishing, 1987), x.

21. Ibid., 4.

22. Philip Goff, "'We Have Heard the Joyful Sound': Charles E. Fuller's Radio Broadcast and the Rise of Modern Evangelicalism," *Religion and American Culture* 9:1 (1999): 86.

23. Lisa McGirr, *Suburban Warriors: The Origins of the New American Right* (Princeton: Princeton University Press, 2001), 53.

24. Ibid., 20.

25. Quoted in Dennis Voskuil, *Mountains into Goldmines: Robert Schuller and the Gospel of Success* (Grand Rapids, MI: William B. Eerdmans Publishing, 1983), 42.

26. Russell E. Richey, "Denominations and Denominationalism: An American Morphology," in Robert Bruce Mullin and Russell E. Richey, eds., *Reimagining Denominationalism: Interpretive Essays* (New York: Oxford University Press, 1994), 89.

27. Donald E. Miller, *Reinventing American Protestantism: Christianity in the New Millennium* (Berkeley: University of California Press, 1997), 11.

28. Ibid., 32.

29. Michael Lienesch, *Redeeming America: Piety and Politics in the New Christian Right* (Chapel Hill: University of North Carolina Press, 1993), 11.

30. Starros Nicholas Akrotirianakis, *Byzantium Comes to Southern California: The Los Angeles Greek Community and the Building of Saint Sophia Cathedral* (Minneapolis: Light and Life, 1994), 74.

31. Moses Rischin, "The Jewish Experience in America: A View from the West," in Moses Rischin and John Livingston, eds., *Jews of the American West* (Detroit: Wayne State University Press, 1990), 34.

32. Akrotirianakis, *Byzantium Comes to Southern California*, 76.

33. Michael Kanin, as quoted in Deborah Dash Moore, *To the Golden Cities: Pursuing the American Jewish Dream in Miami and L.A.* (New York: Free Press, 1994), 21.

34. Moore, *To the Golden Cities*, 264.

35. Neil C. Sandberg, *Jewish Life in Los Angeles: A Window to Tomorrow* (Lanham, MD: University Press of America, 1986), 125.

36. Quote from Moore, *To the Golden Cities*, 269.

37. Maxine Ernst interview in Kit Miller, "Inside the Glitter: Lives of Casino

Workers," in Hal K. Rothman and Mike Davis, eds., *The Grit Beneath the Glitter: Tales from the Real Las Vegas* (Berkeley: University of California Press, 2002), 215-217.

38. Quoted in Hal Rothman, *Neon Metropolis: How Las Vegas Started the Twenty-First Century* (New York: Routledge, 2002), 311.

39. As quoted in Rothman, *Neon Metropolis*, 133.

40. Kenric F. Ward, *Saints in Babylon: Mormons and Las Vegas* (Bloomington, IN: 1st Books, 2002), 50.

41. Rothman, *Neon Metropolis*, 313.

42. Ibid., 319.

43. Walter Nugent, *Into the West: The Story of Its People* (New York: Alfred A. Knopf, 1999), 351.

44. Carl Abbott, *The Metropolitan Frontier: Cities in the Modern West* (Tucson: University of Arizona Press, 1993), 182-183, 184.

45. Bauman, *Liquid Modernity*, 8.

46. Catherine L. Albanese, "Religion and American Experience: A Century After," *Church History* 57 (1988): 345.

47. Moore, *To the Golden Cities*, 271.

48. Thomas Bremer, "Tourists and Religion at Temple Square and Mission San Juan Capistrano," *Journal of American Folklore* 113 (2001): 433, 434.

CHAPTER THREE

NEW PLAYERS AND NEW PATTERNS

David W. Machacek

It is appropriate to begin this examination of new players in Pacific region religion with the cultural ferment of the 1960s and 1970s because that story has much to do with the context in which these new players entered. The history of the counterculture can be traced to a more general liberal trend that began in the 1930s and 1940s. The period following World War II may well have been characterized by a "return to normalcy," as noted by Martin Marty,[1] and a consequent emphasis on conformity to the standards of a middle-class American way of life. But it was also characterized by a growing emphasis on equality and individual rights.

The culture war that characterized the second half of the twentieth century grew out of these conflicting values, perhaps nowhere more evident than in battles surrounding educational institutions. After World War II education came to be seen, rightly, as the primary means of personal advancement, and Americans began investing heavily in higher education. But educational institutions were also socializing agencies that typically emphasized establishment values and institutions. It was perhaps inevitable that these educational institutions would become sites of conflict between expressive individualism and communitarian consensus; this is what happened in the Free Speech, Beat, Hippie, and anti-war movements.

During the post-war era, American universities also began attracting increasing numbers of foreign students, who brought with them new and sometimes critical perspectives on Western culture and institutions. Academic culture shifted from one typically supportive of the establishment to one that actively sought out diverse perspectives, including (some would say especially) those critical of the establishment.

By mid-century the tide of the culture war had moved in favor of individual rights and increased personal freedom and away from a culture of conformity. The counterculture was the most visible evidence of this shift. Less visible, but no less significant, was the emergence of consumerism as the dominant economic culture. The old "Protestant ethic" of hard work, thrift, saving and investment was giving way to an ethic of self-fulfillment and personal gratification; and economic growth, once reliant on savings and investment, became increasingly dependent on consumer spending.

It was this effervescent and fluid milieu that immigrants encountered after 1965. The immigrants themselves had new faces, coming increasingly from East and South Asia, the Middle East, and other parts of the world from which previous U.S. laws had restricted immigration. But while earlier immigrants from those regions had entered the United States at a time when they were expected to assimilate to normative American culture and lifestyles, new immigrants—at least the one-in-four who elected to live in the Pacific region—encountered a culture war.

On one side of this war were those who saw being "American" as a matter of conforming to normative institutions and culture and who saw being a "good American" as a matter doing one's duty to country and respecting the authority of tradition. On the other side were those for whom being "American" meant enjoying the freedom to be different, and those for whom being a "good American" could mean criticizing the establishment and challenging authority. Immigrants thus encountered a culture in which categories of normal, mainstream, mainline, establishment, insiders and outsiders captured little about the reality of social life.

For many immigrant groups, particularly religions of the Middle East, that situation began to change at the turn of the twenty-first century. Beginning in the 1980s, social, political, and religious conservatives gained prominence, and among them were several who pointed to what they saw as the fragmentation of American society along lines of race, ethnicity, and religion. Some social scientists attributed social problems, such as out-of-wedlock pregnancy, welfare dependency, crime, drug abuse, and family violence, to the breakdown of moral consensus. Terrorist attacks on American and United Nations targets in the United States and around the world heightened sensitivity about religious diversity in the United States and led to a renewed emphasis on demonstrating loyalty to American society and institutions, and commitment to core American values.

Immigrants were by no means alone in feeling the pressure to demonstrate their "Americanness"—as evidenced by the response to the 2003 comments of the Dixie Chick Natalie Maines—but immigrants certainly felt that pressure more acutely. For many immigrant religious groups, demonstrating their Americanness meant greater participation in public life. Participation in civic ceremonies, public condemnation of attacks on the United States, demonstrations of patriotism, engagement in social service, lobbying for civil rights, and encouraging members to become citizens and vote were some of the ways immigrant religious groups demonstrated that they were being good Americans.

Interestingly, though, what being a good American meant had changed from what it meant a century earlier. To be sure, the holy trinity of Americanism was still there—Democracy, Capitalism, and Religion. But in the Pacific region the faces of religion had changed, being more diverse than ever before; and, to the core American values to which consent was expected of good Americans had been added the value of religious pluralism. American Muslims who sympathized with those that attacked U.S. targets were deemed un-American, but so were conservative Christians who condemned Islam as a false or evil religion. The religious denominations that, for prior generations, strove for sovereignty over the public culture and urged conformity with the "American way of life" were on the decline; the "new players"—both immigrant groups and home-grown innova-tors—assumed diversity of cultural outlooks and lifestyles.

Here a culture developed that raised happiness, self-fulfillment, and personal empowerment to positive religious values. Being different—"expressing one-self"—was becoming a normative way of fitting in; conformity—associated with being "square"—was decidedly out. To some degree, this was true all over the United States, but it was particularly the case in the Pacific region: outsiders were "in," and insiders were "out."

Immigrant Newcomers

One in every four immigrants to the United States lists California as his or her intended place of residence, according to reports by the U.S. Citizenship and Immigration Services, part of the Department of Homeland Security (formerly the U.S. Immigration and Naturalization Service). That proportion has been ris-ing over the past several years. By a wide margin, California has the largest for-eign-born population of any state. According to U.S. Census figures, 26 percent of California's population are foreign-born. By comparison, New York, the next most popular destination for immigrants, has a foreign-born population of about 20 percent. Hawaii (16 percent) and Nevada (15 percent), the other states of the Pacific region, rank with California, New York, and Florida as the five states in which 15 percent or more of the population are foreign born.

Those numbers rise even further in major population centers. In Los Angeles County, for instance, more than one-in-three residents (36 percent) are foreign born. In the northern part of the state, nearly as many residents of Santa Clara County (34 percent) are foreign born. While 18 percent of all Nevada residents are foreign born, 8 percent of Clark County residents are foreign born, mainly because of the magnetic power of Las Vegas.

In 2000, California received immigrants from 85 percent of the world's coun-tries, making the state's population one of the most diverse in the nation. The state hosts particularly large populations of people who trace their origins to Mexico (about 8.5 million in the 2000 census), China (over 900,000), the Philippines (over 900,000), Vietnam (about 450,000), Korea (over 340,000), India (more than 300,000), and Japan (about 280,000).

Impact on the Mainline

How has this affected the region's religious demographics? Clearly, it has meant a growing Latin influence among Christian denominations, recognized in a profound way by the Pope's designation of Mary as the "evangelist of the Americas." It has also meant growing numbers of Buddhists, Muslims, Hindus, Sikhs, Jains, and other adherents of Eastern religions, although this growth has not been as dramatic as one might expect. A national survey of religious identification, the American Religious Identification Survey (ARIS), conducted in 2000, found that Muslims now account for approximately .4 percent of the region's population and members of "Asian" religions—Buddhism, Hinduism, Sikhism, etc.—collectively account for less than 3 percent. By far, then, the diversification of the region's population has had the greatest impact on Catholicism, Protestantism, and Judaism, contributing to what R. Stephen Warner has called the "de-Europeanization" of these religious families.[2]

Catholicism

The reform in U.S. immigration laws in 1965 coincided with a shift in attitudes among Catholic leaders in America toward diversity within the Church. Until the Second Vatican Council, the Church in America laid heavy emphasis on the Americanization of immigrant Catholics. This was due to a number of circumstances, including anti-Catholic sentiment in the American public, the dominance of the Irish in the American Catholic hierarchy, and a general emphasis on cultural conformity in the American public.

This Americanization policy had a detrimental effect on participation by minority Catholics in the Pacific region. Catholic leadership fretted over the poor rates of participation by Latino and Asian Catholics, especially the large numbers of Mexicans and Filipinos in these states. This was not because Mexican and Filipino Catholics were unobservant. In fact, devotionalism was relatively high among these groups. The problem was that the Church did not recognize or support the vernacular piety of these Catholics.

This situation began to change after the reforms of the Second Vatican Council, which, in addition to making the Mass available in vernacular languages, placed greater emphasis on personal devotion and popular piety. It took some time for the Church to adjust, but in 1984 the U.S. Conference of Bishops formally renounced the old Americanization policy, and adopted an outlook more appreciative of the popular Catholicism manifest in these immigrant communities, emphasizing, in fact, that Americans could learn a lot from the Latino emphasis on the family and personal values. More recently, Pope John Paul II's declaration of Mary as the evangelist of the Americas acknowledged the fact that popular devotion to Mary largely accounts for the revitalization of the Church in America, especially among Latino communities.

This new emphasis on popular devotion has, however, brought new challenges for the Church. The Church, while embracing the value of multiculturalism, must now negotiate the demands of increasingly diverse parishes. According to officials in the Los Angeles archdiocese, the Mass is now said in over 50 languages in the Pacific region. A shortage of priests generally, combined with an even greater shortage of priests from minority ethnic groups, has limited the Church's ability to live up to its commitment to diversity. Furthermore, the parish system itself has limited the Church's ability to respond adequately to the demands of different ethnic groups. Unlike Protestants, Catholics cannot simply choose to join or form a congregation composed of members of their own ethnic identity. They are members of a particular parish by virtue of their place of residence, and in an ethnically diverse region, this necessarily means that a small number of priests must attempt to meet the needs of a large number of groups.

In any case, the Church today publicly advocates multiculturalism and presents itself as a model for others in the region.

Protestantism

The degree to which particular Protestant denominations have been affected by immigration varies widely, as does the response of particular denominations to the demands of diversity. It is not possible here to cover patterns in every Protestant denomination present in the Pacific region. A few representative examples illuminate patterns to watch for.

The voluntary, congregational organization of most Protestant denominations makes it possible for immigrant communities to establish independent congregations tailored to their own tastes, customs, and languages. Korean Presbyterian churches are perhaps the most well known example in the Pacific region.

This is a particularly interesting example because Korean Presbyterians are typically more conservative theologically and politically than their American Presbyterian counterparts in the region, and their growing presence has contributed to a conservative shift at both the regional and national level. However, the ethnic distinctiveness of Korean Presbyterian congregations has a cost, in that many second- and third-generation Korean Americans feel alienated in these congregations because they are less proficient in the Korean language and identify more with American than with Korean culture and customs.

Some later-generation Koreans switch to a different congregation, sometimes even to a different denomination. Others have split off into parallel congregations, affiliated with a Korean Presbyterian church but worshiping in a separate location or at a different time. Because differences of opinion over such matters as gender roles and social values attend these separations, such parallel congregations can be the source of tension within Korean Presbyterian churches.

Much has been written about the success of evangelical Protestantism, and Pentecostalism in particular, among Central and South American Latinos. The fruits of these missionary endeavors are coming home to the United States among immigrants. About one-fourth of all Latinos are Protestant, mostly Pentecostal. Although Pentecostal religion has a long and colorful history in California, as noted by Anderson in this volume, adherents to Pentecostal religion have historically been concentrated in the southern states with large black populations. Latino immigrants to California and Nevada in recent decades have contributed to Pentecostal growth in this region.

A third group of immigrant Protestant congregations is spread across several denominations. While small in number, recent immigrants from Africa have a particularly interesting story. Some of these immigrants were, before emigrating to the United States, members of one of several mainline denominations that engaged in missionary activity in Africa. On arriving in the United States, however, these immigrants often find such mainline congregations to be unwelcoming and unfamiliar. Neither do they find a home in the traditionally black denominations because these immigrants do not share or identify with the history and culture of black Americans. More aggressive conservative, Pentecostal, and evangelical churches have had great success recruiting these immigrants into pan-African congregations, some of which also attract Caribbean immigrants and black Americans. Many of these congregations, interestingly, represent missionary endeavors by indigenous African denominations.

It appears that the more conservative, aggressively proselytizing denominations have an advantage when it comes to immigrants. This is probably due to a variety of factors, but a few major influences stand out.

First, many immigrants, while embracing the educational and economic opportunities available in the Pacific states, are suspicious of these states' liberal, "live and let live" culture. They are concerned, especially, about the impact that exposure to MTV, drugs, and what they perceive as loose sexual mores will have on their children. Churches that promote a conservative message may have a unique appeal to immigrant families because these churches offer a strong sense of belonging and moral order in an environment characterized by libertarian, expressive individualism.

Second, mobility typically breaks the social bonds that tie individuals and families to religious communities. This largely accounts for the fact that the Pacific states host one of the most "unchurched" populations in the country. In such a situation, churches that engage in vigorous evangelism will have an advantage, and these churches tend to be theologically conservative. Such churches, in short, may appear to immigrants as islands of stability in a fluid environment. For a variety of reasons, then, the de-Europeanization of Protestant religion appears to favor conservative, evangelical, and Pentecostal churches. With few exceptions, however, immigrant Protestant churches have developed very little public presence. In part, this is due to theology. As noted above, for many immigrant Protestants, the church is seen as safe haven from the perils of a public culture characterized by moral license. In many of these churches, as in conservative Protestant churches generally, individual moral reform, rather than civic action, is seen as the answer to social problems. Immigrant Protestant churches have not, by and large, aligned with the politically engaged Religious Right.

Other features of these churches also help to explain their lack of civic engagement. A study of African immigrant churches in southern California I conducted in 2002-2003 revealed that churches that desire to become civically engaged often lack the financial, social, and human capital to do so.[3] In other words, not only are these congregations struggling financially, they often lack the social connections and know-how required for successful engagement in civic life.

The Korean Protestant churches are an exception in this regard, but this is only a recent development in response to the September 11 terrorist attacks. Todd Perreira, in a study of the civic life of these churches, reported that in the aftermath of September 11, Koreans in southern California donated almost $450,000 to the American Red Cross. It was the first time the Korean community had engaged in such a civic effort. Before then, Korean Protestant churches had directed their resources to supporting other Koreans, both in the United States and Korea. But September 11 occasioned a shift in the Korean-American identity. One of Perriera's informants, an elder at Young Nak Presbyterian Church in Los Angeles, explained, "Frankly . . . before September 11, I am Korean. But after September 11, I'm no longer Korean. I'm an American."[4] That shift in identity led to civic engagement.

Judaism

Immigration has added diversity to the various expressions of Judaism in the region as well. California today hosts the second-largest population of Jews in the world outside Israel (New York has the largest population). Growth in the Pacific region's Jewish population was fueled by the exodus of Jews from the Middle East as Islamic fundamentalism rose to political prominence there. One of the key events, of course, was the 1979 revolution in Iran, which ejected the pro-Western Shah and installed fundamentalist mullahs, led by the Ayatollah Khomeni, to power. Members of the social elite in Iran under the Shah, many of them Persian Jews, arrived in the United States with considerable economic and human capital and gravitated to the warm and wealthy climate of southern California.

Saba Soomekh reports that the economic success of Persian Jews in southern California had the unexpected effect of deterring them from civic involvement until recently. Economic and social self-sufficiency led Iranian Jews in the region to develop what she described as a "ghetto mentality," with little desire to get involved in civic life.[5]

The shift toward greater civic involvement came during the Clinton administration in the 1990s, when their numbers and financial wherewithal made the Persian Jews an appealing target of political overture. Clinton's campaign, and Al Gore's campaign eight years later, emphasized plans to promote peace in Israel. The Iranian Jews began to realize then that local civic involvement could influence affairs elsewhere in the world. In 2003, for the first time, a Persian Jew, Jimmy Delshad, ran for and won a seat on the Beverly Hills City Council, signaling a new era in the civic life of immigrant Jews in the Pacific region.

The Public Presence of the Religious "Others"

Although not as great as might have been expected, given the large numbers of immigrants from the Middle East and from South and East Asia, post-1965 patterns of immigration have resulted in growing numbers of Buddhists, Hindus, Sikhs, and Muslims. Because of the geographic proximity of the West Coast to Asia, and because of the educational and economic opportunities available on the West Coast, growth in these religious traditions in America has been concentrated in the Pacific region. Mosques, Sikh gurdwaras, and Hindu and Buddhist temples are now prominent features of the landscape. And having hardly registered in polls of religious identification for most of the twentieth century, members of these religions represented just over 3 percent of the region's population in 2000. That number may seem small, but in a state with 34 million residents, it represents a sizable population, and numbers in a participatory democracy translate into civic influence.

The ability to influence civic life varies greatly among individual groups, of course. Research on the effect of religious pluralism on civic life in southern California, reported at a recent conference at the University of California Santa Barbara, identified several variables that influence the social capital (i.e., their participation in and ability to influence civic life) of particular religious groups. Clearly, the presence of economic and human capital in these groups influences social capital. That is, groups with greater economic resources and groups whose members are highly educated and informed about civic issues are more likely to get involved than groups that lack those resources. But just as important is the group's ability to mobilize these resources toward collectively agreed upon civic goals. Groups that are characterized by internal dissent have a harder time mobilizing resources than groups characterized by general consensus about civic issues. Additionally, members of the religious group must develop some sense of the connection between their *religious* identity and their *civic* interests. The lack of such a perceived connection between religious and civic interests prevented many groups, not just Persian Jews, from getting civically involved until recently.

Buddhists

California hosts the nation's largest Buddhist population. About 38 percent of all Buddhists in the United States reside there. That is hardly surprising given the history of immigration patterns on the Pacific coast. Chinese and Japanese Buddhists began arriving in the nineteenth century to labor in the region's mines, railroads, farms, and fishing industry. That immigration came to a virtual halt during the early part of the twentieth century as a series of restrictions on the immigration and naturalization of Asians was enacted.

Until 1965, when the country reopened its borders to immigrants from the East, those Buddhist organizations that existed in the region placed a heavy emphasis on the Americanization of members. The Japan-based Jodo Shinshu, probably the largest such organization, offered members English-language classes and even organized Buddhist youth associations modeled after the Y.M.C.A. The Americanization process was further promoted during World War II, when Japanese Americans living in the region were relocated or confined to internment camps. It was in one such internment camp that leaders decided to change the group's name to the Buddhist Churches of America.

After 1965, the organization experienced another challenge, even as it enjoyed an influx of new-immigrant members. The organization's leadership remained very much tied to Japan, most of its priests being trained there. Furthermore, the new immigrants tended to favor the maintenance of distinctively Japanese practices in the organization, which has tended to alienate the more Americanized members. This sense of alienation, combined with an outmarriage rate of around 50 percent, has led to a real crisis of membership.

The 1965 immigration law reforms opened up the possibility of immigration from other Asian countries as well, and this has meant a significant diversification of Buddhism in the region. The Chinese and Japanese Buddhists are today joined by Buddhists from Thailand, Cambodia, Sri Lanka, Burma, Vietnam, Korea, Taiwan, and Tibet, to name but a few of the largest such groups. The tendency among these groups is to establish their own temples, although some, such as the Wat Thai temple in North Hollywood, have attempted to reach a broader public. The result is that virtually every variety of Buddhism in the world is now represented in California.

They are joined, furthermore, by a growing number of American converts, mostly white, educated, and middle-class. It is impossible to say just how many such convert Buddhists there are in the Pacific region, or nationwide for that matter. Some groups, such as the Japan-based Soka Gakkai, have become predominately American-convert Buddhist movements. Several major Buddhist groups see themselves as having a mission to spread the Dharma in the United States, but there is considerable disagreement among these groups over how best to do that and over how American "American Buddhism" can be while remaining authentically Buddhist.

While "Engaged Buddhism" was not invented in the Pacific region, it has certainly found a home there. In fact, in our study of conversion to Soka Gakkai Buddhism, Phillip Hammond and I found that, while this Buddhist organization's involvement in environmental protection and nuclear disarmament was not what initially attracted people to the religion, these activities were certainly among the reasons they stayed.[6]

Socially engaged Buddhism can take many forms, but running through them all is the notion that the dharma can be an instrument for social change. Of particular importance is the message of Thich Nhat Hanh, a Vietnamese Buddhist teacher whose books are widely read. As explained by the scholar of American Buddhism Richard Hughes Seager, Thich Nhat Hanh emphasizes that "social peace begins with the cultivation of inner peace by individuals. Meditation, chanting the gathas, and other simple ritual practices are all means for the cultivation of love, harmony, and mindfulness, not in order to retreat from the world but as preparation for a deep and thorough engagement with it."[7]

The Buddhist Peace Fellowship, based in San Francisco, began as an attempt by Robert Aitken, Gary Snyder, and Joanna Macy to integrate Buddhist meditation practices with their social activism. Begun in the late 1970s, the Buddhist Peace Fellowship is now a transnational organization that responds to social problems around the world by providing medical services, refugee relief, and by advocating nuclear disarmament.

Hindus

Perhaps more than for any other religious group, the maintenance of Hinduism among immigrants from India has required considerable innovation. That is because religion is so much a part of the mainstream culture and everyday life in India. There, religious shrines dot the landscape, priests are readily available, monks are ubiquitous, and the institution of *samskara* (rites of passage performed over the course of the individual's life) tends to orient the individual lifecycle toward sacred duties and virtuous living. Hinduism is very much a part of the institutional complex in which everyday life is lived.

This is clearly not the case in the United States, where religion tends to be set apart from everyday life. In the United States, worshipers are not able to simply drop by the temple in the course of their everyday activities. Consequently, much religious activity has been moved toward the weekend, and this has meant larger numbers of worshipers gathering at once, rather than individuals coming by at their leisure. Unlike temples in India, therefore, U.S. temples tend to include gathering halls and kitchens, which are used for a variety of religious and cultural events.

Innovation has also been spurred by the fact of the linguistic, cultural, and religious diversity of immigrants from India. Religion in India is a diverse conglomeration of regional cultures, each with distinctive variations of ritual, doctrine, and festival. In the United States, there are generally not a sufficient number of immigrants from a particular region in any one locality to establish separate temples, although that is beginning to change as larger numbers of Indian immigrants arrive. For the most part, the temples that have been established are more ecumenical in spirit, housing several deities rather than only one, as would be the case in India.

Such innovations have, ironically, led to a concern about authenticity, which is reflected in temple architecture. The Shree Venkatsewara Swami Temple in the Malibu hills, for instance, was built by traditionally trained craftsmen brought from India. And plans for building new temples have become the subject of transnational conversation over the Internet.

The ability to import craftsmen and traditional building materials such as marble and granite associated with particular temple sites in India is a luxury that could not be afforded by most immigrant groups. Indian immigrants have been described as perhaps the most successful immigrant group in the country, and with good reason. Many of these immigrants are highly educated professionals who immigrated to the United States in search of better career opportunities than were available in India. Since U.S. immigration laws favored highly skilled individuals and those with private financial resources, these immigrants have done exceedingly well in the United States. Barry Kosmin and Seymour Lachmann report that Hindus are among the most successful religious groups in the nation, as measured by educational attainment, employment, and income.[8]

Although one expects, because education and professional occupation are positively associated with voting, that Hindus participate in the electoral process, they do not appear to have made a link between religious identity and civic action. This may be due to their religious beliefs. One member of the Vedanta Society of West Hollywood explained to me in an interview about Hindu's involvement in interfaith activities that Hindus would not be motivated to civic activism by a desire to right an injustice because, to them, the world "*is* just."

Sikhs

There are really two stories about Sikhs in the Pacific region. The first concerns the very tight-knit, rural, agricultural Sikh communities of northern California; the second, the more recently formed urban professional Sikh communities.

Sikhs began to immigrate to the Pacific region in the early part of the twentieth century, when drought conditions in their Punjabi homeland drove many young Sikh men elsewhere in search of economic opportunity. Despite discrimination in California, those who settled there became very successful agriculturalists. The experience of discrimination, coupled with the Sikh emphasis on community, led these immigrants to form very close communities, often pooling resources in order to advance themselves economically. When U.S. immigration laws began to change in the 1940s, but especially after the 1965 immigration law reforms, these northern California Sikh communities grew, and as they grew they also expanded their efforts into industries associated with agriculture—selling farm implements and agricultural supplies.

Because these early Sikh communities were composed mostly of men and because they focused their efforts on economic success, religion tended to fall by the wayside. In order to avoid discrimination, many of these men stopped wearing the traditional headdress and symbolic dagger that signify initiation. The new wave of immigration, therefore, tended to have a revitalizing effect on the practice of Sikh religion in these communities. The newer immigrants tended to emphasize orthodoxy and orthopraxis, and the old immigrants gradually reclaimed these for themselves as well.

However, recent Sikh immigrants tend to be more scattered across urban environments and are less socially cohesive than the earlier groups. In yet another ironic twist, while these newer immigrant Sikhs stimulated a revival of orthodoxy and orthopraxis among their predecessors in the United States, they also began to emphasize the many ways traditional Sikh values and beliefs cohere with American democratic values, especially as urban professionals in the Sikh community became generally more assimilated into the mainstream society.

This is expressed in a profound way on a poster available from Sikhnet.com, entitled "American Sikh Warrior Defending Freedom." The poster features a very traditional image of a Sikh warrior astride his horse in front of an American flag. A flyer about Sikh Americans produced after September 11 features photographs of Sikh leaders with President Bush and a Sikh child holding an American flag. It reads, in part, "The Sikh faith teaches us the humanitarian principles of freedom, equality, and justice —the same principles this great democracy is founded on."

Muslims

Circumstances of history have created unique challenges for Muslims in the United States. As a religious movement among urban black Americans during the Civil Rights Movement, Islam in America developed an image as militantly anti-establishment. Although African-American Muslims later turned toward a more orthodox understanding of Islam, the image stuck. In the minds of many

NEW PLAYERS AND NEW PATTERNS

Americans, that image was reinforced by political-religious movements in post-colonial societies of North Africa, the Middle East, and South Asia that began in the second half of the twentieth century and continue to the present.

The unconventional but highly dramatic tactics of some of the most militant of these movements, generally described as "terrorist," have led in the minds of many Americans to an association of Islam with violence and hatred of the United States. While most Americans associate Buddhism with the Dalai Lama, and Hinduism with Ghandi, they associate Islam with Osama bin Laden. Muslims in the United States are consequently very image-conscious, and they have gone to great lengths to promote a more positive image.

In California, the Islamic Center of Southern California, the Council on American-Islamic Relations, and the Muslim American Society work not only to propagate Islam but also to establish positive public relations. The Web site for the Muslim American Society of Southern California, for instance, emphasizes such values as "brotherhood, equality, justice, mercy, compassion, and peace"—genuine Muslim values expressed in terms drawn from the lexicon of American civil culture. The mission statement of the Council on American-Islamic Relations makes its purpose explicit: "to promote a positive image of Islam and Muslims in America." These organizations have well-developed public relations machinery and regularly issue press releases addressing a wide variety of local, national, and international events and issues. Muslim leaders are also involved in the many different interfaith associations active in the Pacific region.

Historical circumstances propelled Muslims in the region into the civic arena. When the Federal Building in Oklahoma City was bombed in 1995 and public suspicion automatically fell on Muslim radicals, American Muslims realized they had a public relations problem. Muslim organizations soon became involved in not only promoting a positive image of Islam in America, but also in advocating civil rights. More recently, civil rights activism among American Muslims has been fueled by responses to the September 11 attacks by Muslim extremists on American targets. Muslim-American organizations were quick not only to condemn the attacks but also to call attention to the spate of hate crimes against people of Middle-Eastern heritage in the United States.

But Muslim civic activism has not only been motivated by self interest. Muslims in the Pacific region have interpreted the third pillar of Islam, the duty to give alms, as a civic religious duty. One particularly notable and creative expression of this is the University Muslim Medical Association Clinic in South-Central Los Angeles.

The clinic was founded in 1996 in response to the medical needs of the population in this poor neighborhood and to try and improve relationships between immigrant Muslims and black Americans in the aftermath of the 1992 riots. The two UCLA students who founded the clinic initially envisioned a medical trailer that would drive through the city offering blood pressure exams and other minor services. But the students' project came to the attention of a Los Angeles City Councilwoman, who helped them obtain a grant from federal housing authorities to renovate an abandoned building on Florence Avenue. The city itself ponied up a grant to cover the cost of operations for the first four years.

When, in the fall of 2000, the clinic faced closure because of a funding shortage, a story by Theresa Watanabe in *The Los Angeles Times* stimulated a surge of Muslim philanthropy. Within days, Watanabe reported, donations of more than $284,000 came in, enough to keep the clinic open for another year. Today, it serves thousands of patients every year and is the only free medical clinic in South-Central Los Angeles. The clinic has served as a model for similar charitable efforts by Muslims across the country. Such activities are sincere, but also strategic in that they attempt to counter widespread stereotypes about Islam and to promote an image of Muslims as desirable friends, neighbors, colleagues, and citizens.

As in all large religious groups in the region, there is considerable variation among Muslims, mosques, and Islamic organizations in attitudes about American culture, society, and politics. Some emphasize adherence to Islamic traditions associated with their own ethnic culture. Others place the emphasis on Americanness, and argue that Islam is a universal religion not bound to any particular ethnicity, nationality, or political ideology. Although there has not been an Islamic "Reformation," the difference between these two perspectives resembles that between Catholic and Protestant Christians. The former tend to be more tradition-oriented, place more emphasis on orthodoxy and orthopraxis, and are generally less willing to compromise with American mainstream culture and institutions. The latter tend to emphasize knowledge of the Quran, personal conscientious judgment in matters of faith and morality, and generally adopt a more accommodative stance toward mainstream culture and institutions.

On the whole, Muslims in the Pacific region have been very successful in negotiating a positive public identity. Dramatic evidence of this came in the aftermath of the attacks on U.S. targets on September 11, 2001. To be sure, there were repercussions, as hate crimes against people and religions from the Middle East increased, and the U.S. government began detaining Muslims and scrutinizing the activities of mosques and Islamic benevolent societies.

However, at the same time, Americans of all different faiths were carefully scrutinizing the behavior of the U.S. government toward Muslims and perhaps their own feelings about their Muslim friends, colleagues, and neighbors. Muslims in the region responded by speaking out against violence, keeping track of hate crimes against Muslims, and forming alliances with other religious leaders to advocate for the rights of Muslims in the United States. The participation of Muslim leaders in interfaith memorials and public appearances with political officials dramatized the fact that most Muslims in the region condemned the violence, supported U.S. efforts to combat terrorism, and grieved for those whose lives were lost. There were certainly negative consequences of the September 11 attacks for Muslims, but in some ways events in the aftermath of those attacks demonstrated just how well established Muslims in the region had become.

Organizational Innovation

Robert Wuthnow's suspicion that the United States is moving toward a post-denominational era is certainly true in the Pacific region.[9] If denominationalism relies on relatively stable and enduring social ties, religious organizations in the Pacific region that are growing are those that emphasize the forming of community out of erstwhile autonomous individuals. Additionally, whereas the mainline denominations, as mentioned earlier in this chapter, were associated with conformity to a normative American culture, the post-denominational or "new paradigm" churches represent different ways of adapting to cultural diversity.

Niche Churches

One very effective way that religious organizations can attract members and promote involvement is to capitalize on mutual interests. Some such organizations become highly specialized to a particular interest group, giving rise to what I am here calling "niche churches." The most common such niches are based on ethnicity and lifestyle.

Ethnic congregations are nothing new on the American scene, of course. However, earlier immigrant communities tended to settle in geographically defined locales, and the ethnic congregation—be it Protestant, Catholic, Jewish, Sikh or other—was often a defining feature of the ethnic neighborhood. Today's immigrants, by contrast, especially in the Pacific region, tend to be more geographically dispersed. While some immigrant groups still settle primarily in geographically defined enclaves, the trend is toward settlement in ethnically mixed suburbs. What distinguishes today's ethnic niche congregations from earlier ethnic neighborhood congregations is the assumption of mobility, the assumption that members will have to drive, sometimes considerable distances, in order to partake. This has the effect of eroding the religion-ethnicity tie, making both relatively more voluntary and expressive of individual priorities.

More innovative than these ethnic congregations are what might be called "lifestyle congregations." Here what ties the congregants together is not ethnicity but lifestyle choices. The most obvious examples are the growing number of gay and lesbian religious organizations. Melissa Wilcox has identified at least four types of gay and lesbian religious organizations, all of which can be observed in the Pacific region:

1) Internal groups, such as Integrity (Episcopalian), Affirmation (Latter-day Saints), and Dignity (Catholic), take the form of support groups within normatively heterosexual religions

2) Exit groups, such as Common Bond (Jehovah's Witnesses), are designed to support gay and lesbian people who have left organizations that are hostile to homosexuals

3) Safe space groups, such as the Universal Fellowship of Metropolitan Community Churches, "provide support, community, and religious services within a wholly or mostly (lesbian, gay, bisexual, transgender) LGBT congregation"

4) Alternative space groups, such as Dianic Wicca and the Radical Faeries, represent wholly innovative forms of gay and lesbian spirituality.[10]

Some nondenominational evangelical churches also fall into the category of lifestyle churches. Rock Harbor church, a megachurch in Costa Mesa, California, for instance, has been described as a "Gen X" church because of its upbeat style of worship and appeal to a younger, hipper generational constituency. More common are nondenominational "community" churches. Here, the lifestyle emphasis is usually not community, so much as family, as these churches tend to appeal mainly to young adults who are marrying and starting families. In addition to worship services, such churches may offer a variety of activities that mimic those of a traditional extended family: camping trips, basketball games, and so on. In keeping with these observations, one surmises that it is the desire for membership in a supportive community that draws young families to these congregations.

Niche organizations come in a variety of forms and sizes, but all share the tendency to opt for particularity over catholicity, or universality. Instead of trying to meet the needs of the entire population, whether defined by neighborhood, community, or nation, these churches target their services to a particular market niche defined by ethnicity or lifestyle choices.

Multicongregational Churches

Discussions about "pluralism" and "multiculturalism" suggest a desire by diverse groups to share civic space. But some religious groups find themselves sharing sacred space as well. Much of the Pacific region is densely populated, and religious diversity is concentrated in the most heavily populated areas. Space for religious activity is therefore at a premium. Because of movement to the suburbs and declining adherence to the mainline Protestant churches, many once-prominent neighborhood churches find themselves tethered to large urban edifices that are often both expensive to maintain and underutilized. One solution to the problem is the multicongregational church.

Multicongregational churches are those in which more than one faith group worship under the same roof. A Lutheran church in Anaheim, for instance, also houses an Ethiopian evangelical congregation. Even more dramatic is the case of the Irvine United Church of Christ, whose sanctuary is also used by Jewish and Muslim congregations. Such space-sharing decreases the costs to individual congregations of maintaining a place of worship, but also tends to promote a spirit of religious civility.

Different social forces have given rise to a variation on the multi-congregational church, the parallel congregation. The term "parallel congregation" was coined by Paul Numrich to describe small groups of American converts to Buddhism who study with monks at the Theravadan temples he studied.[11] Although studying Buddhism with monks at the temples, these American converts did not participate in the cultural life of the temples' immigrant communities, giving rise to two distinct congregations that interacted little with each other.

Such parallel congregations are not unique to Buddhist organizations; they can be found in many religious organizations in the Pacific region. Typically, parallel congregations form along either generational or ethnic lines. In immigrant religious organizations, for instance, such parallel congregations may form when second- and third-generation Americans stop identifying with the ethnic traditions emphasized by the organization's immigrant founders, or stop speaking the native tongue well enough to participate meaningfully in worship services. The development of separate services for the more Americanized members expresses a desire to maintain a religious-ethnic identity in an environment where, as we have seen, powerful forces tend to disrupt it. The opposite pattern also applies. When an existing American congregation experiences a sudden influx of new-immigrant members, they may begin to offer separate services tailored to the needs and demands of the immigrant group(s). Parallel congregations may also form along lines of theology. The obvious example is that of charismatic Catholics, who often hold services independent of the regular Mass.

Finally, multi-ethnic churches merit mention here as a further subtype. The typical pattern in such churches is to create separate services for separate constituencies. This is the predominant strategy employed by multi-ethnic Catholic parishes. Some, however, strive to bring the diverse constituencies together for worship, encouraging all to share in celebrating the ethnic traditions of particular constituencies. More often than not, this means holding services in English, but emphasizing the ethnic traditions—costume, music, etc.—of particular constituencies on a revolving basis.

Megachurches

At the opposite end of the spectrum from the niche church is the "megachurch." If the niche church emphasizes particularity, the megachurch strives for catholicity, attempting to serve large numbers of diverse people. A megachurch is generally defined as a church with more than 2,000 members. Although that number is clearly arbitrary, it suggests the defining feature of these churches: size. While megachurches are found throughout the United States, they are especially prominent in the Pacific region. The Hartford Institute for Religion Research, which maintains a thorough list of megachurches in the United States, records 125 megachurches in California, four in Nevada, and four in Hawaii.[12]

Although there is considerable variance in the degree of internal diversity in megachurches, in most it is theology rather than ethnicity or lifestyle that ties the congregation together. For the most part, these churches are nondenominational, evangelical, and Pentecostal, emphasizing lively worship that often incorporates sophisticated multi-media devices. More interesting is the fact that many of these churches are multi-ethnic and deliberately work to form bonds of spiritual community that cross lines of race, class, and ethnicity. Thus, the cultural diversity of congregants is another way of emphasizing the universality of these churches' theology.

Conclusion

Membership in a religious organization and participation in collective forms of worship, we know from decades of sociological study, are sustained by enduring social ties—to family, friends, neighborhoods, and communities. Mobility, one of the dominant forces shaping the Pacific region's religious culture, disrupts those ties. In a region where, according to U.S. Census data, about half of the population moves at least once in five years, it is hardly surprising to find that "new players" (i.e., those religious groups that appear up and coming) are those religious organizations that emphasize the formation of networks of interpersonal support, whether among recent immigrants or among the highly mobile American-born portion of the region's population.

In such an environment, old ideas about religious insiders and outsiders, religious establishments and marginal religious groups, indeed "new" and "old," make little sense. This makes the region perhaps uniquely hospitable to religious newcomers, whether imported from another nation or representing an innovation from within. Pluralism thus defines the public culture here in much the way that Mormonism defines public culture in Utah or Baptist religion defines public culture in the southern states.

Endnotes

1. *Modern American Religion, Volume 2: The Noise of Conflict, 1919-1941* (Berkeley: University of California Press, 1991).

2. "Approaching religious diversity: Barriers, byways, and beginnings," *Sociology of Religion* 59 (1998): 193-216.

3. David W. Machacek, "Prayer warriors: African immigrant religions," presented at the Religious Pluralism in Southern California Conference, University of California Santa Barbara (May 10, 2003), http://www.religion. ucsb.edu/projects/newpluralism/PrayerWarriors.doc.

4. "From Confucian Korea to Protestant America: Negotiating status and identity in the city of angels," presented at the American Academy of Religion (November, 2002), http://www.religion.ucsb.edu/projects/newpluralism/ConfucianKorea.doc.

5. "Tehrangeles: Capital, culture, and faith," presented at the Religious Pluralism in Southern California Conference, University of California Santa Barbara (May 10, 2003), http://www.religion.ucsb.edu/projects/newpluralism/tehrangeles.doc.

6. Phillip E. Hammond and David W. Machacek, *Soka Gakkai in America: Accommodation and Conversion* (Oxford: Oxford University Press, 1999).

7. *Buddhism in America* (New York: Columbia University Press, 1999), 203.

8. Barry A. Kosmin and Seymour P. Lachman, *One Nation Under God: Religion in Contemporary American Society* (New York: Harmony Books, 1993), 258-60.

9. *The Restructuring of American Religion: Society and Faith since World War II* (Princeton, NJ: Princeton University Press, 1988).

10. "Innovation in exile: Religion and spirituality in lesbian, gay, bisexual, and transgender communities," in David W. Machacek and Melissa M. Wilcox (ed.), *Sexuality and the World's Religions* (Santa Barbara, CA: ABC-CLIO, 2003), 232-57.

11. *Old Wisdom in the New World: Americanization in Two Immigrant Theravada Buddhist Temples* (Knoxville: University of Tennessee Press, 1996), 63ff.

12. http://hirr.hartsem.edu/org/faith_megachurches.html.

CHAPTER FOUR

THE INFLUENCE OF ALTERNATIVE RELIGIONS

Tamar Frankiel

The Pacific Region and New Age Spirituality

In January 2003, the front cover of *Whole Life Times* out of Malibu, California, blazoned the headline "Prayer and Politics." The accompanying friendly photograph was of Marianne Williamson, a spiritual teacher and resident of California for many years (she now lives in Detroit). Author of three *New York Times* bestsellers and a number of other books, she began purveying prayers of consolation and encouragement in her *Illuminata* books in the mid-1990s. She wrote widely on the principles of the popular "Course in Miracles," which energized the spiritual side of the self-improvement movement during the 1980s and 1990s. In *A Return to Love* and *Enchanted Love* she explained the Course in Miracles further by developing a "mystical" perspective on interpersonal relationships. In the late 1990s, however, she turned to politics, writing *The Healing of America,* followed by a new improved version, *Healing the Soul of America,* published in 2000.

Williamson's political books, advocating a citizen's democracy to further liberal policies, have not been as popular as her personalist works. Nevertheless she continues, as in the *Whole Life Times* interview, to push her new agenda. In this respect, Williamson can point to some important dimensions of religion in public life in the Pacific region.[1]

First, many people, especially in California, continue to move beyond traditional religious affiliations (Christian, Jewish) into non-institutional teachings and practices comparable to the Course in Miracles and popularly called "spirituality."

Second, most of the new groups and teachings focus on personal development and relationships.

Third, some practitioners of alternative spirituality want to translate their work into public life, but they generally have a great deal of difficulty doing so.

Historical Perspectives

This twenty-first century phenomenon has deep roots in California and Nevada history. California was built with relatively little input from the highly politicized Puritan religious streak of New England or the more genteel Episcopalian influence of the Southeast. Ever since Anglos arrived in California in the Gold Rush years, it has been a home for alternative religions and anti-institutionalism.[2] Not only the Roman Catholic population (Latino and immigrant Irish and Italian) but also Chinese, Jews, sectarians such as Seventh-day Adventists, and secularists all resisted mainline Protestant domination.

The fate of institutional Protestantism is perhaps represented by California's most popular nineteenth-century religious figure, the Unitarian minister Thomas Starr King. He stirred Californians to support the North during the Civil War; yet he was remembered in later generations not for his politics but for his inspirational sermons, expressing a transcendental Unitarian philosophy deeply influenced by Emerson. The history of nineteenth-century religion in the region suggests that Californians cared little for institutional religion, and even less for religious institutions' involvement in politics. Nevertheless, religious interest did not die; it just changed.

The predominant changes throughout the twentieth century were in the direction of a highly personal, individualistic approach to religion and an insistence on tolerance of others' views, even the very unusual. Much of the Pacific region's population developed an acceptance of shifting memberships and even mixing religions eclectically. One could belong to a mainstream church and also dabble in Christian Science, at least until one's minister found out. Eccentrics like George Wharton James, who preached Methodist warmth combined with Native-American ceremonies, commanded a considerable following on the lecture circuit in the early decades of the twentieth century. In the same period, Eastern religions entered California with a message for the Anglo elite and found highly receptive audiences (a development that must be distinguished from Asian immigrants practicing their religions). After World War II, California was inundated by a wave of "new religions," and by the 1970s California had become almost synonymous with unusual "cults."

California did go through a period of greater conservatism in religion in the 1920s-1950s. During that period, the southern part of the state—from Los Angeles to San Diego, and inland to San Bernadino and Fresno—grew in population and dominance, with the new arrivals coming from the Midwest and South and bringing more conservative, even fundamentalist, attitudes. Today, the Inland Empire and Central Valley of California remain similar to the rural heartlands of the United States in religious viewpoint. But tolerance and pluralism are still the watchwords everywhere, personalist approaches to religion have become enormously important, and "cults" continue to emerge. Unfortunately, it is very difficult to get reliable statistical information about how such influences affect public life. Many people adopt alternative religious approaches—for example, personal spiritual transformation or Eastern forms of meditation—without actually joining permanent organizations. They may still belong to traditional groups within Christianity or Judaism, or they may report themselves as "unaffiliated" in the U.S. Census or other polls. Even if they report an affiliation, they may be recorded as "other." The situation is a little better for some non-Western traditions; there are now statistics for Bah'ai, Zoroastrian, Buddhist, Hindu, Taoist, Sikh, and Jain memberships. But these probably represent only the tip of an iceberg.

Yet the spiritually inclined, even when unaffiliated, clearly have had a formative influence on the region's religious culture.[3] Is it also possible that alternative religions are affecting people's public participation and attitudes on matters of politics and public concern? This chapter explores what can be known from the statistics available, and what can be reasonably guessed at from current developments, as reported in the media.

The Data

For the purposes of this chapter, data on alternative spirituality consist of those who are unaffiliated—that is, they apparently have no religious connection—and those who report themselves members of an "Eastern religion." Looking at the maps of California and Nevada in the North American Religion Atlas (NARA) with those categories in mind, some interesting patterns emerge.[4]

The number of unaffiliated in California is particularly large, ranging from 29 percent in the most religious county (San Benito, a small county with a 44 percent Latino population), to 80.8 percent in the least religious (Calaveras, in the old mining district made famous by Mark Twain's "Jumping Frog" story). Only one county, in Nevada (Storey), has a higher percentage of unaffiliated, a whopping 93.1 percent. Rural southern California tends to have higher percentages of affiliation than the north, a product both of a larger Latino population and a greater influence of conservative Christians. Rates in urban areas range from 32.4 percent unaffiliated in Los Angeles and 42.7 percent in San Francisco to 49.5 percent in San Diego and 56.1 percent in Sacramento counties.

California may differ from other states in that many of its rural counties in the northern and mountain areas show a very large percentage of unaffiliated. These are not heavily populated areas; some are forest and farmland (Trinity, Shasta, Lassen, Modoc, and Butte), while many are the old mining areas in the foothills of the Sierras (El Dorado, Amador, Calaveras, Madera, Mono). These regions show a *minimum* of

69 percent of the population either unaffiliated or uncounted. The statistics reflect Californians' famed independence and anti-institutionalism in matters of religion. Because of their relatively small population—perhaps 500,000 altogether—they have relatively little overt political impact. However, as seen later in the section on nature religion, they do draw attention for environmental concerns, especially related to the logging and fishing industries on which many inhabitants are dependent. In the past, some of the more "religious" environmentalists like Earth First! have drawn a following here, but there is no consistent pattern of adherence to such groups.

Overall, in 23 of California's 58 counties, 60 percent or more of the population are unaffiliated; in another 15 the unaffiliated range between 50 percent and 59.9 percent of the population, notably higher than the Pacific region's average and more like that of the Pacific Northwest. Unfortunately, it is difficult to say more because the generality of the data does not permit the "other and unaffiliated" to be categorized in definitive terms.

Patterns of affiliation with Eastern religions are more revealing. Theoretically, these would include Hindu, Buddhist, Jain, Sikh, and Taoist groups at a minimum, but the best supported interpretive data among non-immigrants is from Buddhist groups. While the overall percentage of the California and Nevada populations belonging to these religions is only about 3 percent, the county-by-county data show some fascinating patterns. In nine counties, over 10 percent of the population report that they adhere to an Eastern religion, while a tenth county records 8.9 percent. This is certainly enough to be a "swing vote," or at least to have an impact on public policy.

A few of these counties have high populations of East Asian immigrants. Connections to the native country may not always be reflected in "Eastern" religious adherence, however, since many Asian immigrant communities have a high population of Christians. A good example of where immigration is a significant factor is the Yuba City area of agricultural Sutter County, north of Sacramento. The city has one of the largest Punjabi (East Indian) communities in the United States, as well as an old and respected Chinese community. The 2000 U.S. Census identified 11.3 percent of the 77,000 population as Asian in "race." This certainly contributes to the remarkable 16.6 percent of the population who are adherents to an Eastern religion, the state's second highest rate.

Still, a high percentage of Asian nationality is not necessarily a predictor of religious affiliation. San Francisco County, for example, boasts a 30.8 percent Asian population, but only a 13.1 percent adherence to Eastern religions; Alameda County (which includes Oakland and environs) is 20.4 percent Asian, but has only 8.9 percent Eastern religious affiliation; Contra Costa, just to the north, has 11 percent Asian and 3.9 percent in Eastern religions.

Figure 4.1   Eastern Religion Adherents in 11 Counties (NARA)

County	% Asian population	% Eastern religious adherence
Lake	0.8	4.1
Marin	4.5	10.8
Mendocino	1.2	13.0
Napa	3.0	7.1
Nevada	0.8	13.2
Santa Cruz	3.4	14.8
Siskiyou	1.2	11.3
Sonoma	3.1	5.1
Sutter	11.3	16.6
Trinity	0.5	19.6
Tuolumne	0.7	4.9

These data suggest that what might help most in trying to identify the potential influence of Eastern religions on public life is locating areas where the percentage of adherence to Eastern religions is above the state average of 3 percent and also significantly exceeds the percentage of Asian-heritage population. **Figure 4.1** shows the 11 counties that meet these criteria:

Sutter County, because of its large Asian population, should probably be considered a special case, as it is possible that its non-Asian adherents may be either married into or culturally affected by the presence of traditional Asian communities, either Punjabi or Chinese.

Marin, Sonoma, and Mendocino counties occupy a band along the California coast, beginning just north of San Francisco's Golden Gate Bridge and extending halfway to the Oregon border. Lake and Napa are smaller counties bordering those three on their inland sides. The five counties together appear to be the center of non-Asian adherence to Eastern religions in California, particularly Buddhism. Institutionally, several important centers are located there. Tibetan and Chinese Buddhist organizations own land and operate retreat centers in Mendocino County.[5] In Marin, Spirit Rock Meditation Center is a well-known retreat center for American Vipassana Buddhism.[6] A sixth county, Santa Cruz, lying south of the San Francisco peninsula along the coast, is culturally similar as a home to religious and cultural alternatives.

Siskiyou and Trinity counties are neighbors in the far north of the state. Mt. Shasta, an important base of alternative religion for the last 70 years, is in Siskiyou County. This is also an important area for environmental activism.

These two counties, along with the five mentioned earlier, also have high percentages of religiously unaffiliated.

Nevada County is near Reno, Nevada, but its neighbors, Sierra and Placer counties, do not have its level of Eastern-religion adherents. Tuolumne similarly stands alone among neighboring counties. This leads to suspicion that these areas must have special attractions for adherents of Eastern religions; indeed, that is the case. Grass Valley in Nevada County is the home of one of the branches of Shambhala, an international community that has built a network of more than 165 Tibetan Buddhist meditation centers worldwide.[7] Tuolumne County, advertised as the "gateway to Yosemite," hosts a Soto Zen Buddhist Sangha for laypeople as well as a family-oriented Buddhist community known as "Acorn Sangha," which is affiliated with an eclectic group of Buddhist groups known as the Unitarian-Universalist Buddhist Fellowship. These two would certainly help account for the higher-than-usual percentage of Eastern-religion adherents, especially in counties with small overall population (Tuolumne 55,000; Nevada 94,000).

A number of these counties—particularly Marin and Santa Cruz—are regarded as "ultra-liberal" politically and ultra-permissive culturally. Certainly on the political side, Marin, Sonoma, and Santa Cruz, which have the largest population and the most voters in the counties being considered here, voted on the liberal side in the presidential election of 2000, according to State of California data.[8] The Democratic candidate, Al Gore, received between 59.6 percent and 64.3 percent of the total vote, well above the statewide average of 53.5 percent. Napa, Mendocino, and Lake, all of which have a more sizable rural population and a smaller population overall, were more in line with the state average (48.4-54.4 percent). But all six counties voted higher than the state average of 3.9 percent for Ralph Nader, the Green Party candidate, between 4.8 percent (Napa) and an astounding 14.7 percent (Mendocino). Marin and Sonoma gave him 6.8 percent and 7.3 percent of the vote, respectively, while Santa Cruz voters for Nader represented 10.1 percent of the county's total. The three largest of these counties gave Bush and Buchanan, the two most conservative candidates, only 29.4 percent to 32.5 percent of their vote. The California 2000 voting data thus support the notion that these coastal counties are "ultra-liberal." The inland/mountain counties (Siskiyou, Trinity, Nevada, Tuolumne), with their small and largely rural populations, went strongly for Bush, but even they voted more for Nader than the state average, from 4.0 percent in Tuolumne to 6.9 percent in Nevada County.

In public life, this suggests a strong correlation between a significant population of Eastern-religion adherents and liberal politics. Hypothetically, those two characteristics may be associated with cultural permissiveness as well. Marin County was accused of just this when one of its young people, John Walker Lindh, was captured in Afghanistan in 2001, apparently fighting for the Taliban regime.[9] Marin residents generally found it difficult to comprehend how one of their own could have grown up to become a radical, anti-American Muslim. Besides cultural permissiveness, another explanation might be the increasing tendency of liberals to be harsh critics of American foreign policy. Another illuminating perspective on the issue comes from a woman interviewed by the *Christian Science Monitor*, who said she had consciously avoided the news about Walker because she was trying to stay "on a higher plane."[10] It is worth pondering whether a strongly spiritual orientation might lead ultimately to either an apathetic attitude to politics, or to a superficial approach to social issues because of an unwillingness to set aside time to study such issues in depth.

The data suggest two foci for investigation: a large number of unaffiliated, who might be practicing alternative religiosity and may be relatively removed from politics, and a possible "swing vote" population in certain areas, who may be Buddhist or of other backgrounds, but politically are known to support Green Party or other liberal causes.

Personalism: The Route to Health, Happiness, and Creativity

The unaffiliated who practice no religion but consider themselves "spiritual" are truly an uncounted force in Pacific-region religious life. Most of them seem to practice what I call "personalism," a Marianne Williamson-type of approach to religion and spirituality that focuses on personal improvement, variously termed self-discovery, self-development, self-actualization, or manifestation of the higher self. Because it is highly individualistic, this religious practice seems at first glance unlikely to affect public life. But does that first glance convey the correct impression?

The direction of personalistic religion in the early days was established by Christian Science, New Thought, and Religious Science, all of which had strong bases in California even though they originated elsewhere. The anarchistic tendencies of the entire "positive thinking" movement inevitably led to a proliferation of organizations that promised health, wealth, and happiness if one only followed their program. By the 1960s, however, this movement was modified by the growth of a "therapeutic culture" in California, due to the increasing use of psychiatrists and psychotherapists. This grew by leaps and bounds over the next several decades. This culture was clearly not based in any religious orientation and, in most of its manifestations such as Rogerian, Gestalt psychology, or the more 'alternative' approach of R. D. Laing, was not even spiritual. One might have expected psychology to replace religion completely were it not for several new developments.

Scientology and the Science of Religiosity

In the 1950s, L. Ron Hubbard, a science fiction writer, founded what came to be the Church of Scientology. Inventing a unique technical language to describe psychological processes, Hubbard produced a theory of humanity and its evolution into higher states of being. He designed methods, the best-known being "auditing," for each individual to become a "clear."

Through a hierarchical series of rather expensive classes, tightly controlled by the church, a person can achieve a higher level of evolution for himself. The church was harshly criticized for its secrecy and its ability to accumulate large sums of money that it claimed were not taxable. After many years of dispute with the IRS, Scientology reached a settlement in 1993, as a result of which about 150 churches in the United States were allowed to practice as non-profit ecclesiastical organizations. Most important for our purposes is that Scientology pioneered the idea of a specific set of techniques to achieve what were described as spiritual goals. This became a prototype for other movements.

In the 1960s Werner Earhart developed another technology, known as EST and delivered in seminar form, which was oriented toward empowering individuals but was not religious in orientation. (Its methods might be regarded as similar to neuro-linguistic programming, or NLP, except that EST used disorienting and challenging approaches to startle the individual out of complacency.) EST was the predecessor of other seminar trainings that increasingly emphasized "personal transformation," such as Forum, Landmark, and Avatar. The last-mentioned, drawing on a specifically religious term from Hinduism, suggests the direction of the programs. As one becomes more advanced, one comes to believe in the potential of humans to be free creators, activating a "divine" aspect of the self.

Recovery and Spirituality

Another factor was the enormous growth of 12-step programs between the mid-1960s and the end of the twentieth century. Founded in the 1930s as an approach to alcoholism, the 12-step method and system of support groups came to be used for a variety of programs to conquer intractable problems of addiction and develop a mentally healthy approach to life. Because the 12 steps emphasize both healing and spiritual teachings (including practices like "inventory," which are clearly related to confession), the programs provide a framework through which people who want to overcome addictions can incorporate religious (or "spiritual") practices as well. Unlike the psychologically based seminar model, 12-step programs emphasize humility, service, and a regular practice of prayer or meditation to develop a relationship with a "Higher Power" (which could be understood as God). Many people who have gone through a 12-step program have re-affiliated or strengthened their connection with traditional churches, but many also began alternative practices such as Eastern meditation or found their way into other supportive spiritual programs.

Mysticism in Daily Life

In the 1970s, the Course in Miracles became widely known, as a foundation was established to support and spread the teachings. The original material was claimed to be "channeled" or dictated by a "Voice" to a formerly secular psychologist, Helen Schucman, a professor of medical psychology at Columbia University. Despite some dissension within the movement, the foundation eventually evolved into an institute and teaching center, which by 2000 was located in Temecula, south of Los Angeles.

It was presented as Christian in a loose sense, with the Holy Spirit and Jesus as central figures. The Course never abandoned its Christian background, but the later teaching center sees itself as inspired by Plato's Academy. The teachings, studied and practiced on an individual basis, are regarded as the foundation for a life of love, forgiveness, peace, healing, and "miracles" in daily living. The course, presented almost entirely through texts and workbooks, was perhaps the most personal and least institutional program of any described. Unlike 12-step programs or self-improvement seminars, the Course does not require group meetings. It does require self-discipline to study, pray, and meditate, and eventually to integrate the teachings into daily life, to become a "normal mystic."[11]

In Judaism, the Jewish Renewal movement offers a similar approach, emphasizing Hasidic teachings to bring mysticism into ordinary life. (This movement must be distinguished from Orthodox Hasidism, which also had a considerable impact on late-twentieth-century Judaism.) Jewish Renewal began on the East Coast, in large centers of Jewish population in Boston, Philadelphia, and Washington, D.C. However, it became well known in California too, especially through the Aquarian Minyan in Berkeley, founded in the mid-1970s.

Other mystically informed Jewish movements sprouted in the 1990s, particularly Metivta in West Los Angeles, emphasizing meditation and spiritual counseling, and Chochmat HaLev in Marin County, north of San Francisco. More communal in nature than the Course in Miracles approach, Jewish Renewal emphasizes celebration in worship and the development of a personal relationship with God through mystical study and practice. Probably more than any other form of Judaism, the movement emphasizes concern for physical and emotional healing, even creating special healing services. This is undoubtedly related to the therapeutic culture and recent interest in alternative medicine, both of which are prominent in California.

These and many similar approaches to teaching "spirituality" are extraordinary forces in Pacific-region culture today. Collectively they have created an entire language for relationships and for describing spiritual growth. They insist on the divine potential, "spirit," "spark," or "higher self" within each person. They require a considerable commitment to a spiritual discipline, in return offering a support system. Some, like Scientology, require considerable financial resources; others, like the 12-step programs, operate on the basis of small contributions with a tremendous volunteer effort. They all provide means of orienting a person to what might be called the "big picture"—a spiritualized cosmos, a Higher Power, or a Divine Creator—and teach that this force is at work in everyone's personal life. They suggest means of connecting to, and in some cases becoming adept in using, this force. Perhaps most surprisingly, they market traditional techniques of confession and forgiveness in quite new forms, enabling practitioners to leave their old lives and start anew.

Conscious Living and Activism

There seems to be no question that the practitioners of all these forms of spirituality—and there are many other variations—attest to major changes in their attitudes toward life and, in many cases, actual changes they believe they could not have otherwise made—in relationships, financial matters, family matters, health, or career. The question at hand, however, is whether and to what extent their personal changes affect public life.

When one looks at the activities sponsored by most of these movements, it becomes clear that most of the members' energy goes directly back into the movement itself. Of the examples discussed here, only 12-step programs encourage participants also to support a church, synagogue, or mosque of their choice. Most, like Scientology, Kabbalah Center, and Avatar, urge individuals to become group leaders within the religion. (This is not necessarily a negative—so did early Methodism.) But aside from some high-profile members such as the film star Tom Cruise (a Scientologist) or the singer Madonna (an adherent of the Kabbalah Center), there is little public activism.

Some of these movements do include social-service programs. Scientology in particular seems to have worked to develop such programs. A great deal of its members' effort goes into drug-addiction programs, because Scientology claims that its religious program helps addicts. In 1996, the organization sponsored a program in which its members contributed more than 60,000 hours of work to the Los Angeles County Department of Children and Family Services, particularly in helping foster children. A presidential commendation stated that the Scientologists' effort gave "energy and dedication to provide solutions to the many problems that government alone cannot fix . . . , inspiring all who seek to improve our world." Scientology thus promotes an old American tradition of volunteerism in a way that captures the emphasis on the personalistic, combined with some social but not political concern:

> Although the primary emphasis of Scientology remains on bettering
> the individual, on bringing him to greater heights of spiritual aware-

ness, the long-range aim has always been the same—a civilization without insanity, without criminals and without war, where the able can prosper and honest beings can have rights, and where man is free to rise to greater heights. And so, as the numbers of Scientologists continue to grow, so, too, is their presence increasingly felt as a vital force in the community.[12]

What kinds of changes might practitioners of personalist spirituality and "greater heights of spiritual awareness" make in their lives that might have an indirect impact on public life? It is possible to gain some insight by turning to what may be the best snapshot of contemporary California spirituality available, a popular annual event known as the Conscious Living Exposition. The most recent such conference occurred in February, 2003, in Los Angeles, where participants were treated to a variety of seminars on such topics as animal rights, animal communication, vegan eating, alternative medicine, mercury in food and water, forgiveness, relationships (many spoke on this subject, as it was Valentine's Day weekend), tantric yoga, crop circles and UFOs, near-death experiences, getting messages from the "other side" [of death], messages from "Spirit," and healing prayer.

The seminars about animal communications and animal rights are at least partly political, and fall under the discussion of nature religion and environmentalism, as does the seminar on mercury in the water. These could clearly lead to political activism. Most of the seminars, however—15 out of 22, not counting entertainment events—dealt with strictly personal issues such as healing, yoga, and unusual spiritual experiences. Four had explicitly to do with political issues: the animal rights presentation, Marianne Williamson speaking on spiritual struggles and current events, Arianna Huffington discussing "conscious politics," and Michael Lerner stressing peace activism. Williamson has already been discussed. Huffington is well known in southern California as a conservative-turned-liberal, with no particular spiritual message. Lerner has a definite religious orientation in traditional Judaism, influenced by Jewish Renewal; he edits a political and literary magazine based in northern California. All of these were explicitly liberal presenters and presumably, like most of the seminar leaders, "preaching to the choir." This suggests that in the swirl of California's personalistic spirituality, there is indeed a political bias: a gentle liberal activism.

That personalism comes out on the side of liberalism is interesting. Theoretically, if one believes in personal change facilitated by minimal institutional interference, one might adopt a strong libertarian or conservative ideology—a counterpart to the evangelical right but with a different religious message. Personalism could also be simply in political default, promoting political apathy and allowing secular positions to override religious preferences. Certainly California is not filled with politically dedicated activists: fewer than half of eligible California voters went to the polls in 2000, despite a highly contested election.

Nevertheless, the Conscious Living Expo suggests that apathy is not the only result of personalism. Proponents of personalism sit easily with prominent left-wing liberals at conferences, as though those liberals represent the social con-science of "conscious living." In this light, it is interesting that California was the only state to go strongly Democratic in the 2002 mid-term elections. Could this reflect the indirect influence of personalism? It could also be that the high Nader vote in 2000, following Nader's proclamation that "there's no difference between Gore and Bush," registered among other things a protest vote against politics as a complex institutional battlefield. Under an ideology that the self-development of the individual is the goal as well as the means to social harmony, conflict-filled political realities and competing interest groups, even in the Democratic Party, may go against the personalist grain.

Buddhism

In the late 1960s, representatives of Eastern religions began to teach more widely in the United States. Prominent figures led major organizations in California: the San Francisco Zen Center (Buddhist), the Self-Realization Fellowship (Hindu) in southern California, and the Hindu-based movement at Ojai featuring Krishnamurti (all of which were established long before the 1960s). Since the 1980s, the "Free Tibet" movement has attracted many political liberals and has exposed thousands to messages from the exiled Dalai Lama.

Buddhism in its classic forms was both a cosmic statement and a personal path. The world as we know it is full of illusions; we are full of craving and desire, spending our lives to achieve things that are illusory and transitory. Our ignorant craving causes us all to suffer; the world continues through countless eons like this. The only path out of suffering is the struggle to see clearly the true reality of existence, the arising and passing-away of everything. When one reaches that clarity of insight, known as enlightenment, one also will have compassion for all beings, even the smallest, who continue to suffer.

In its Indian origins, Buddhism was one of several sixth-century BCE protests against Brahmin Hinduism. After several centuries, however, Buddhism essen-tially died out in India (which had developed other philosophies of liberation) and planted itself securely in Southeast Asia, Tibet, China, and eventually Japan. Although some Buddhist influences may have reached western Europe occasion-ally, Buddhism did not become widely known in Europe or the United States until the nineteenth century, and then only among an elite. In the 1960s, however, its message of seeing clearly through the illusoriness of existence reached many who had become, during the era of the Civil Rights Movement and the Vietnam War, quite disillusioned with government and society (of course, it is possible these movements may be related only coincidentally, not causally). The message of inner peace reflected a deep hope for external peace as well.

Yet the primary effort of Buddhist practice is inner work; its external effects emerge from living one's own life on a moral basis. There are few if any prescriptions for political or large social projects; compassion, the primary social virtue, can take many forms. Buddhist leaders tend to offer ethical but not political positions. For example, at the height of anti-war protests preceding the 2003 Iraq War, thousands of people received an e-mail proclaiming the position of "His Holiness the Dalai Lama's views on war and [the] Iraq conflict":

> War, or . . . organized fighting, is something that came with the development of human civilization. It seems to have become part and parcel of human history or human temperament. [Yet] . . . we have seen that we cannot solve human problems by fighting. Problems resulting from differences in opinion must be resolved through the gradual process of dialogue. Undoubtedly, wars produce victors and losers; but only temporarily. Victory or defeat resulting from wars cannot be long-lasting . . . War . . . should be relegated to the dustbin of history.
>
> . . . But what can we do? What can we do when big powers have already made up their minds? All we can do is to pray for a gradual end to the tradition of wars.
>
> The real losers will be the poor and defenseless, ones who are completely innocent, and those who lead a hand-to-mouth existence. On the positive side, we now have people volunteer medical care, aid, and other humanitarian assistance in war-torn regions. This is a heart-winning development of the modern age.
>
> Okay, now, let us pray that there be no war at all, if possible. However, if a war does break out, let us pray that there be a minimum of bloodshed and hardship. I don't know whether our prayers will be of any practical help. But this is all we can do for the moment.[13]

The Dalai Lama proposes no political action, either for his immediate audiences in Dharmsala or for others around the world; not protests, letters to government officials, or stances on either side. He does not admit to the possibility of benefit, either in terms of social liberation from tyranny or ridding a country of weapons, as viable goals of war. Rather, war is presented as an unfortunate problem in human evolution. Moreover, he sets forth clearly that the big powers are making the decisions, and that only in the long term will the need and desire for war be erased. If one can offer humanitarian help, this is good (but he does not insist his followers do so). Prayer is the main thing—"all we can do for the moment."

This suggests that Buddhism, like the personalistic forms of alternative spirituality, may not serve as a direct force in public life. Still, by inculcating in its followers compassionate and tolerant attitudes, it may indirectly contribute to the shaping of public opinion tendencies. Because of compassion for "the poor and defenseless," the direction is likely to be liberal-Democratic.

Nature Religion and Sacred Ecology

Despite personalism's anti-institutional tendencies, the strong showing of the Green Party in the 2002 elections in many California counties, including several with strong Eastern-religion affiliations, suggests one possible avenue of connection between alternative religiosity and public life: concern for the environment. Since John Muir's efforts around the turn of the twentieth century, Californians have taken nature and conservation very seriously. Although Muir himself felt that his spiritual bonds with nature were an important part of his motivation to preserve Yosemite and other wilderness sites, most of his successors, from the Sierra Club to legislative lobbies, have been secular. A change occurred in the 1980s, when some groups tried to give environmental concerns a spiritual foundation, particularly in organizations like Earth First!, in neo-paganism, and in some movements led or inspired by Native Americans. This movement is multi-dimensional, however, and not all organizations that seem nature oriented are politically active.

Saving the Forests

In California, one of the most important movements was begun by Julia "Butterfly" Hill's two-year camping on top of an ancient redwood tree (1997-1998), in protest against logging of old wood. Not only did she engage many people in further protest and other forms of environmental activism, she gave voice to a spirituality underlying the movement, institutionalized in her Circle of Life Foundation dedicated to continue saving forests. Hill's father was an itinerant preacher, and she spent her youth living in trailers. She began her spiritual journey after a devastating automobile accident. In her "Butterfly's Tale," she wrote the following, stressing her spiritual approach to the environment:

> The first time I entered into a redwood forest—it was Grizzly Creek—I dropped to my knees and began crying because the spirit of the forest just gripped me. The knowledge, the spirituality, the power that has no words, that power that makes your hair stand on end, see? the power that gives you goosebumps even to remember. When I entered what I call the majestic cathedral of the redwoods, the spirituality of the holiest of holy temples which are these forests, dropped me to my knees because trying to rationalize what happens in these forests intelligently doesn't work.[14]

The very personal sense of the holiness of nature harks back to Muir, and it has energized many Californians whose religious affiliation may be otherwise nonexistent. Their efforts, however, do not go into religious institution building because their "church" is nature itself. Rather, they work on influencing public opinion and the legislative process.

More recently, environmental activists have tried to attract support from religious organizations, recognizing perhaps that the earth is not an object of worship for most Californians. For example, the Trees Foundation, a secular environmental organization based in Arcata, California, was formed in 1991 as a means of networking among various environmental activists. They supported not only Julia Hill but also David "Gypsy" Chain, killed while attempting to halt illegal logging, and other activists. Now the organization promotes cooperation with religious groups.

A publication by the group featured an article on the Religious Campaign for Forest Conservation, supported by a wide range of religious groups, including Christian evangelicals and Pentecostals, Jews, Roman Catholics, and Greek Orthodox. In cooperation with the National Forest Protection Alliance (NFPA), based in Montana, the religious campaign has sponsored formal briefings of Congressional staff on the issue of forest protection on federal land. They emphasize that forest conservation is a religious mandate for our times and argue the moral and ethical reasons for saving our nation's public forests. For example, they use readily available data to point out that the current level of logging in national forests is unsustainable, and that proceeds from logging do not remain in the local community, but are concentrated in large metropolitan areas where the timber companies maintain offices. They also argue from poll data, trying to convince Congressmen that 70 percent of Americans support an end to commercial logging on the public's forests, but large campaign contributions from the timber industry have overridden public sentiment.[15]

Animal Rights

Another significant California movement that is spiritually based in part is the animal-rights movement. This movement promotes vegetarianism, protests against medical experimentation on animals, and expresses concern for how animals are treated on farms, in shelters, and at zoos. Its organizers recognize explicitly that most of its supporters are outside the mainstream traditions of Judaism and Christianity, and for them secular-humanistic and scientific reasons to be in favor of animal rights are sufficient. Some are anti-religious because of the long history of religious animal sacrifice (which continues in groups like Santeria). On the other hand, some are seeking more support within churches.[16] Those who do base their animal-rights advocacy in spiritual beliefs generally emphasize compassion as a universal virtue and the reality of feelings and certain levels of consciousness in animals.

Animal-rights movements are strong in Europe as well as in the United States, and California does not stand out among states with an unusual proportion of animal-rights advocates relative to its large population. The country's largest animal-rights organization, People for the Ethical Treatment of Animals (PETA), is headquartered in Norfolk, Virginia; the Great Ape Project begun by Peter Singer, designed to establish legal rights for non-human primates, has its offices in Portland, Oregon. However, California activists have been successful in affecting environmental laws by allying with other conservation groups.

The Endangered Species Act, for example, enabled animal-rights advocates in 1991 to gain protection for a 30-square-mile area of habitat for an endangered kangaroo rat. Whales and whaling have also been important causes for more than two decades. A small but important Farm Sanctuary run by Gene & Lorri Bauston exists in the area of Orland in northern California (they also administer a sanctuary in upstate New York), which not only rescues neglected animals and campaigns against farm abuses, but also sponsors conferences and promotes a vegan lifestyle. Most recently, they began a "Sentient Beings Campaign," whose honorary chairperson is the television star Mary Tyler Moore.[17]

Neo-Paganism

Other religious attitudes related to the land and environment have emerged in neo-pagan religions. In many places in the United States and Europe one can find popularizers of Celtic, Druid, old European, and "witchcraft" traditions as options for moderns. The most active in pro-environmental causes are some Druid organizations, which emphasize planting "sacred groves" of trees, among other conservation activities. Perhaps surprisingly, Druidism has not taken a strong hold in the Pacific region.

The most prominent neo-pagan movement in California is Wicca, a revived name for witchcraft. Wicca sprouted in England in the late nineteenth century, but attracted attention in the post-1970 era when its female members openly called themselves "witches" who practiced "magick" and criticized Christianity, Judaism, and modern culture. Like Druids, Wiccans promote an intense ritual life and religious teachings that honor a "natural" approach to religion, with celebrations tuned to the natural seasons and usually named after old English ceremonies such as Beltane (May Day). Wicca has been more deeply influenced by radical feminism than some other neo-pagan movements. Goddesses borrowed from many religions predominate in the ceremonies, and certain female mystics, like Hildegard of Bingen, are "saints." Wiccan teachings among California groups range from Tarot and astrology to herbalism. They even affiliate, on occasion, with Unitarian-Universalist fellowships.

It is difficult to assess the membership or impact of this movement in the Pacific region. Wiccan groups span the nation and the globe, but are quite small in terms of actual membership; California, according to one widely accessed Wiccan Web site, has the largest reported affiliation (surpassing England and Michigan), but still has fewer than 2,000 members. In public, their influence seems even smaller, except on the occasions when one of their rituals attracts attention or they make a public protest. Despite their predilection for nature-based ceremonies, they have not been an important influence in the environmental movement. In California, their focus is primarily on creating small, supportive communities ("covens") and, increasingly, on family life.

Sacred Sites

A fourth way in which the environment receives attention in California and Nevada is through the ritual appropriation of "sacred space." Throughout the region's alternative religious movements, one finds strong interest in "sacred sites," often ones that were used or remembered by Native Americans. Perhaps the most prominent is Mt. Shasta in Siskiyou County. On one of the county's Web sites, one finds an astrologer and a psychic advertising tours of the mountain's sacred sites. The psychic, known simply as Ashalyn, offers a committee of colleagues to enhance one's visit to Shasta, including "philosophical counseling with Alexander, animal communication and healing with Kahanna, . . . lifeforce balancing and rejuvenation retreats with Shahan, [and] angelic healings and angel readings with Rayleen," while Ashalyn herself provides "soul communications and guided vision quests."[18] This kind of program is similar to many others, most of which claim great spiritual benefits. One guide and teacher, a former nurse from France, conveys an alternative spiritual message in language that is typical of these groups:

> Journeys to sacred sites offer us these deeply impacting moments by radiating specific frequencies that activate the memories of our spiritual nature and our connection with all life. When one embarks on a spiritual pilgrimage, what can be experienced by the heart in a sacred moment can help expand our consciousness, accelerate our spiritual growth, heal the past, and change the course of our future. During a guided spiritual pilgrimage, mother earth will embrace us and open the doorways to higher levels of awareness.

Besides her training as a nurse, Josiane Antoinette claims authority by her shaman-grandmother in Corsica and her own near-death experience. As a result, she founded the Bernadette Foundation and now offers her clients clairvoyant readings, afterlife/funerals, and sacred ceremonies connected with tours of Shasta.[19]

The Shasta tours are an example of how sacred-site religiosity becomes a purveyor of personalism. Another example is Ojai, near Santa Barbara in southern California. Ojai was immortalized in Frank Capra's classic 1937 film *Lost Horizon*, where he used the site to represent the lost Tibetan paradise, "Shangri-La." Native Americans of the region, known as the Chumash, called the Ojai Valley the Valley of the Moon and believed that it was a gateway to the land of spirits.[20] It was chosen by Annie Besant as the headquarters of her branch of the Theosophical Society, and she brought Krishnamurti there as a child to train him to be the world's messiah, a job he later declined. Numerous retreat centers and camps have been established in the area, whether for strictly recreational or more spiritual purposes. Most of these would be manifestations of personalism, whether sacred or secular.

Ojai has also become significant, however, as the center of many environmental movements. Recently, according to Martin Jones Westlin in the *Ventura County Reporter*,[21] it has become the headquarters of a group called the Rainbow Ark Foundation, established by Heather Foxhall, a former theater and healing-arts specialist, "to create a global culture of peace and healing of the earth." The group began holding conferences in 1998, emphasizing the use of media, including theater, film, and journalism, to further the movement. Foxhall says this is not ordinary pacifism, but part of "sacred ecology, . . . the idea that all life is interconnected" and that all are citizens of the planet. Well-known members of her "Global Wisdom Council" include the oceanographer Jean-Michel Cousteau and two grandsons of Nelson Mandela.

Environmentalists at another ancient sacred site, Lake Tahoe, have established a cooperative educational and research program with activists working in the Lake Baikal watershed in Russia and Mongolia. (Lake Baikal is the world's largest and deepest fresh-water lake.) The Tahoe-Baikal Institute organizes projects on such matters as reintroduction of native species, industry in stream environment zones, erosion, and forest health. However, its associates are not merely scientific or political in orientation. A recent leadership conference in Russia spent three days studying Buddhist and indigenous views on the preservation of sensitive lands and found many similarities between the relationship the Buryats, on the eastern shore of Lake Baikal, have with their sacred lake and that of the Washoe with Lake Tahoe (to be considered further in the section on Native Americans). In addition, members of the institute have served as the chair of the "Light of Sacred Lands" program at the Sacred Earth Network (Amherst, Massachusetts), putting them in the forefront of the "sacred ecology" movement.[22] This institute and its projects are quite remarkable in scope and awareness, both ecological and spiritual, and—because of the enormous value of the comparative enterprise—have the potential to become a model for other such international projects.

The Future: Apocalyptic Scenarios

Another source of attitudes toward public life well represented in California is predictors of the future. They are quite prolific: even in *California Journal,* a promotional magazine, an astrologer promised to "anticipate Gray Davis' next step." This authority predicted that in January 2003 the Governor would focus on agriculture, in February on transportation, and in March on education. One learns less about Davis and more about California, that it would even jokingly print a sidebar about astrology.

There are, however, serious religious futurists. These are not the utopians of old who raved about the "California Dream," but rather apocalypticists of a new order. Almost any follower of the California spiritual scene can tell you about the Mayan prophecy that the present world will come to an end in 2012. He or she often will add that ancient traditions from all over the world predict that our current time is one of great turmoil and transformation. We will look at one of these "prophetic" figures below.

Futurism in Film

Apocalypse is probably best known in Hollywood. In the 1990s, several significant films appeared with apocalyptic imagery and themes. Perhaps *Independence Day,* a 1996 film portraying the threat of an alien civilization from outer space, marks the beginning of this recent era. There, earthlings managed to overcome their disunity to fight off the invaders just in time (as also in *Deep Impact* and *Armageddon,* both released in 1998). However, there were no explicitly spiritual or religious themes in these films.

The very popular 1997 film *Contact* was different. While also presenting the alien civilization as a possible threat, it opened up discussion of the existence of God and the role of science. Significantly, *Contact* ridiculed traditional Christian apocalypticism as the work of fanatics, while extolling scientists with their faith in humanity over both religion and politics, which operated by generating fear. As Conrad Ostwalt has pointed out in his discussion of apocalyptic films, the alien contact in this film is "benign, fatherly, even divine-like to the secular, scientific mind where God is functionally absent."[23] In contrast, the lesser-known *Postman* (1997) portrayed the redemptive rebuilding of civilization after a devastating war, led by a messianic figure who epitomized many traditional religious values.

A different angle appeared in a 1999 blockbuster movie, *Matrix.* A brave-new-world type story, the film invoked religious language of "Zion" and kabbalistic allusions, while naming the hero/messiah "Neo," explicitly chosen as the "One" who would fight the overwhelming power of the computer, which had enslaved nearly everyone. As Ostwalt observes, Neo was one of the strongest messiah figures in contemporary apocalyptic movies, and he added martial arts expertise and mind control to his skills, "bringing an eastern religious element into the picture."[24]

The theme of technology out of control (or controlled by evil people) is not new, of course, going back to *2001: A Space Odyssey* and even further, to *Frankenstein*. The threat of nuclear annihilation preoccupied secular apocalyptics in the 1960s, but there are many other fears, such as global warming or vicious viruses (*Waterworld* and *Outbreak*, both 1995), that not infrequently replace it. In film, *Minority Report* also portrayed the dangers of the tyranny of the majority, while *The Truman Show* suggested social control by the media itself, in the form of a television show that entraps a man in a totally controlled virtual reality.

Ostwalt agrees with Daniel Wojcik that apocalypticism is rampant in American society,[25] and thus Hollywood has a good market to sell such ideas in various forms. It is not merely a Pacific region phenomenon, nor is it present only in marginal religious groups. Nevertheless, when Christian or Jewish religious apocalypse are marginalized, as they certainly are in the Pacific region, the media, centered in Hollywood, take on the responsibility for what Ostwalt calls "dealing with issues like human finitude. . . . Particularly with the development of realistic and sophisticated special effects, the ability to portray massive destruction and virtual realities on the screen has grown and added fuel to the creative element of artists who want to revive the apocalyptic form."[26] This means that a major industry of southern California, employing artists and technicians on a massive scale, can market not only ordinary sex and violence, but also promulgate ideas and fears that can permeate the everyday life and conversation of multitudes in the region.

However, we would be ill-advised to portray Hollywood as overly afflicted with apocalypticism. Other alternative religious themes appear in film, and they tend to support personalism rather than social or cosmic disaster. Angels, life after death, and the enduring quality of relationships were probably just as common in spiritually based films as was apocalyptic during the 1980s and 1990s. Self-discovery in the context of the common good was also an important theme in several 1990s films, like the surprise hit produced by the young independent filmmakers Ben Affleck and Matt Damon, *Goodwill Hunting* (1997).

Real-Life Prophets

Yet, while apocalypticism is sometimes merely a "what if?" horror story or the stage for a hero myth, there is significant support in the alternative religious communities for self-proclaimed prophets. One of the most dramatic of these purveyors is Sean David Morton, who appeared at the Conscious Living Expo as a speaker on the "Exodus Generation." While he has been publishing a newsletter under the name Delphi Associates since 1993, he gained fame (or notoriety) for claiming to reveal the secrets of "Area 51," a site in the Nevada desert where some believe the American government was covering up evidence of extra-terrestrial contact. He has received media publicity since at least 1997 as an accurate predictor of events, and was interviewed on a national radio show, Coast-to-Coast, as recently as September 2002.[27] Although a number of critics have claimed he fabricated his predictions, what is significant for our purposes is that such individuals can gain considerable following.

Morton claims to be an "Earth sensitive," able to make accurate predictions of the future, although most of the so-called predictions could be garnered from current newspaper opinion sections or from other new-age writers. For example, writing from his base in Hermosa Beach in the "California Republic," he portrays the coming decade as one of terrorism, heralded by the World Trade Center attacks on September 11, 2001. Those were "harsh lessons in the effects of globalization with regards to technique, target and motivation," while the WTC itself was a "literal Tower of Babel, constructed in SHIN-AR, or BUSH-LAND, with 65 nations represented among the 3,014 victims." He "foresees" the eventual triumph of globalization, producing a "Monoculture" modeled on American lifestyles. This world culture will be ruled by a brutal centralized power, a "corporate global plantation," in which any protesters will be labeled terrorists. Yet, says Morton, a different force will also emerge:

> A gigantic surge in psychic energy will manifest worldwide in people who have natural ESP ability or have been working with intuitive and esoteric matters. A truly wireless global network without the need for computers or cell phones will begin to materialize. A truly planetary mind will begin to take shape as we experience a network of connected brain patterns strung across the world. The Internet, pagers, cell phones and satellite and cable TV have been just the kindergarten for what is to come![28]

In short, the good guys will rise up to battle the bad guys, just as in a Hollywood apocalyptic film (it is worth noting that one of Morton's career ventures was as a screenwriter—perhaps parallel to L. Ron Hubbard's being a science fiction writer before founding Scientology).

Morton's practical contribution is to offer courses in "Spiritual Remote Viewing" techniques, which help students become "sensitives" and even have prophetic experiences. Eventually this will, he claims, create a web of minds that will also be enhanced by computer chips and nanotechnology. He warns those who do not attune to their higher selves, as well as become open to herbal treatments and spiritual healing, that they will die in viral plagues that will hit the world between 2004 and 2006, killing perhaps 1 billion people.

According to Morton, not only will the Middle East be fragmented and virtu-ally disempowered by multiple wars, astronomical and geological events will also change the face of the earth. One must simply be ready for massive change and prepared to join the "heroes" and "angels." Of course Morton offers teach-ings in meditation and special initiations at a significant price.[29]

It is difficult to see enterprises like Morton's as more than an attempt by the capitalist spirit to cash in on the apocalyptic spirit. Yet, while Morton may be an extreme example because of his tendency to be over-dramatic, many such prophetic figures continue to attract attention in the region. The main import of such predictions is to create anxiety, largely by repeating slogans about global-ization, big business, and technology. Such apocalypticism encourages no action to make public impact. On the contrary, even more than the Hollywood writers, it espouses a fatalistic, "save yourself" attitude. In this respect, it too collapses into the personalism that characterizes so much of the Pacific region's alternative religiosity.

Native-American Issues in Public Life

Although Native Americans in the Pacific region make up a small percentage of the population compared to that of the Southwest, they do wield significant influence in certain areas. Most familiar since the 1970s are claims to tribal land. Since most tribes long ago lost the lands they inhabited before Spanish and Anglo conquest, their first major efforts in the 1970s were to reclaim sacred land, whether burial sites, natural sites of tribal significance, or archeological sites.

This has been an important cause in California because the consciousness of Native-American history and religion plays an important part in alternative spirituality in the Pacific region. Education in the state, even down to the pri-mary grades, has made students aware of the moral problems raised by Native-American history. In 2000, a film called *American Holocaust: When It's All Over, I'll Still Be Indian* appeared to tell the natives' story. It was nominated for an Oscar and, although it did not receive wide distribution, was featured at the 2003 Conscious Living Expo. The term "holocaust," with its evocation of the horrors of extermination of Jews in World War II, was certainly intended to awaken the American conscience, as well as to draw attention to the continu-ing problems of Native-American life. This is an important background for any consideration of Native-American issues.

Tribal Land: Sacred or Recreational

The issue of reclaiming land is exemplified by debates concerning the Lake Tahoe area. Much of this land, once sacred to the Washoe and other tribes, has long ago fallen victim to intense commercial (including tourist) and residential development. Efforts of the local tribes to regain control of what remains have met resistance. For example, as David B. Parker reported in the *Reno Gazette-Journal*, the U.S. Forest Service in December 2002 proposed to help the tribe by restricting climbing on Cave Rock, an ancient sacred site that, before Anglo contact, was so holy it was used only by shamans.[30] Climbers, picnickers, and other recreational users protested the Forest Service action, insisting that Cave Rock was public land, not a "church."

On the other hand, the Paiute have been able to preserve much of the Pyramid Lake area, where their ancestors fought off Anglo settlers, because their ownership was eventually recognized by the government. Yet they too come in conflict with those who want to use it for recreation. Because they do not believe in fencing off the land, they do not want to keep whites out entirely, but extensive vehicle use has damaged places like Sand Mountain and Needle Rocks. In some cases, the tribe works with recreational groups to devise ways to keep the sites in good condition. In others, like Needle Rock, the tribe has restricted access to tribe members alone. They have so far kept the whole area free of casinos.

Tribal Survival, Economics, and Politics

The casino issue has become a major issue in Native-American politics and what might be called anti-spirituality. Since the 1990s, many Native-American communities have tried to establish their tribal identity and their access to some piece of land, however small, because this gives them special rights. Indian tribes are, by act of Congress, treated as sovereign nations. If they have a reservation, the land is under their control and they are not subject to federal or state sovereignty, or taxation. This was intended to make it possible for them to establish commercial or industrial activities that would return all their profits to the tribe, as a kind of implicit reparation for the occupation of native land by Americans. However, most of the existing reservations are poor in resources. In California the industry that has brought the greatest income to Native-American communities is gambling.

The gambling industry is not, of course, directly connected to Native-American religious practices. It is merely an economic mechanism that arose due to several unique factors. First, many Native Americans wished to maintain a distinct community on whatever portion was left of their land. This is the primary religious and communal bond that generated the initial situation: people simply did not wish to leave. That meant, however, that they would have to create a niche in the American economy either by farming or by manufacturing and trade. Neither of these turned out to be viable—farming because of the poor lands given to Native-American communities, manufacturing due to lack of capital. Many Native Americans did try to earn a living through trade in traditional arts and crafts, but these home-based businesses did not have a dependable market and their growth was inherently limited.

Gambling turned out to be an economic area in which Native-American communities could compete, first because it required low capitalization—essentially only enough money to rent a small location, buy machines, and pay employees. With the increasing investment of Californians in travel and entertainment (including to Las Vegas and Reno/Lake Tahoe), it could attract a wider segment of the population. The special laws concerning Indian tribes enabled a lucrative business to be created with little regulation. At the same time, non-Native communities did not wish to get involved in gambling, for moral and social reasons, so there was little competition. In California, the industry became essentially a Native-American monopoly (this was not true in Nevada). For once, Native-American communities had a real and dependable source of income.

Any industry protects its own turf. Many states sought to regulate the gambling industry and, in California, Native Americans worked to ensure that regulation be as light as possible. In addition to negotiating agreements that allowed tribes largely to regulate themselves, they supported candidates who were willing to follow a hands-off policy as far as state government agencies were concerned. A considerable portion of tribal revenues went into campaigns for various legislative propositions as well as for specific candidates. Fred Dickey reported in the *Los Angeles Times* magazine that by 2003 the "Indian lobby," as it had come to be called, was the largest single contributor to state candidates and ballot initiatives, having given $122.6 million over the previous five years.[31]

The general live-and-let-live attitude of Californians toward Native Americans, indeed their sympathy for Native-American causes, allowed casinos to grow enormously during the 1990s. However, as the economy turned sour in 2001, questions arose as to agreements that had been made with the tribes. They were allowed to self regulate like sovereign governments, free from taxation. Even though they could collect California state sales and hotel taxes from customers, the state had no way of retrieving the funds from tribes. At the same time they were permitted to contribute to campaigns, which other sovereign governments are not allowed to do.

The agreements negotiated in 2000 between Governor Gray Davis and 61 tribes seemed wholly to favor the tribes and gained the state nothing. "Governor Dances-With-Donors," Steve Lopez called him in the *Los Angeles Times* of January 17, 2003, noting with anger the tribes' generosity to the Davis campaign fund, to the tune of just under $1 million. Critics claimed that no one was monitoring or even examining consumer complaints regarding tribal casinos. Some have charged that casinos are being built carelessly because their owners, the tribes, are free even from environmental protection laws—ironically, since Native Americans supposedly cherish the land. Meanwhile, as Dickey has reported, more Native-American communities are trying to gain federal status so they can operate casinos, to swap their own land for sites closer to cities, and to build casinos on tiny Native-American sites (for example, a reservation whose total size is six acres). A number of tribes who were not part of the original agreements are seeking inclusion, and legal questions have been raised about some of those efforts.

When tribal agreements were renegotiated in the spring of 2003, with the state government under pressure to get more money from tribes, the outcome was unclear. However, the negative publicity surrounding the issue has shifted Californians' perceptions of Native Americans, raising new questions about their influence on public affairs. For decades, other Californians have seen them as a downtrodden minority, seeking only to honor their ancestral past and to make a living with dignity. Although that view was partly mythical—for all communities contain individuals of various temperaments and inclinations—some now perceive a more sinister element governing the economic life of thousands of Native Americans. It is estimated that only abut 10 percent of Californians of Native-American descent (36,000 out of 333,000 total) receive income from the casinos, but it is clear that some Indians—and some tribes—are becoming wealthy while many remain very poor. This affects Native Americans themselves, but also clearly will affect their relations with not only the government but also all Californians in the future.

Native-American Spirituality in the New Age

At the same time, interest in and appropriation of Native-American themes and ceremonies continue to play a role in alternative spirituality. Such appropriation can be traced back to the beginning of the twentieth century, when a former Methodist preacher, George Wharton James, taught Native "house-blessing" ceremonies to wealthy Anglo housewives. The latest wave of appropriation was the strong interest in shamans, dreaming, and Native ceremonies in California and the West in the 1980s and 1990s. Much of this was an outgrowth of Carlos Castaneda's popularization of his Yaqui hero, Don Juan, in a series of books published in the 1970s. In some cases, Native-American teachers themselves have transmitted traditional teachings to outsiders. More commonly, however, non-natives are the teachers of an expanded and re-defined form of archaic tradition.

An example of a currently popular "shamanic" figure—this time for women—is Lynn Andrews, author of *Medicine Woman* (reprinted 39 times by 2003). She describes herself as teaching the "mysteries" of conscious living through books, lectures, and a well-known annual retreat at Joshua Tree National Monument in the southern California desert. Andrews claims to have been initiated in to the secrets of "Spider Woman" (a Native-American spirit) by a secret society of 44 women known as the Sisterhood of the Shields, who now have decided to allow their wisdom to be taught to the world. Andrews explains:

> Throughout time, shamans have practiced the art of choreographing energy in a nonlinear field. Shamanic knowledge and practice is at the very heart of creation. As 21st Century shamans we learn to create a sacred circle in which we transform our ordinary life into a life of power.[32]

Andrews has appropriated Native-American terminology, and presumably some authentic teachings, into a more familiar California style of spiritual self-development.

Native Americans often are ambivalent about such appropriation. On one hand, they see it can be beneficial for their cultures to be acknowledged for contributing to the spiritual legacy of humankind. On the other hand, many hardly recognize the teachings transmitted by Anglos and sometimes object to their own teachers offering to teach non-natives. Tracking that conflict would, however, take this chapter afield from its main purpose. It is sufficient to note that most of the Native-American teachings transmitted to whites, with the possible exception of honoring the natural environment, are channeled into personalism and have little direct impact on public life.

Politics, Anyone?

This survey shows that leaders who connect spirituality to politics are few. Marianne Williamson was noted at the outset, but one must cast a broad net to find individuals who both espouse a personalist spirituality and promote political activism. An important northern California presence has been Michael Lerner, an observant Jew who has espoused many liberal causes in America and Israel. Through the vehicle of *Tikkun* (Hebrew for "mending"), the leftist journal he founded, Lerner has been one of the rare voices who has made a specific connection between spirituality and politics. However, many writers for the magazine have not been so willing to connect Jewish observance to their espousal of leftist causes, while most observant Jews have found Lerner's extremism on social issues and the Israeli peace process far to the left of their positions. On the other hand, Lerner's support of Israel also has offended some far-left groups. He is an example of how difficult it is to live both in the practical world of interest-group politics and in the spiritual world.

Nevertheless, the potential for public activism within alternative religiosities exists. A few educational enterprises are attempting to bring spirituality to the forefront, and some are explicitly connecting this effort with the idea of a new politics or new communal formations. The most notable for its faculty and curriculum style is the University of Creation Spirituality, founded by Matthew Fox, a former Roman Catholic priest dismissed from the Dominican order for his radicalism, who is now an Episcopal priest. This school offers Doctor of Ministry degrees to people of varied religious backgrounds, offering courses in the world's mystical and spiritual traditions, as well as in the "new cosmology" emerging from modern science. Pantheistic in theology, its teaching emphasizes the blessings of creation and the idea that everyone is a "mystic" with a mission to advance goodness and justice.

A more traditional, but still spiritually oriented, program for advanced students has appeared in Judaism as well. The Academy of Jewish Religion in Los Angeles, originally started as a branch of a similar program in New York, became independent in 2002 and already has 40 rabbinical and cantorial students (the New York branch after 40 years has about 60 students). It is unique among rabbinical seminaries in that it is nondemoninational (not Orthodox, Reform, Conservative, or Reconstructionist) and that it requires studies in Jewish mysticism, including Kabbalah and Hasidic spirituality. While its demanding five-year program includes traditional biblical and talmudic studies, its primary focus is producing religious leaders who are outstanding in their own spiritual and moral development, and who can help their congregations move in that direction. In the near future, the school plans to initiate a spiritual counseling program as well.

Interestingly, both these schools have tended to attract older students, often those who are beginning a second career or who have moved into spiritual work within their first career. This differentiates them from many seminaries in the traditional denominations and also points to a new emphasis on spiritual education among adults. When one looks for such education among younger people, however, the region has not produced anything of similar import.

Both Judaism and Christianity have nondenominational elementary and secondary schools, but only the Kabbalah Center in Los Angeles—itself controversial within Judaism because it rejects all mystical authorities except the lineage of its founder—has established a school for young people with a spiritual emphasis. The curriculum is similar to Orthodox Jewish day schools, except for additional emphasis on spirituality and a personal relationship to God.

The leaders and institutions mentioned above are alternative offshoots from traditional religion. So are Native Americans who teach non-natives in the new-age movements. But it is possible that new institutions will emerge from other sources. This chapter has pointed out that ecological concerns have become a way to connect personal spirituality, in either eclectic or Buddhist forms, to larger social concerns. Many of the personalists, including Buddhists, emphasize the "interconnectedness" of all beings, including animals and plants, as well as humans. This sense of connection may generate ethical and spiritual concerns that extend to such areas as animal rights or restoration and beautification of natural environments. Very few organizations now include spirituality as well as serious work projects and in-depth education, as does the Tahoe-Baikal Institute discussed earlier. Most are far more superficial, but this may change as Pacific-region residents are exposed to more possibilities. In addition, the desire of some environmental groups to interact with churches and other religious institutions reflects a social maturity on the part of environmentalists and a willingness to cooperate on issues of common moral concern.

In the meantime, it is a matter of serious concern in a state as large and influential as California, in a region so pivotal nationally and internationally, that large numbers of individuals seem to adopt a spiritual orientation that can lead to political apathy. The echo of detached spirituality—"I try to live on a higher plane"—may come to haunt Californians. But it is also possible that eventually, people will respond to Marianne Williamson's call for an engaged citizenry that bases its work on spiritual values, studies issues, and carefully acts for the benefit of a larger whole.

Endnotes

1. While technically this article includes Nevada as well, I will usually refer simply to "California." This is particularly appropriate for this essay, as the only areas of Nevada that have a significant population involved in alternative religions are a couple of counties abutting California (particularly in the Las Vegas area).

2. See Tamar (Sandra S.) Frankiel, *California's Spiritual Frontiers: Alternatives to Anglo-Protestantism 1850-1915* (Berkeley: University of California Press, 1988).

3. Ibid., chapter 5, which discusses the influence of spiritual language even on a conservative church like the Church of the Nazarenes.

4. General census data is from U.S. Census Bureau, State and County Quick Facts, at the Web site http://quickfacts.census.gov/qfd/states.

5. Dharma Realm Buddhist Association constructed a campus called City of Ten Thousand Buddhas in Ukiah Valley in 1976 and recently won approval to expand its village by building an Institute of Philosophy and Ethics (http://www.drba.org/). A Kagyu school of Tibetan Buddhists headquartered in St. Louis, Missouri, has a retreat center in Mendocino County.

6. Spirit Rock is related to an East Coast center in Barre, Massachusetts, but has operated independently for some time. Its major teachers include Jack Greenfield, trained in Thailand and widely known as an author and teacher.

7. According to Shambala's own publicity, this network was founded in 1973 by Chögyam Trungpa Rinpoche, a meditation master, artist, author, and poet, and the tradition is carried on by Trungpa Rinpoche's son Sakyong Mipham Rinpoche. It is a form of Vajrayana Mahayana Buddhism of the Tibetan Kagyu school. See http://www.lighthousewoods.com/buddhist_shambala.html.

8. See results at the California Secretary of State Web site http://vote2000.ss.ca.gov/Returns/pres/44.htm; hereafter referred to in the text as "California 2000 voting data."

9. He was indicted in February 2003 for conspiracy to murder U.S. citizens, conspiracy to provide support to terrorist organizations, and providing services to the Taliban.

10. December 20, 2001, online edition.

11. See the Course in Miracles Foundation (also Institute for Teaching Inner Peace) Web site at http://www.facim.org/acim/description.htm.

12. http://www.scientologytoday.org/corp/.

13. Transcript of the Dalai Lama's speech is available at http://www.tibet.com/NewsRoom/iraq1.htm (accessed December 22, 2004).

14. "Butterfly's Tale" http://www.circleoflifefoundation.org/scrapbook/butter-flys_tale.

15. Sue Maloney, "Religion and the Forests," Environmental Protection Information Center (EPIC) [Arcata, CA] April 28, 2000, http://www.treesfoundation.org/html/publications_article_7.html (accessed 3/23/03).

16. Frank L. and Mary T. Hoffman, "Can Animal Rights and Vegetarianism (Veganism) Succeed Without Church Support?" June 2002, http://www.all-creatures.org/articles/succeed-rc.html (accessed May 4, 2003).

17. http://www.sentientbeings.org, http://www.famsanctuary.org.

18. The Siskiyou County visitors' Web site is http://www.visitiskiyou.org/guides.htm; Ashalyn's "Shasta Vortex Adventures" site is http://www.shastavortex.com. The astrologer is Claudia Balashi offering "Sacred Mountain Tours," http://www.shastaspirit.com/Claudia; she is part of a larger organization known as Shasta Spirit.

19. See the Web site of the Bernadette Foundation, www.awakeningthesoul.com (accessed May 1, 2003).

20. Colin Wilson and Rand Flem-Ath, *The Atlantis Blueprint* (London: Little, Brown & Company, 2000), 342. While this fits with the sacralization of space in recent spiritual movements, I do not claim it is an accurate reflection of Chumash mythology, which seems to have been much more specific about its sacred 'gates.' See, for example, John Anderson's commentary on Chumash 'gates,' which he states included Point Conception and certain sacred mountains (http://www.angelfire.com/id/newpubs/conception.html).

21. October 17, 2002.

22. http://www.tahoebaikal.org/about/report2001.

23. Conrad Ostwalt, "*Armageddon* at the Millennial Dawn," *The Journal of Religion and Film* 4.1 (April 2000) http://www.unomaha.edu/~wwwjrf/armagedd.htm (accessed 4/27/03), paragraph 6.

24. Ibid., paragraph 10.

25. Daniel Wojcik, *The End of the World as We Know It: Faith, Fatalism, and Apocalypse in America* (New York: New York University Press, 1997).

26. Ostwalt, "*Armageddon* at the Millenial Dawn," paragraph 18.

27. http://www.coasttocoastam.com/shows/2002/09/27.html.

28. Sean David Morton, "The Last Ten Years," December 2001, www.delphiassoicates.org (accessed March 26, 2003).

29. Ibid.

30. March 3, 2003.

31. February 16, 2003.

32. http://www.lynnandrews.com (accessed April 30, 2003).

CHAPTER FIVE

PONO AND KAPU:
RIGHTEOUSNESS AND TABOO IN HAWAII

George J. Tanabe, Jr.

When Hiram Bingham and his party of Congregationalist missionaries landed in Hawaii in 1820, their shock at the sight of "destitution, degradation and barbarism"[1] was lightened by the astonishing news from the returning shore party that the native gods and the *kapu* (taboo) system had been overthrown by the ruling chiefs themselves. Kamehameha the Great, unifier of the islands by force of arms, had died 10 months before the missionaries arrived, and Kaʻahumanu, his favorite wife, forced the new but weak king Liholiho to feast with female chiefs, thus breaking the *'Aikapu* or taboo against mixed-gender eating that excluded women from feasts at which important decisions were made.

Seeing that white men suffered no divine retribution from eating with women, Kaʻahumanu and other female chiefs had repeatedly broken the taboo, but never had the king himself openly transgressed. While the *kapu* system was not so easily swept away, and many beliefs and practices continued,[2] Kaʻahumanu had mounted a successful challenge that called into question the power and authority of the native gods. The gods, said the native historian David Malo, had lied, and Liholiho and Kaʻahumanu set about destroying the old gods at the temples. Jehovah, said the missionaries, had prepared the way for their mission.[3]

As with other traditional societies, "Hawaiian polity was religious and Hawaiian religion, at the level of the chiefs, was political. The two were inseparably entwined and their purpose was to keep the universe in a state of *pono*, or 'perfect equilibrium.'"[4] Even before the arrival of the missionaries, it was evident that Hawaii was not in balance: how could there be divine justice when white people broke the taboos and lived, while native Hawaiians were dying in droves from foreign diseases the gods obviously were powerless to prevent? The new

139

god Jehovah showed himself to be potent, and it was not long before Liholiho's mother and thereafter Ka'ahumanu herself, the de facto ruler, converted to Christianity. *Pono* required religion and "Ka'ahumanu's strategy was to return religion to the center of law and chiefly power, with herself as the delineator of law and of *hewa* (sin)—refashioning Christianity to meet her Hawaiian ends."[5] With the new *pono* came new *kapu*, and Ka'ahumanu forbade illicit lovemaking, dancing, gambling, and drinking. Bingham's strict Calvinist taboos now defined public life.

Changing versions of *pono* and *kapu* continue to make up the intersections of religion with public life in Hawaii. *Pono* has a broad range of meanings: harmony, balance, righteousness, correctness, goodness, virtue, well-being, welfare, perfect order. It is a social and political equilibrium defined by a religious view of the world. *Kapu* are taboos, regulations and prohibitions designed to structure, secure, and enforce *pono*. Both are inherently religious, fundamentally social. Together they describe a preferred society theologically envisioned.

Pono can be thought of as the correct integration of religion and public life, and *kapu* forbids anything that disrupts the equilibrium. Unlike the Hawaii of Ka'ahumanu and Bingham, modern Hawaii adheres to an American polity that forbids government from the establishment of religion and any prohibition of its free exercise. In practice, however, *pono* persists even at the legislative level because religion cannot be divorced from life, and life cannot always be split into private and public spheres having nothing to do with each other. The constitutional mandate separating church from state is not designed to drive religion into the closet of privatism, but to ensure the free expression of religion in public without government interference. While traditional Hawaiian *pono* at the social level was a government responsibility, American *pono* is a citizen's right. But that right, many still insist, must be guaranteed by government through official restraints from interference or establishment of religion.

In the modern state of Hawaii, *pono* and *kapu* are defined by citizens, many of whom use the legislative process to institute their versions of religious righteousness. In this effort, they seek not only to protect their private morality but also to extend it to the public as a whole. Garret Hashimoto, president of the Hawaii Christian Coalition, reminds members that past church leaders campaigned against slavery, worked for government reform, and called for the American revolution. "Sincere repentance," he says, "leads to renewed righteousness in government and laws. The Hawaii state motto is a call to Christian obedience: *"The life of the land is perpetuated in righteousness* [pono]."[6]

The Hawaii Christian Coalition is but one of many groups seeking to perpetuate righteousness in the land. Like the coalition, which is part of the national Christian Coalition founded by Pat Robertson in 1989, many local groups are affiliated with national and international organizations. Institutional networks are extensive, and alliances are made and unmade according to issues. Certain alliances fall into repeated and predictable patterns, but so do they arise among unlikely bedfellows. At times conservatives line up against liberals, and at other times both sides join forces to oppose a common enemy. Unlike the Assemblies of God or the Church of Jesus Christ of Latter-day Saints, for example, the Hawaii Buddhist Peace Fellowship protested the war in Iraq, but all three groups are united in their opposition to legalized gambling.

It is difficult to gain an analytical footing on these shifting alliances through the usual categories of religious organizations, ethnic identities, political parties, conservative orientations, or liberal leanings. The clearest way to chart the dynamic interactions between religion and public life is through issues of righteousness and taboo, religious ideals and prohibitions that partisans seek to make the life of the land through social action, and, whenever possible, the sanction of law. But with each particular struggle for the control of public morality, the exact definitions of *pono* and *kapu* are hotly contested. What follows therefore is a consideration of the major issues surrounding the pursuit of *pono*, which is affirmative in vision, and the battles over *kapu*, prohibitions of evils that stand in the way of righteousness.

The Pursuit of Pono

Politics and Public Policy

Concerned about how humanists and atheists have swept American life of its Christian values, Garret Hashimoto has called on fellow Christians to "retake America, not by the sword but by our God-given duty to vote."[7] Hashimoto expresses a great sense of crisis and warns that "Americans are engaged in a great civil war, arguably the most important in our history." The war is being waged over whether or not Christianity will prevail as the legal and cultural standard for American society and government. He argues that the founding fathers "did not want an institutional state church like the Church of England, but to them a separation of Christianity from government would have been a certain recipe for national suicide!"[8]

Many evangelicals are convinced that America has lost its Christian *pono*. According to Daniel Kikawa of the Aloha Ke Akua (God Is Love) Christian ministry, Hawaii in particular has forgotten that the saying adopted by the state as its official motto was first uttered by Ke'opuolani, Liholiho's mother and the first Christian convert, in explicit reference to Jesus Christ. In 1843 Ke'opuolani's second son, Kamehameha III, dropped "Jesus Christ" from the saying when he reiterated it upon the restoration of the kingdom, which had been seized briefly and then returned by the British.

Adopted as the state motto, Kamehameha III's rendition ironically is set in the context of native Hawaiian sovereignty, but for Kikawa the motto has been truncated and should read in Ke'opuolani's original words, "The life of the land is perpetuated by the righteousness (*pono*) of Jesus Christ."[9] Kikawa is convinced that Christian *pono* has been usurped and is badly in need of restoration.

In a 2000 newsletter, the Hawaii Christian Coalition reported on its general meeting in which

> ... six of our members gave testimonies about how they were led to run for public office for the first time in this election. God is on the move! As these candidates spoke from their hearts, they emboldened us and encouraged and strengthened each other. We salute these Christian leaders' willingness to devote so much time and effort to serve their communities by running for public office, and pray that their example will inspire others to step forward to help shape the government policies that affect Hawaii's families.[10]

In his message, Hashimoto urged members to "recapture our Christian freedom and heritage and once again be one nation under God, for the glory of God."[11]

The coalition's general meeting was held at Calvary Chapel, one of Honolulu's megachurches. Founded by Pastor Bill Stonebraker, who became a Christian while living as a surfer on Oahu's north shore, Calvary Chapel has its main sanctuary in a former theater building and is affiliated with other Calvary Chapels throughout the United States and in many other countries. Having outgrown the theater building, Calvary Chapel is building a huge campus in central Oahu that will include a gym and a school. There are 15 other Calvary Chapels throughout the state, and the organization also owns and operates its own radio station. Deeply concerned with touching the lives of people where they are at, Calvary Chapel has a wide array of special ministries for teens, women, single parents, married couples, and men.

"Pastor Bill" partially credits his success to being able to fill the spiritual vacuum created by the "post-Christian age" in which Christianity, particularly mainline Protestantism, no longer provides the dominant system of values in America. Stonebreaker believes the mainline declined because of its failure to reach people at their spiritual core. Instead of staid traditional liturgy and formalism, evangelicals offer a faith in Jesus that is lively, personal, relevant, and in tune with contemporary tastes. The old-time hymns, for example, are hard to sing and are out of tune with modern musical fashions. A new Christian music has replaced the old standards, and its rhythm and lyrics resonate with contemporary ears. "I have never," Stonebreaker said in an interview, "sung a hymn in my life."

For him, the retaking of America is to be accomplished by reaching the hearts, minds, and spirits of individuals, one by one. His ministry focuses on the personal lives of his parishioners, who face immediate problems at home, school, and work. Interested in reaching as many people as possible, Pastor Bill does not generally preach politics from the pulpit since every political stand is bound to turn someone away. The only political stand he took from the pulpit had a characteristically personal touch: "I don't know who you are voting for, but as for me I am voting for Bud." Knowing that Bud is his son, the congregation took his political endorsement in the humorous spirit in which it was given.

William "Bud" Stonebraker is a Calvary Chapel pastor like his father, and was elected to the State House of Representatives in 2000 and reelected in 2002. As a first-time candidate, he was aware of how little he knew about politics and government, but was reassured by those who said that the best guide was to do what is right. Rep. Stonebraker has a very clear sense of *pono*, informed by his Christian faith. But he is realistic about the government's inability to change people's hearts and minds in moral terms. The church is best suited for moral persuasion, and, he said in an interview, "My job as legislator has very little to do with changing someone's morals."

Recognizing that he deals with people who have different values, Stonebraker welcomes debate in the political process, which is the primary mechanism for change at the public level. While he shares the concern about the erosion of family values in a post-Christian society, Rep. Stonebraker does not feel a similar sense of crisis about America's basic foundation, which is the opportunity to get involved. Open access to politics is still intact, and the fundamental problem is that not enough Christians exercise their right and privilege to vote. The spiritual side of the church is very well developed, he says, but the political side is underdeveloped. He is committed to mastering the political process, making others aware of it, and encouraging them to use it.

Despite the rising numbers of evangelical Christians, Rep. Stonebraker is certain they are far from where they should be in the political landscape. While Rep. Stonebraker is directly involved with the legislative process, his father prefers the indirect route of supporting organizations such as the Hawaii Christian Coalition and the Hawaii Family Forum.

In the years since its founding in 1998, the Hawaii Family Forum has had a significant impact on local politics. The organization is affiliated with James Dobson's Focus on the Family in Colorado Springs and is part of a multi-state network of Family Policy Councils. It is supported primarily by evangelical organizations such as Calvary Chapel and Hawaiian Islands Ministries. Some of the most prominent people in Hawaii serve on its board of directors.

The president is Francis S. Oda, Chairman and CEO of Group 70 International, a leading architectural firm. All of the board members are business and community leaders, and include Mitchell D'Olier, President and CEO of Victoria

Ward Limited, and Bill Paty, a respected sugar plantation manager who also served, among other positions, as president of the 1978 Hawaii Constitutional Convention and chairman of the State Department of Land and Natural Resources under Governor John Waiheʻe.

Under the leadership of its former executive director, Kelly Rosati, the forum played a key role in blocking legislation to allow legalized gambling and physician-assisted suicide. It helped enact laws protecting minors from sexual exploitation in strip clubs, and in raising the age of sexual consent from 14 to 16. The forum also campaigns against same-sex marriage, domestic violence, access to Internet pornography sites at public libraries, and the State Board of Education's sex education policy that counsels abstinence but also teaches safe-sex techniques. The forum supports total premarital abstinence.[12] For her work in changing the age of consent—an effort that involved intensive lobbying to override Governor Benjamin Cayetano's veto—Kelly Rosati was named by the *Honolulu Star-Bulletin* one of 10 people who made a difference in Hawaii in 2001.[13]

As of June 2003, J. Denice von Gnechten became the forum's new executive director. Like Rosati, von Gnechten is a lawyer and is committed to the ideals and strategies of James Dobson, whom she admires for being willing to get involved with politics. Her own engagement in the political process represents a complete reorientation from the apolitical Christianity she grew up with in Appalachia where politics, a dirty word, was shunned by Christians. Like Hashimoto, the Stonebrakers, and others, von Gnechten believes that Christianity must be returned to the center stage of public life, especially since it is the necessary if not the only foundation of democracy.

Von Gnechten believes America is still in a post-Christian age of moral relativism, and the battle to restore Christianity is an uphill fight, although the events of 9/11 may have turned the tide. A member of Dan Chun's First Presbyterian Church, von Gnechten is also the new president of the Christian Legal Society of Hawaii, and believes that the practice of law must be based on Christian principles. The legal profession, she believes, has contributed its share to the erosion of values, as has the educational system, popular (especially Hollywood) culture, and even mainline institutional religion. The forum has a well-defined agenda, enjoys good support, and under von Gnechten will continue to be the leading lobbyist based on religious values.

It is symptomatic of the state's liberal Protestant anemia that its lobbying organization, the Hawaii Council of Churches, died recently. Twenty years ago the Council's voice carried great influence, not only because it represented the mainline churches but also because of its affiliations with the Jewish and Buddhist communities. One of its last major achievements was a 1997 interfaith resolution supporting same-sex marriage that was signed by leaders of the United Church of Christ, the Episcopal Church, the United Methodist Church, the Disciples of Christ, the Unitarian Universalist Association, the Presbyterian Church, the Honganji Buddhist Mission, the Hawaii Association of International Buddhists, and Temple Emanu-El (Reform). The resolution argued that in a religiously diverse community, no single religious point of view should be the basis of public law, and gays and lesbians should be accorded the same rights and recognition even in civil union.

In their shared social morality, liberal Protestants have more in common with their Buddhist counterparts than they do with evangelical Christians. Once active, the interfaith movement, however, has gone the way of the Hawaii Council of Churches, and liberals such as Jory Watland, a Lutheran minister and community activist, note its demise with dismay. New interfaith alliances such as Open Table are active, but they remain committed more to dialogue than action. Interfaith coalitions, however, have emerged around particular concerns such as gambling, but they constitute themselves as single-issue groups.

To some degree, the Hawaii Council of Churches has been succeeded by the Faith Action for Community Equity. Emerging from an earlier interfaith community organization, the group was formed in 1996 as an association of individual Methodist, United Church of Christ (UCC), Catholic, and Episcopal churches. The First Unitarian Church and the Korean Mu-Ryang-Sa Buddhist Temple are also members. Its current president is Rev. Neal MacPherson of the Church of the Crossroads (UCC), which has a long history of activism, particularly during the Vietnam War when the military police once entered its premises to arrest deserters it was harboring. Like the Stonebrakers and von Gnechten, MacPherson also describes current society with the words "post-Christian," but for him the term indicates the new religious diversity in which Christianity is but one religion among many. Unlike his evangelical counterparts, MacPherson is not galvanized to return Christianity to its preeminent position, but is committed to embracing other religious values and insights into cooperative arrangements.

Recognizing that his pluralistic approach is at odds with the popularity of the Jesus-centered movements, MacPherson accepts the mainline Protestant decline, and in particular the outsider "out-of-synch" status of his own church. MacPherson builds on the liberal, even radical, tradition of Church of the Crossroads, and sees the post-Christian world as an "opportunity for us to reclaim a kind of minority status as the early Christian movement had up until Constantine."

Crossroads is not interested in membership numbers, but in returning to its minority prophetic heritage. Post-Christian churches, MacPherson believes, should all be small, and exert their influence through alliances with other churches and faiths. Faith Action is an interfaith coalition that determines its agenda according to its grassroots membership. Most of its issues have been localized, non-controversial, and winnable: traffic safety signs, priority bus seating for seniors, long-term care, minimum living wage ($12 per hour plus medical insurance), and banning cigarette and alcohol ads around schools.

Faith Action avoids controversial issues that would threaten its broad-based consensus, and is paying more attention to public education and universal health care. MacPherson also noted in an interview that many mainline Protestant churches pulled back from controversial issues out of fear of losing more members. "When you are in a survival mode," he said, "you don't want to make waves."

In major and minor ways, religious groups across the spectrum—and there are many more than have been covered here—are actively pursuing *pono* in public life. From their respective theological and moral standpoints, as they told the *Honolulu Star-Bulletin*, they would agree with Bishop Francis DiLorenzo of the Catholic Diocese of Hawaii, that "those who tell us that religious beliefs have no place in the exercise of citizenship" are wrong since "it is precisely because of our religious beliefs that we must advocate for justice, for human dignity and the good of the community." Even as small a group as the International Society for Krishna Consciousness (Hare Krishnas) formed a third political party, Independents for Godly Government, and successfully ran candidates for office at the state and city levels on the same conviction that religion should inform politics.

Notably absent from the political landscape are the Buddhists. Although there are over 50 Buddhist temples and organizations on Oahu alone, Buddhists have seldom organized themselves to exert political influence as a group. Certain individuals and temples have taken public stands on political issues or have participated in initiatives sponsored by ecumenical organizations, but on the whole the Buddhist community has been passive. Even Soka Gakkai International-USA (SGI) has not followed the path of its Japanese parent organization, which founded the Komeito, a national political party. SGI has chosen a less partisan approach to the pursuit of *pono,* and, like other Buddhist organizations, prefers community engagement through service rather than politics.

Festivals and Parades

The importance of keeping religion in the background of motivation for public engagement is not lost upon religious organizations seeking broad support for community events. Carol Pelekai, staff member of the SGI and leader of the Wai'anae SGI group, developed an idea into a major festival celebrating the strengths of a community with a reputation for social and economic problems. Under the theme of "Show Your Treasures," SGI Westside, the Spark Matsunaga Institute for Peace, Makaha Ahupua'a, and Nanakuli Ahupua'a joined forces to organize the Westside Youth Festival with the support of nearly 100 businesses and over 30 community groups. The public schools and the Army 25th Infantry Division played key roles in the 1999 event, which featured singing, dancing, educational exhibits, youth craft booths, entertainment, and other activities aimed at creating a "drug free, abuse free, trash free" community. Touching a nerve of real need, the festival was a tremendous success and has become an annual event.

Peace and nonviolence are major initiatives of SGI, a Buddhist organization based on the teachings of the Lotus Sutra and the medieval Japanese Buddhist monk Nichiren. The Westside Youth Festival has incorporated the theme of "Victory Over Violence," and has developed lesson plans to help students understand different kinds of violence and the nature of nonviolence. The lessons are cast in social terms and do not promote any explicitly Buddhist teachings.

Carol Pelekai explained in an interview that none of the activities are designed to promote religion, and that churches are required to refrain from preaching if they are to participate. Most of the supporting churches are evangelical Christian—the mainline Protestants have been reticent—and they understand drugs, trash, and abuse well enough to accept SGI's lead in keeping religious preferences from getting in the way of building a network. Broad support depends on theological neutrality, and the festival must also be religion-free to succeed. As with federal funding, religion must be kept private to make it easier for different religious organizations to cooperate in public. No one complained about the active involvement of city, state and federal agencies in the Westside Youth Festival, and SGI is particularly comfortable with its own religious neutrality since it does not have a rigid moral ideology that compels it to transform its religious vision into public policy. Accordingly, SGI is not involved with efforts to make sin into crime.

The Family Day Kid's Parade presents a different case of a coalition, one that ignited controversy and lawsuits. The Hawaii Christian Coalition sponsored a Kid's Day Parade in Waikiki as part of the City of Honolulu's Family Day celebrations for the 2003 Independence Day weekend. When the coalition denied the applications of several gay rights groups to join the parade, the state's chapter of the American Civil Liberties Union (ACLU) filed suit in federal court asking for an injunction against the parade.

The issue centered on whether or not the parade was co-sponsored by the city or whether it was a private event of the Christian Coalition. "If it's a private event," asked Brent White, legal director for the ACLU, in a *Honolulu Star-Bulletin* article, "why is city administrator Alvin Au on city time and using a city phone taking applications for the parade?" U.S. District Court Judge Helen Gillmor rejected the ACLU's request for a temporary restraining order, determining that the city was not a co-sponsor and that it gave no more help to the Christian Coalition than it did to other parade organizers.

"I'm so happy for the children of Hawaii," the Hawaii Christian Coalition Chairman Garret Hashimoto told the *Star-Bulletin*. "The city is doing exactly what they're supposed to be doing by helping the community, and we are helping the community and we're not doing anything wrong." The parade went on as scheduled, and gay-rights supporters heckled Mayor Jeremy Harris as he rode in a convertible through Waikiki.

The controversy was revived with another ACLU suit against the city, this one on behalf of Rev. Vaughn Beckman, senior minister of the First Christian Church, and other plaintiffs. The focus in this case was not so much on whether the city was a supporter or sponsor, but on the "intermingling" or "alignment" between the city and the Christian Coalition. "I think I speak for a lot of religious leaders in Hawaii that we do not want to see the state and the religious community intermingling in such a way to cause people to feel excluded or to pay for people to be excluded," Beckman said.[14] "We strongly believe in freedom of religion but that it is improper for the city to be aligning itself with one particular branch of religion," White said. For Beckman, the city should not be promoting fundamentalist religious beliefs of one segment of our society to the exclusion of all others. Although he admitted that there might have been religious messages in the parade, Garret Hashimoto did not think that it was a religious event.[15]

Is the denial of a parade application on the basis of one's views on homosexuality a religious, parareligious, or secular act? All three judgments apply, depending on who is doing the judging. The nonreligious critics of the parade say it was religious, while the religious sponsor says it was not. Like so many other church-state issues, religion shows itself to be fluid, capable of passing in many guises.

Good Friday is still a state holiday, and the U.S. Ninth Circuit Court of Appeals ruled in 1991 that its purpose was essentially secular in providing an extended spring holiday for workers. The ACLU has questioned whether a city-built Shinto *torii* gate is religious or not, but it still stands, deemed to be a purely cultural symbol of Japan. Much is at stake in the ambiguities of defining religion, and religious groups chart different courses in the public arena, ranging from self-restraint (SGI) to self-assertion (Christian Coalition). Public assertions of religion as well as restrictions against them have both been attacked as forms of unfair discrimination. The issue is particularly sensitive with those who feel that a country founded on Christian principles should not restrict the establishment of those principles and values as laws and public policy.

Faith-based Social Services

Pono is the motive and objective of many religious groups providing social services to the community at large. The extent of services provided by religious institutions is truly remarkable, and it is difficult to find a church or temple that is not involved with projects to promote public well-being, especially of those in need. According to Pastor Dan Chun of the First Presbyterian Church of Honolulu, 80 percent of charitable food distributions and 34 percent of day-care services are provided by churches. The Salvation Army has been active since 1894, and Catholic Charities runs an $18 million operation. Churches and para-church organizations play major roles in Hawaii, just as they do in other states.

While the impetus and structures for helping others are natural extensions of religious organizations, specific actions often take place only with the initiative of a small group of people or even a single individual. In 1989 Ivy Olson, wife of the pastor of Calvary-by-the-Sea Lutheran Church, inspired her congregation to provide a temporary home for homeless single mothers. Eventually the church founded dozens of homes, which they called "Ohana Houses" after the Hawaiian word for extended family. Olson expanded their support from donations and volunteers to include a state contract to house and help homeless people get back on their own feet. The Lutheran Angel Network Charities now operates 46 Ohana Houses with the cooperation of 14 other churches.

In June 1989 Shimeji Kanazawa and Rose Nakamura conversed with each other while they prepared food for volunteers at the Moiliili Hongwanji Mission, an ethnic Japanese Buddhist temple in Honolulu. On being told by Nakamura, who had just retired from the East-West Center, about her desire to do volunteer work, Kanazawa knew that she had found a leader for a caregiver program that was until then just an idea. As a trustee of the National Federation of Interfaith Volunteer Caregivers, Kanazawa decided that a Buddhist temple should also be caring for the elderly and disabled, especially since Buddhist teachings call for the promotion of the well-being of society through *dana*, a Sanskrit term meaning selfless giving. With a startup grant from the Public Welfare Foundation in Washington, D.C., Project Dana began its operations. Ten years later, Project Dana had 650 trained volunteers serving more that 750 individuals and their families at 22 interfaith sites. The success of the program inspired Buddhist temples in Fresno and Venice, California, to start their own Project Dana. The project has received numerous awards, and Rose Nakamura, who continues to serve as administrative leader, was the first recipient of the Rosalynn Carter Caregiving Award, in 1997.[16]

Lutheran Angel Network Charities and Project Dana are just two examples of organizations providing faith-based social services. For some groups like Project Dana, religion is the motivation for services provided with no regard for propagation or conversion. Other groups, like the River of Life Mission, disseminate religious teachings to those who receive their services. A member of the Association of Gospel Rescue Missions, the River of Life Mission distributed 1.6 million pounds of food in 2001, received 9,400 visits, served 125,329 hot meals, gave out 63,300 articles of clothing, provided 6,000 showers, haircuts, and shaves, and managed 30,000 hours donated by volunteers.

The mission seeks to rehabilitate and integrate people back into society, and there must be a fundamental change in perspective for this to happen. "The only means to effectively and progressively accomplish change is through one's relationship with Jesus Christ," according to the mission's Web site. The mission therefore "receives no governmental funding of any kind in order to preserve the faith-based foundation of all of its ministry and services."

President Bush's faith-based initiative has received mixed responses from religious organizations. Many share the River of Life Mission's preference for protecting their religious priorities in providing services. Even parachurch organizations that do not proselytize and therefore qualify for federal funding are concerned that wider competition will shrink their share of resources. Reynold Feldman of the Lutheran Angel Network Charities told the *Honolulu Star-Bulletin* that "the only difference for us is that it will give us more competitors." On the other hand, the president of the International Society for Krishna Consciousness (Hare Krishnas) in Hawaii welcomes Bush's initiative and hopes his food program will qualify.

Rev. Neal MacPherson of Church of the Crossroads (United Church of Christ) is concerned that federal faith-based support will muzzle the voice of the church and also violate the separation of church and state. The White House initiative is relatively new and evolving, and the local reactions reflect uncertainty about what can and cannot be done with federal dollars.

The federal agencies involved in the initiative are less troubled by these uncertainties and welcome the new opportunity to work directly with faith-based organizations, which include churches as well as parachurch 501(c)(3) not-for-profit organizations. The term itself avoids the taint of "religion" or even "religious," and stakes out an area of allowable activity that is not inherently religious. Representatives from the Departments of Health and Human Services, Housing and Urban Development, Public Health Service, Labor, and Justice have formed a faith-based work group that meets regularly to plan and act. For them, the federal grants are not as important as the new opportunities to do outreach work in churches as well as parachurch organizations, and faith-based organizations provide as much in resources as they consume.

Alfred Valles, State Director of the Bureau of Apprenticeship and Training of the Department of Labor, is looking at churches as venues for his programs, while Maile Kanemaru, Weed & Seed Director, has cooperated with churches as part of her anti-drug efforts and is planning on other partnerships. These programs do not involve federal grants to faith-based organizations.

While federal programs like Head Start have cooperated with churches before, most of the agencies in the working group are doing so for the first time and are delighted with the new opportunities.

On the issue of whether or not any faith-based organizations receiving federal funds can refuse to hire someone it deems religiously objectionable, the working group follows guidelines issued by the White House. While the White House denied in July 2001 that it had made a deal with the Salvation Army to allow it to discriminate against hiring homosexuals in return for its support of the faith-based initiative, then-White House Press Secretary Ari Fleischer and Vice President Dick Cheney consistently insisted that the initiative does not require faith-based organizations to make fundamental changes in their underlying principles and organizing doctrines.

The President's Executive Order on Equal Protection of the Laws for Faith-based and Community Organizations affirms that the government cannot discriminate against charitable organizations because of their religious affiliation. The White House booklet on protecting religious liberty is subtitled "Why Religious Hiring Rights Must be Preserved," and quotes the President: "And when government gives that support, charities and faith-based programs should not be forced to change their character or compromise their mission." Therefore, if a church discriminates against a gay person by refusing to hire him, the government will respect that decision, which will not be reason to withhold federal funding. So, despite public statements by the White House to the contrary, in the faith-based organization program there is to be no government discrimination against religious discrimination. Or, to put it in terms of liberty, churches are free to discriminate on the basis of their faith.

The booklet also affirms the separatist principle that organizations cannot use government funds to support "inherently religious" activities, such as worship, religious instruction, and proselytization.[17] But faith-based organizations may and should retain their religious identity and cannot be prohibited from taking their faith into account in employment decisions. This practice is also allowable under the Civil Rights Act of 1964 and has been upheld by subsequent Supreme Court decision. Hiring is not an inherently religious act, and faith-based hiring is not subject to restrictions against federal support of religion. Just as parachurches are not intrinsic churches, faith-based organizations are parareligious and can act in seemingly but not inherently religious ways.

The distinctions are both semantic and real. Government agencies are reaching out to churches in unprecedented ways, and religious groups understand that church-state relations are being redefined with greater flexibility. Pastor Dan Chun, who describes himself and the First Presbyterian Church as evangelical, dates the visible turning point to 9/11.

Before the attack on the World Trade Center, he said, churches did not have a significant seat at the public table except for ceremonial roles played in events such as the annual opening of the state legislative session. This was particularly true for the evangelical Christian churches, which preferred to stay away from politics. But since the early 1990s the evangelical churches have burgeoned, and with their immense religious success have stepped out or responded to invitations into the public arena. In the aftermath of 9/11, the new evangelical dominance gained notable legitimacy when government and military officials turned to Dan Chun and others for help in coming to grips with the national tragedy.

In October 2001 Governor Benjamin Cayetano assembled a task force to deal with the economic and employment impact that 9/11 had on an already struggling economy, and the result was Hawaii Together, a group headed by Dan Chun and Susan Au Doyle of Aloha United Way. With a grant from the governor, Hawaii Together provides information, services, and coordination among agencies to help the community transform tragedy into strength. This is to be accomplished by working together and "with God's help," according to the group's Web site.

Pastor Chun is a major religious leader serving in a Presbyterian church that is an exception to the mainline Protestant trend of malaise. Under his leadership the church has flourished and is outgrowing its present site. In March 2003, his Hawaiian Islands Ministries sponsored its Fifteenth Annual Conference, hosting over 5,000 people at the State Convention Center with a schedule of about 100 workshops, seminars, meetings, and lectures covering topics ranging from coping with depression to energizing the spirit, from inner life to community involvement. Together with the University of Hawaii Center on the Family and the Hawaii Community Foundation, a secular philanthropic organization, the Hawaiian Islands Ministries organized the Hawaii Moving Forward project to help faith-based organizations and other community organizations build a network for strengthening Hawaii's families. It received a grant of $600,000 from the federal Compassion Capital Fund, established to support faith-based initiatives.

The White House guidelines define wider latitudes for religious organizations, some of which are now seeking and being sought for funding opportunities. Bob Marchant, Executive Director of the River of Life Mission, has turned down a number of requests from nonreligious organizations wishing to affiliate with the Mission in order to apply for faith-based grants. Marchant has already met with the federal faith-based working group to discuss a grant for a project of his own. His interest represents a change in his understanding of federal grants from several years ago when he turned down an offer to apply for a government grant that required one-third of his building to be placed off-limits to religious activities.

"Our feeling as a board and staff," he told the *Honolulu Star-Bulletin* at that time, "is that if we're doing what God wants us to do, he'll provide for us through donations and foundations." The recent faith-based initiative, however, is more tolerant of religious activities, and Marchant feels comfortable about living within the current guidelines. He is no longer opposed in principle to receiving federal funds, and his main reservation is not religious restrictions but the bureaucratic thicket involved with applying for and administering federal grants.

When religion is the motive for social services, it is possible to keep private faith invisible from public action. Under the pre-faith-based-organization construct, churches often institutionalized their good intentions by forming 501(c)(3) corporations (such as Catholic Charities and Lutheran Angel Network Charities) to provide services free of inherent religion. This voluntary separation of church and state allows government funding, and these organizations, though founded on religious conviction, operate like secular agencies.

But when religion is not just the motive for, but the mode of, rendering services to those whose rehabilitation must take advantage of inherently religious resources, then federal funds could not be used. The prohibition, however, is no longer a blanket rule, and new definitions of when and where the prohibition applies allow an ingenious combination of public funds and religious services.

The White House-issued "Guidance to Faith-Based and Community Organizations on Partnering with the Federal Government" states clearly that "organizations may use government money only to support the non-religious social services that they provide." Religious services, however, can still be provided, as long as they take place at a separate "time or location" that does not involve federal support. Job training, for example, can take place in one room while Bible study is conducted in another room. Or training can be given in the sanctuary as long as worship takes place at another time. Religious and nonreligious services, therefore, can be provided in the same room as long as they are sequential and not concurrent, or they can be concurrent as long as they are not in the same room. The distinctions are clear and liberating, and both service providers and recipients can engage voluntarily in inherent religious activities by judiciously moving between appropriately defined times and places. It is this understanding that persuades Bob Marchant to be interested in the federal support he shunned only a few years ago. The wall separating church and state now has a new, regulated, doorway through it.

Hawaiian Sovereignty

The doorway between *pono* and politics is wide open in the Native-Hawaiian sovereignty movement. The political meaning of *pono* involves restoration of a Native-Hawaiian polity, the details of which are vigorously debated, and the lines of the arguments can be drawn directly through American annexation back to the times of Kaʻahumanu and Bingham. Like Kaʻahumanu, Native Hawaiians seek to correct an imbalance. Hawaiian sovereignty is much too complex an issue to deal with briefly, and here it is sufficient only to point out the religious element of *aloha'ina*, reverence for the land.

Both the traditional *kapu* system and its replacement, Christian law, have been superseded by state and national constitutions and statutes, and the sovereignty movement is complicated by differing assessments of the degree, if any, to which current laws apply to the possible forms of restoration. Are state and federal entitlements sufficient? Should the nation be within the nation? Should it be independent from America? While the debates over these divisions continue, there is a definable consensus about the spiritual nature of the cause. The religious foundation of sovereignty in whatever form it might take lies in the idea of *aloha'ina*, reverence for the sanctity of the land. *Aloha'ina* forms a bedrock of inalienability: ownership of the land can be usurped, but its sanctity can never be stolen. "Hawaiian religion," say two sovereignty leaders, "is also a sovereign claim."[18]

The revival of *aloha'ina* occurred with the rise of the modern sovereignty movement, which took dramatic shape on January 3, 1976, when a group of native Hawaiians led by Walter Ritte and Emmett Aluli defied warnings of U.S. marines and landed by boat on the barren island of Kaho'olawe. Used for target practice by the American military, which seized the island in 1941, Kaho'olawe was seen as the epitome of American abuse and destruction, and the group sought to reclaim her. Several other landings followed with increasing controversy as more people joined in the illegal crossings. The writer, poet, and singer George Helm emerged as another leader, and "breaking with the greatest taboo of Hawaiian experience in Western time he, more than any of the other activists, turned to the ancient gods, and to figures as Emma DeFries for religious guidance."[19] George Helm resurrected the gods Ka'ahumanu had undone.

Helm did not restore a religion that had been completely obliterated—Emma DeFries and others kept ancient traditions alive—but he clearly construed the land as sacred within a political context. Helm and the Protect Kaho'olawe 'Ohana transformed what had been a movement seeking federal assistance into a "spiritual and nationalistic movement."[20]

For Davianna McGregor, another sovereignty leader and professor of ethnic studies at the University of Hawaii, the spiritual ceremonies held on Kaho'olawe connected her to the ancestors, their beliefs, and their gods. "Christianity has taken away our soul as a people. Kaho'olawe provided a way for us to get reconnected with that soul."[21] The gods are the life force of the land, and being in touch with their mana was an experience of spiritual and political empowerment. At his 1977 trial, Walter Ritte refused to separate his political actions from his religious convictions, and in response to the prosecutor's question about his motivation being political as well as—or rather than—religious, Ritte replied, "I was motivated because I am Hawaiian."[22]

McGregor uses *aloha 'ina* as a category to identify those sovereignty groups practicing the traditional spiritual customs and beliefs, which along with the land have to be defended as well as reclaimed. In opposing geothermal development in the Puna district on the island of Hawaii, protesters sought to protect the goddess Pele and the rain forest from the forces of development.[23] The gods, the land, the Hawaiian people and the nation are one, and modern landowners who do not respect this unity are trespassers. Transgressions are particularly egregious when graves and bones are involved, for ancestors are also a part of the unity. The building of the H-3 freeway through Halawa Valley on Oahu, and other construction sites as well, were delayed by protesters demanding cessation of the project or major re-routings to avoid desecration of sacred sites. One of the protesters chose to give birth to her child at one of the temple sites in the valley, saying that it was an act of *pono*. Nearly 40 years in the making, the 16-mile freeway underwent major design changes, and by the time of its dedication in 1997 its final cost came to a staggering $80 million per mile.

Reverence for the land is not unique to Hawaiian religion, and is a characteristic of many native traditions. The modern Hawaiian version, however, is distinguished by its political nature and is also to be differentiated from other religious nationalisms because of its nonviolence. It has its own context in *pono*. The fluidity of *pono*, however, allows the political edge and religious meaning of *aloha ' ina* to be diluted and abstracted, and the concept is often reduced to a kind of environmentalism. In the sovereignty movement, the secure alignment of *aloha ' ina* with *pono* sanctifies the land and the political effort to restore it to native Hawaiians.

Pono is righteousness but there is considerable argument over just what is right, and the fault lines, shifting from issue to issue, can be seen most clearly in the flip side to what is right, that is, in what is wrong. Modern taboos are as hotly contested as they were in Ka'ahumanu's time, and partisans, knowing that *pono* requires *kapu*, wage battles for public prohibitions that safeguard righteousness.

Contesting Kapu

Gambling

Gambling is popular among residents of Hawaii, not only by illegal means such as sports betting and cock fighting, but through travel to Las Vegas, whose hotels and casinos offer special deals to islanders. With a struggling tourist industry and an economy that missed even the high times of the 1990's bubble, Hawaii has considered numerous proposals for legalizing gambling, but none so far have been approved. While the public is split on the issue, the anti-gambling forces have kept legalized gaming out, and Hawaii remains one of only two states (the other is Utah) without permissible games of chance. Gambling is taboo.

Former Governor Benjamin Cayetano was open to some form of regulated gambling, but insisted that the people should decide. Attempts to let the people speak through a constitutional amendment or advisory referendum have failed, and the issue will regularly reemerge as it has in the past. In the 2003 legislative session, gambling was involved in 14 House bills and 13 Senate bills. At the top of the political pyramid, Republican Governor Linda Lingle and Democratic U.S. Senator Daniel Inouye are opposed to any form of legalization, and at the grassroots level a diverse set of members make up the Hawaii Coalition Against Legalized Gambling.

The coalition cooperates with the National Coalition Against Legalized Gambling, and among single-issue organizations in Hawaii it enjoys the broadest interfaith cooperation. In addition to community groups and government agencies such as the Honolulu Police Department, the religious members are liberal Protestant, evangelical Christian, Jewish, Mormon, Unitarian, Muslim, Quaker, Catholic, and Buddhist. The Church of Perfect Liberty, a Japanese new religion, is also a member.

In his address to church representatives of the state coalition, Tom Grey, executive director of the national coalition, said, "Liberals and conservatives can fight side by side on this one." O.W. Efurd, executive director for the Hawaii Pacific Baptist Convention, noted in the *Honolulu Star-Bulletin* that "there's a lot of folks you wouldn't see united in other issues, [but] this is one they agree on." These diverse groups share common ground on the mostly non-religious reasons why gambling should be banned. Judy Rantala, a member of the Church of the Crossroads and the state coalition's current president, argues that legalized gambling contributes to child neglect, domestic violence, the cannibalization of small businesses, traffic congestion, gaming addiction, bankruptcy, and crime. It is, she told the *Star-Bulletin,* "a stupid use of hard-earned money." Kikue Takagi, another Crossroads member, recalled in an interview Rantala's observation that tremendous cooperation can be gained if people set aside their theologies.

Most members, however, object to gambling for moral as well as social reasons, and can turn to church teachings to make their point. The Methodists, for instance, cite their Book of Discipline: "Gambling is a menace to society, deadly to the best interests of moral, social, economic and spiritual life, and destructive of good government. As an act of faith and concern, Christians should abstain from gambling and should strive to minister to those victimized by the practice." A slightly different view is given by Catholic Bishop Francis X. DiLorenzo, who told the *Star-Bulletin* that gambling is "not considered morally wrong in itself, but it may become morally wrong when it interferes with one's other duties or responsibilities." The difference is not significant enough, however, to affect their common stance against legalized gaming.

Physician-assisted Suicide

In 1996 Governor Benjamin Cayetano created the Blue Ribbon Panel on Living and Dying With Dignity. The Panel consisted of 18 members from various fields, and was charged with developing guidelines for a state policy on end-of-life issues. The religious community was represented by a rabbi, a United Church of Christ minister, a Catholic nun, and a Buddhist priest. In 1998, the panel issued a report recommending the legalization of both physician-assisted suicide and physician-assisted death (active euthanasia). The report was approved by an 11-7 vote of the panel members.

Concerned about the governor's and the panel's support for physician-assisted suicide and euthanasia, the Hawaii Family Forum teamed with the Hawaii Medical Association to form Hawaii's Partnership for Appropriate and Compassionate Care. Members include other health care associations, the Hawaii Catholic Conference, and local chapters of national disability organizations such as The Arc and Not Dead Yet devoted to resisting legalized medical killing.

With the active support of Governor Cayetano in 2002, the House of Representatives passed a bill to legalize physician-assisted suicide by a 30 to 20 vote. But the bill was bottled up in the Senate Health Committee by its chairman, David Matsuura, a Senator with publicly professed Christian beliefs, who called the measure a "dumb bill." Pointing to former Governor John Burns, who allowed an abortion bill to become law even though he privately had his own Catholic objections, Cayetano said he hoped Matsuura would be able to set aside his own religious beliefs and schedule a hearing. The Senate took the unusual step of recalling the stalled bill from Matsuura's committee, and after lengthy debate the Death With Dignity Act was defeated on the Senate floor by three votes.

Partnership lobbying was a significant factor in stopping the measure. While many mainline Protestant and Buddhist churches supported in principle the right of people to make their own choices in end-of-life issues, they did not campaign as vigorously as those opposed to the bill. The Unitarians took a more active role, and Roland Halpern, a member of the First Unitarian Church and executive director of Compassion in Dying of Hawaii, said he was "naturally disappointed that the bill didn't pass, [but] we are nonetheless appreciative that the debate has come this far...All we were hoping for was a fair hearing, and I think we got one." The First Unitarian Church supported the bill, having already passed a "right to die" resolution in 1988.[24]

In the 2003 legislative session, Senator Colleen Hanabusa introduced a right-to-die bill in the Senate. Medical and healthcare groups took the lead in having the bill killed in committee, but an internist, James McCoy, M.D., one of the leaders of the movement, credited the Christian Medical and Dental Associations with providing him materials and information.

"It's basically for all intents and purposes—no pun intended—dead in the Senate," Senator Hanabusa told the press. "It was mostly the doctors who took the lead. It was a different [public relations] campaign this time around. It wasn't framed in a church kind of presentation." [25] While the religious arguments did not play as significant a role as they did in 2002, it is still notable that conservative Christian voices were as audible as liberal churches have been silent.

Same-sex Marriage

All sides of the liberal-conservative spectrum have been very vocal on same-sex marriage, the most controversial issue at the intersection of religion and public life. Those opposed to it invoke deeply rooted taboos against homosexuality, while those in favor of it argue that since homosexuals are equal to others in the eyes of God they should be treated similarly by the laws of the land.

In 1991 three same-sex couples sued the state for the right to marry, thus challenging the statute reserving marriage to one man and one woman. In 1993 the Hawaii State Supreme Court ruled that the one man-one woman statute violated the State Constitution's equal protection clause and said that the statute could be upheld only if the state could demonstrate a "compelling state interest" in maintaining the law supporting traditional marriage. The Supreme Court returned the case to the lower court, and in a 1996 bench trial Circuit Court Judge Kevin Chang ruled that the state failed to demonstrate a compelling interest, and ordered the State Department of Health to cease its practice of denying marriage licenses solely because the applicants were of the same sex. The state asked for and received a stay of the order as it appealed the decision to the State Supreme Court.

During the three years the Supreme Court took to consider the case, the legislature passed a bill in 1997 that called for the people of Hawaii to vote on a constitutional amendment giving the legislature the right to reserve marriage to opposite-sex couples. It also passed a reciprocal beneficiaries law that granted unmarried homosexual couples some of the rights and benefits enjoyed by married heterosexuals. These benefits covered insurance, property inheritance, health, and retirement. In 1998, after a high-publicity campaign in which the Mormons alone spent $600,000, 70 percent of voters approved the constitutional amendment giving the legislature the sole right to define marriage, which existing statutes already limited to heterosexual couples. In 1999 the Supreme Court finally issued its ruling and declared the original lawsuit moot since the constitutional amendment took "the statute out of the ambit of the equal protection clause of the Hawaii Constitution." The Supreme Court thereby reversed Judge Chang's ruling, and the traditional marriage law was given "full force and effect." [26]

Throughout the controversy, but especially during the constitutional amendment campaign, religious views were prominently aired. The Catholics, Mormons and evangelical Christian churches opposed same-sex marriage on grounds that the traditional family ordained by God would be destroyed, religious liberty would be denied to those who should be free to discriminate against married homosexuals, and healthy child raising would be threatened by unnatural and sinful parental models. A Baptist minister, Rick Lazor, called homosexuality a "grievous sin," while Hawaii Episcopal Bishop Richard Chang voted against the Lambeth resolution that declared homosexuality was incompatible with scripture.

Bishop Chang did not, however, take an activist stand during the constitutional amendment campaign, and recognized the deep divisions within the Episcopal Church. The Hawaii Association of International Buddhists opposed the attempt to use the constitution to discriminate against homosexuals and affirmed the equality of all people, regardless of gender orientation. Rabbi Avi Magid of Temple Emanu-el noted that while Reform Jews have taken both sides of the issue, he was in favor of same-sex marriage. Rev. Joan Ishibashi of the United Church of Christ also affirmed homosexual marriage, she told the *Honolulu Star-Bulletin,* because "the gay and lesbian community is just as much a part of God's creation." All of the Christian groups claimed, of course, that their respective and divergent views were based on the teachings of Jesus Christ.

With seemingly endless energy, the founder of the Alliance for Traditional Marriage and Values emerged as the leading opponent of same-sex marriage. Mike Gabbard has been described as a fair and quiet man of integrity, and alternatively as an angry hatemonger and homophobic zealot. A range of labels has also been used to describe his religious identity: a Christian activist, a Catholic, and a devotee of the Hindu god Krishna.

Gabbard was a student of Chris Butler, known as Jagad Guru, who broke away from the Krishna movement in Hawaii to form Honolulu Mantra Meditation Hawaii in the 1970s. Butler was the inspiration for the Independents for Godly Government, a political party with which Maui state senator Rick Reed was associated. Gabbard supported Reed, who was a staunch opponent of abortion and alternative sexual lifestyles. Appearing regularly on cable television during the constitutional amendment campaign, Gabbard became involved when he realized how the media was presenting unnatural and immoral activity as normal. "I believe," he told *Honolulu Weekly,* "that all of our problems—be they environmental, crime, health, economic, wars, etc.—can be traced to people holding on to and living by [a] hedonistic and therefore selfish worldview. ... This is why [homosexuality] is such an important issue to me."

Under Gabbard's leadership, the alliance has been influential in local politics. In 1996, the alliance campaigned successfully against legislators who supported same-sex marriage, joining other groups in defeating gay-friendly incumbents. Jack Hoag, a Mormon leader and co-vice chairman of Hawaii's Future Today, thinks the incumbents, who are normally difficult to defeat, lost because of their support for same-sex marriage. The veteran political analyst Richard Borreca dates the revival of the Republican Party in Hawaii to the 1996 election and the ouster of the Democratic incumbents. He also predicted that the issue would raise its head again in the 2004 elections (which, in fact, it did). Linda Lingle, the state's first Republican Governor after 40 years of Democratic Party control, is firmly against gay marriage. Gov. Lingle is also the first woman to serve in that office, as well as the first Jew.

In their friend of the court brief submitted to the State Supreme Court, lawyers for Agudath Israel America, a national Orthodox Jewish organization with members in Hawaii, argued that laws of marriage are founded on moral judgments and taboos.

If "taboos" and "moral judgments about improper marriage relationships" by themselves furnish a sufficient state interest as to justify government's refusal to accept the "marriages" of certain non-blood related relatives, they also furnish a sufficient state interest as to justify government's refusal to accept the "marriages" of persons of the same gender.[27]

The *pono* of the traditional family must be protected by a *kapu* against same-sex marriage.

Drugs

Known for Maui wowie (marijuana) and a beach culture of pleasure, Hawaii has serious issues involving both drug use and trafficking. Even though the Religion of Jesus Church in Kona preaches the spiritual virtues of marijuana and its power to "bring us closer to God and our Heavenly Father closer to us," such religious groups are in a very small minority. On the scale of religious controversy, the drug issue is at the very bottom, even below gambling: few are openly for drugs. The only arguments waged have to do with whether funding, eradication and treatment are adequate or not. The growing use of drugs is evident to many, and there is a continuing sense of crisis over a problem that seems beyond control. The use of ice (crystal methamphetamine) has reached such alarming proportions that the director of the State Department of Human Services calls Hawaii the "ice capital of the universe."[28]

Religious and parachurch organizations have long been involved with combating drugs. Some use medical treatments and counseling, while others include spiritual techniques. The surfing culture that condones drug use is also the arena in which drug rehabilitation through religious conversion has taken place. The testimony of Pastor Leroy Metzger of Hope Chapel Kauai is not uncommon: while living with a group of surfers on Maui, "little did we know our lives were about to be invaded by the power of God's Love and Forgiveness." Through the intercession of his wife, "Christ then brought out His big bolt cutters and cut the chains from my heart and freed me from a long time drug habit, and immoral life style, instantly gone! WOW!"[29]

Testimonies like Metzger's are seldom heard in mainline churches. Rehabilitation through conversion is mostly an evangelical phenomenon, taking place in churches, often small and located in neighborhoods where economic and social conditions breed drug usage. Rev. Bob Nakata, an ordained Methodist minister and a veteran of the state House and Senate, became increasingly concerned about the ice problem in his 2002 reelection campaign. Recognizing that the evangelical churches were addressing the problem actively, Nakata visited many of those churches in his windward Oahu district. The evangelical ministers in the area already had a coalition, Ke Kumu Ola O Kahaluu (The Lifeline of Kahaluu), to address community issues, and held weekly prayer meetings in parks and other places where drugs were sold.

"The liberal churches," Nakata said in an interview, "are better at issues concerning the salvation of the world, but the evangelicals do a much better job with individuals and families, the ones whose lives are often in chaos." Nakata spent more time with establishing relationships with evangelical churches than he did on his campaign, and lost the election by a narrow margin. He returned to the pulpit of Kahaluu Methodist Church in his hometown, and also became the director of the KEY Project, which provides community social services.

In collaboration with a drug treatment program, Nakata organized a public forum in May 2003 at the KEY Project facility, inviting representatives from government agencies to speak with the community. What started as an ordinary town meeting with outside experts unexpectedly turned into an outpouring of frustration, anger, and sadness over the toll that drugs had taken on families and friends. Person after person stood up and told of loved ones ruined and lost. The emotional tenor was heightened by the recent suicide of a young man whose family refused to admit that he had a drug problem. The testimonies were riveting, and Nakata realized that the testimonies expressed conversion: a corner had been turned. "The denial," Nakata said later, "was over." What followed was a commitment to action.

In subsequent meetings, the community decided that it would organize a sign-waving campaign on a three-quarter-mile stretch of a road in Kahaluu. Word of the campaign spread, neighboring communities signed on, and on May 2, 2003 over 1,000 people went out to cover the entire windward and northshore areas with signs saying no to drugs. The event sparked other sign wavings in other communities and the neighbor islands. The surge of sentiment at the grass roots elicited responses from government agencies, and the lieutenant governor organized a huge statewide meeting for late 2003.

A liberal Protestant himself, Nakata is critical of liberal churches for failing to address the drug problem as a social and spiritual issue. He works with people who let Jesus cut the chains from their hearts to free them from drugs. The evangelicals understand the power of religion to change lives from within, and know, as Bud Stonebraker put it, that laws can only change external behavior but not people's hearts. Drugs can be legally prohibited but illegally obtained and used as long as opiates function as a substitute for religion. But when God and Jesus Christ fill the empty center, as popular Hawaiian singer Kelly Boy Delima told Nakata, then religion and the sense of the divine leave no room for drugs. A powerful voluntary *kapu* for drugs is the *pono* of religion.

Church and State

For those who hold to a strict separation between church and state, religion itself is a taboo in government life. For those who find it impossible to separate private religion from public life, any attempt to prevent the public exercise of religion is an infringement of their religious freedom. Much of the controversy arising from both the pursuit of righteousness and the battle for prohibitions involves the questions of separation and liberty.

The state chapter of the ACLU and the Hawaii Citizens for the Separation of State and Church have been most vigilant about any crossing of the line. Mitch Kahle, who founded the citizens for separation in 1997, has been effective in forcing government and the military to remove religious symbols and words from the workplace.

In 1997, he succeeded in getting the U.S. Army to dismantle a 37-foot-high steel cross at Schofield Barracks and has had churches take down crosses erected in violation of building codes. He successfully campaigned against the teaching of creationism in the public schools, and has brought an end to prayers at official functions. Kahle caused the removal of "God Bless America" signs from the Health and Taxation departments, and forced the Honolulu Police Department to drop the phrase "so help me God" from the swearing-in oath. Because of his efforts, the U.S. Navy had to drop the phrase "I believe in God" from youth recreation cards, and McKinley High School had to remove "Love of God" from the student honor code.

He has not won all of his battles, and Good Friday still remains a state holiday with a court-defined secular meaning even though he dressed as Jesus with a crown of thorns and a cross bearing a sign saying "Stop Celebrating My Murder" and debated Representative Bud Stonebraker. For the most part, however, Mitch

Kahle has been a successful activist, and (like Kelly Rosati of the Hawaii Family Forum in 2001) was named by the *Honolulu Star-Bulletin* one of 10 people who made a difference in 2002.

Patrick Downes, of the Catholic Diocese of Hawaii calls Kahle "hostile to Christianity" and told the *Honolulu Advertiser* he thinks Kahle "goes out of his way...to reassert his faith-phobia." Kahle has his own supporters, but many agree with Downes.

When Kahle attacked Senator David Matsuura for having a Christian fish symbol on his capitol office door, Matsuura replied that Kahle was denying him his right to free speech. The Hawaii Family Forum defended Matsuura, and, turning around a charge often levied at the group itself, asked rhetorically, "Where is the tolerance for diversity and pluralism?" The family forum complained that Kahle was picking on Christianity again, noting that he seldom if ever criticized other religions. The editorial writers of the *Honolulu Star-Bulletin* agreed with the HFF, and opined that "total separation is neither required by the Constitution nor desirable."

For Representative Bud Stonebraker, separation is required to prevent government from interfering with religious practice and expression. But the term "separation of church and state" does not appear in the Constitution, he says, and separation does not mean that Christianity must stay out of government. Stonebraker notes that 95 percent of the founding fathers were Christians who would not agree with the modern watchdogs' strict interpretation of separation. For Kahle, religion is taboo in government, and for Stonebraker government is taboo for religion.

In its suit against the city over the Family Day Parade, the ACLU, a close ally of Kahle, charged that the city is favoring Christianity over other religions. Alfred Bloom, a retired University of Hawaii professor of religion and a prominent Buddhist, agreed and observed that the Family Day Parade showed once again that Christian opponents of separation charge that their religion is being ignored and insist that "their beliefs about society must be the norm for the community." Bloom charges them with trying to foist their Christianity on all citizens with no regard for differences. Ironically, both the Christian activists and their critics feel marginalized—the former by a post-Christian secular society and the latter by Christians themselves.

Those wishing to retake America and return it to its Christian foundation are fond of citing the founding fathers, the Constitution, and the Declaration of Independence to demonstrate not only that the early history of the nation but the very nature of the country are rooted in Christianity and the Bible. Christianity, they argue, therefore can no more be removed from the foundation of America than can the founding fathers and their documents be cast aside.

"I just love this country," says Bud Stonebraker, "and I love it because I believe that at its source it's based on sound things not necessarily spiritual but Biblical." Aware that this privileged position of Christianity could be seen as religious imperialism or even—as Alfred Bloom suggests—totalitarianism, Garret Hashimoto, president of the Hawaii Christian Coalition, refers to the works of David Barton, who shows that "United States institutions were intended to honor and advance nondenominational Christianity while allowing freedom of worship for all." He also cites Orthodox Rabbi Daniel Lapin, who is grateful to Christianity for enabling American Jews to prosper.[30] Far from creating inequality, Christianity guarantees equal freedom of worship for all religions. Therein lies a justification for the Christian insistence that their beliefs about society must be the norm for the community.

Non-Christians like Alfred Bloom are not convinced that priority given to one religion is a formulation of equality for all. The debates over whether to make religion a taboo in government are controversial because they pit two deeply cherished virtues, freedom and equality, against each other.

In being prevented from praying in public schools or the legislature, evangelical Christians feel their religious freedom denied, and therefore seek to regain the liberty not only of public expression but of reestablishing Christianity as the righteousness of the land. Freedom in this case includes the freedom to give priority to one religion over others.

Equality, on the other hand, denies the freedom to establish unequal priorities. Since equality requires that one religion cannot be made more important than others, then either all religions must be given equal seating at the public table, including the foundation on which it stands; or all religions should be excluded from public life.

Total inclusion is a practical impossibility and even undesirable—should Shinto and all other religions be part of America's foundation? Strict separation, however, is possible, though clearly undesirable to many, and is the only means to equality, which is incompatible with the freedom to prioritize. In theory freedom should guarantee equality, but its practice allows inequality; that is why equality disallows freedom in practice.

Caught between the incompatibility of these two fundamental values, the question of whether religion should be separated or established in government life cannot be settled unless one is sacrificed for the other. If religion is *pono*, why should it be *kapu*? If religion is *kapu*, how can it be *pono*?

Conclusions

The intersections between religion and public life in Hawaii involve many groups and issues that have not been covered in this overview. The Catholic and Mormon formulations of *pono*, for example, deserve more attention, and *kapu* such as abortion and pornography need to be explored. Traffic through the intersections is heavy, and while every vehicle has not been stopped and searched, certain conclusions can still be drawn.

It is clear that what is happening in Hawaii is related to national trends. This is epitomized by the fact that most of the groups examined here are affiliated with national organizations. The arguments and controversies also reflect national debates. Regional religion is interregional as well.

The level of activity, however, would seem uniquely high. It may be that the greater visibility is due to the smaller size of the state. But religious organizations large and small, old and new, liberal and conservative, and Asian, Pacific, and Western, are actively engaged in pursuing *pono* and contesting *kapu*. The level of activity also seems to have increased in recent years, and some, like Dan Chun, date the change specifically to 9/11. Even Chabad (a Jewish traditionalist movement), usually reticent in Hawaii, is suddenly active.

Many churches, of course, have never been engaged with public life and continue to stay quiet. What is significant, however, is the clear drift of the mainline Protestants, once the dominant players, toward the quiet corners. Taking their place are the evangelical Christians, still a minority but growing rapidly. The evangelicals, once in the background, are now stepping into center stage. Though sometimes loud with protest and truth claims, the evangelicals are acting with increasing political sophistication. The Hawaii Family Forum in particular is a major force moving to marshal not only evangelicals but a broader consensus of conservatives in general. Krishna devotees too are against abortion and same-sex marriage.

For some issues, especially those involving sexuality, the liberal-conservative line separates the antagonists. Other issues, such as gambling, bridge the divide and bring together diverse groups. In all cases, the real players are coalitions whose members change according to the issues. Churches and temples know that networks and alliances are essential to effectiveness in public life. The game is played by teams, and the field is crowded with acronyms.

Though the modern state is vastly different from the Hawaiian nation of the nineteenth century, Ka'ahumanu and Hiram Bingham would be familiar with the role of religion in public life. They too placed *kapu* on gambling and other vices. Despite the revolutions and changes, the state motto, an embracing platitude, expresses the common ground on which they and the modern citizens of Hawaii can stand: the life of the land is perpetuated in righteousness. No one is against righteousness, but many struggle against others to perpetuate their version of righteousness in the life of the land.

Endnotes

1. Hiram Bingham cited by Gavan Daws, *Shoal of Time: A History of the Hawaiian Islands* (New York: Macmillan, 1968), 64.

2. John Charlot describes the complexities of this religious change in detail and uses the term "royalist" to describe the syncretist religion that emerged as a result of Ka'ahumanu's actions. After the arrival of the missionaries, three groups of native Hawaiians can be discerned in relationship to Christianity: the traditionalists who opposed it, the pro-Christian party, and a large number of people who were undecided. See John Charlot, "The Feather Skirt of Nhi'ena'ena: An Innovation in Postcontact Hawaiian Art," *The Journal of the Polynesian Society*, 100, (June 1991): 119-165.

3. Lilikal Kame'eleihiwa, *Native Land and Foreign Desires* (Honolulu: Bishop Museum Press, 1992), 67-82.

4. Ibid., 13.

5. Sally Engle Merry, *Colonizing Hawaii: The Cultural Power of Law* (Princeton: Princeton University Press, 2000), 70.

6. *The HCC Report*, vol. 1, no. 1 (July, 1999): 1.

7. *The HCC Report*, vol. 2, no. 2 (May, 2000).

8. *The HCC Report*, vol. 1, no. 2 (October, 1999).

9. Daniel I. Kikawa, *Perpetuated in Righteousness: The Journey of the Hawaiian People from Eden to the Present Time* (Kea'au, Hawaii: Aloha Ke Akua Publishing, 1994), 193.

10. *The HCC Report*, vol. 2, no. 3 (October 2000).

11. Ibid.

12. http://www.Hawaiifamilyforum.org.

13. *Honolulu Star-Bulletin* (December 30, 2001).

14. http://www.kgmb.com, July 14, 2003.

15. http://www.kgmb.com, July 17, 2003.

16. Project Dana 10th Anniversary booklet, 1999.

17. Protecting the Civil Rights and Religious Liberty of Faith-Based Organizations, http://www.whitehouse.gov.

18. Noa Emmett Aluli and Daviana Pmaika'i McGregor cited by Houston Wood, *Displacing Natives: The Rhetorical Production of Hawaii* (Lanham: Rowman and Littlefield, 1999), 129.

19. Tom Coffman, *The Island Edge of America: A Political History of Hawaii* (Honolulu: University of Hawaii Press, 2003), 303.

20. Ibid., 304.

21. Davianna McGregor in Robert H. Mast and Anne B. Mast, eds., *Autobiography of Protest in Hawaii* (Honolulu: University of Hawaii Press, 1996), 404.

22. Cited by Wood, *Displacing Natives*, 132.

23. Davianna McGregor in Mast and Mast, *Autobiography of Protest in Hawaii*, 405.

24. LaTonya Taylor, "Physician-Assisted Suicide Bill Dies in Hawaii Senate," *Christianity Today* (April 29, 2002), http://www.christianitytoday.com/ct/2002/116/55.0.html.

25. http://www.ama-assn.org/sci-pubs/amnews/pick_03/prsd0310.htm.

26. Summary Disposition Order, http://www.Hawaii.gov/jud/20371.htm.

27. Brief of Amicus Curiae Agudath Israel of America, No. 20371, State Supreme Court of Hawaii, http://www.Hawaiilawyer.com.

28. http://www.hawaiinews.com/archives/crime/000142.shtml.

29. http://www.hopechapelkauai.com.

30. *The HCC Report*, vol. 1, no. 2 (October, 1999).

CHAPTER SIX

CONCLUSION: FAITH AND SPIRITUALITY IN A FLUID ENVIRONMENT

Wade Clark Roof

A theme running throughout these essays is the fluid, ever-changing character of faith and spirituality in the Pacific region. It has been so since the early days. A hundred years ago, in 1906, *Sunset Magazine* published an article entitled," Is California Irreligious?"[1] The answer given was an ambivalent "yes" and "no."

If the many and varied types of faiths and spiritualities in the state—and, by extension, the region—are any basis for judgment, then it is indeed very religious. There are more religious denominations, sectarian groups split off the world religions, and new spiritual and therapeutic movements here than anywhere else in the United States. And yet, the region has a distinctively secular ethos. It has a lasting legacy shaped by a frontier heritage with its individualism, free thinking, and religious indifference. And religion has had no option but to adapt to this pervasive secular ethos. Chameleon-like, it adjusts by taking on the colors of its surrounding environment. Except in the most extreme religious forms, where boundaries with the culture are carefully guarded, this adaptive strategy is also the key to religion's continuing vitality and public company.

Outsiders see the region as peculiarly different. California is, of course, the butt of jokes everywhere in the country and in much of the world: it is a land of cults, religious fanatics, and new spiritual fads; or as Jacob Needleman says, a place that fosters "what is unusual, and often downright weird, in American life."[2] Nevada and Hawaii likewise have long been viewed through suspicious eyes—Nevada for its gambling and brothels, Hawaii for its many "alien religionists," such as Buddhists, whose beliefs and practices seemed strange from a Christian perspective.

Americans outside the region judge it by Judeo-Christian standards, which, in turn, often seem to people within the three states as rather narrow and confining.

Viewed as hostile to true religion, the region from the early days of the country's founding has been looked upon as a prime mission field for Christian evangelizing. Here of all places—in America's Babylon—the Gospel should be professed and converts won. Today the region, and California in particular, remains a challenge to those seeking to make converts.

So much enterprising missionary endeavor in the face of so much secularity is a clue to the region's religious distinctiveness. Over the years Christian missionaries have faced challenges to proselytizing, and even when successful their converts often have later either "backslided" —that is, became apostates— or joined other faith communities. For 150 years missionaries have vigorously sought through successive migrations and outreach to make California into "the image of New England, or the South, or the Mid-West,"[3] but without much lasting success. Yet the challenges they faced forced them to find innovative ways for spreading the Gospel.

Today, evangelical Christians are at the forefront of this innovative spirit in framing their message in a culturally current fashion. But creative missionary and outreach efforts are hardly limited to Christians. As these essays make clear, religious and spiritual movements of all kinds are conscious of the need to continuously "work at" recruiting members and followers. New immigrant religions recognize that they must adapt to the environment not only in order to grow, but also to gain acceptance and enhance their public presence.

Likewise, religious groups transported to California from other parts of the United States, and especially from the South, succeed to the extent they accommodate and become transformed by the popular culture—a pattern Mark Shibley describes as the "Californication" of religion.[4] Cultural transformation is essential to their influence in a particular setting. So-called cults and new spiritual movements differ in that they can maintain themselves as recognizably different, maintaining somewhat more rigid boundaries but knowing that as small groups they can find a sufficient following in a religiously pluralistic environment.

Hence we are led to ask: How do we explain this conundrum of so much religion in such a secular place? And in what ways has this environment shaped distinctive religious and spiritual styles? If, as Wallace Stegner once said, the West Coast is "pretty much like the rest of the United States, only more so," how do we describe the religious quality, or set of qualities, that makes it "more so"? It is a complex question of course, but the following three considerations shed some light.

Early Modernization

The most important consideration is one of timing. As the historian Elden G. Ernst has observed, California "emerged in a relatively well advanced stage of modernization (some would say secularization) from the beginning of its statehood in 1850." To illustrate the point, he notes:

On the wall of the Santa Barbara Mission, for example, is a photograph of the mission community in 1882, with the following medley of names: Fathers Francisco Arbondin, Bonaventure Fox, Joseph Jeremias O'Keefe, Jose Maria Romo, Francisco Sanchez, Anthony Gallagher, Joseph O'Malley, and Dominic Reid.

Even at this early date, there was considerable ethnic variety in California. Elsewhere as well the region was attracting Catholics from both Europe and Mexico. Culturally diverse people were moving in rapidly and in large numbers, creating a mosaic of traditions that continued over time to expand. Unlike other regions that had a longer history prior to major settlements and where urbanization occurred more gradually, California society thus emerged quite quickly as a pluralist society. "Conventional western European-rooted churches," as Ernst says, "have had to learn how to live in a more advanced state of the post-Christian era, where other ancient religions flower alongside the new ones."[5] It was a setting that encouraged a philosophy of "live and let live," or a stance toward religious pluralism that was favorable. While not all religious groups were theologically inclusive, overall the culture sustained, and continues to sustain, an approach to religion that is far more open and accepting than aggressively defensive.

This was less true for Nevada, but it too had a considerable mix of religious traditions in its early statehood—Mexicans from the south, Mormons from the north, Anglos from the east and some spilling over from California. Hawaii had one after another succession of migrant-labor groups who brought with them many religions during this same period, and for a lengthy period of time before becoming a state. With all three states lacking in a religious establishment and shaped by the cross-pressures of competing religions and cultures, the Pacific region came onto the American scene almost from the beginning as a prematurely modern religious environment.

For this reason, Christianity has simply not had the influence here that it enjoyed in most other regions of the country. Its lack of imprint on the culture is evident in its weak hold upon major social institutions. Bible reading in public schools, for example, was never as pronounced on the West Coast as elsewhere in the United States. In the Cold War years before the Supreme Court ruled this practice unconstitutional, only 2.4 percent of schools throughout the western region held devotional services; however, 76.8 percent of the public schools in the southern states, where there was a dominate Protestant culture, did so.[6] Religion in the Pacific region—as for the West Coast generally—continues to have far less of a constraining public presence.

To get to the heart of the argument, with modernization has come a fundamental shift in the role of religion in society. Unlike in earlier, more traditional societies, religion in the modern, pluralist world is less of a unifying force with regard to beliefs and moral values; and individuals are more autonomous and free in their pursuit of religious and spiritual interests. As tradition loses much of its hold on society, there is greater fluidity and more dynamic, often contested, encounters over values, beliefs, and practices. What we have is Zymunt Bauman's "liquid modernity" (quoted in Douglas Firth Anderson's chapters), or a situation characterized by individually tailored meaning systems and frequent shifts in popular outlook, and hence much less of a collectively shared sense of religious groundedness. In this important respect, the Pacific region has always been greatly distanced from the European religious heritage as it took root early in the United States, and particularly on the East Coast.

Modern religious consciousness also entails a sense of self as malleable and capable of growth and transformation. Since the 1960s a particular type of self-oriented culture has flourished, described sometimes as "expressive individualism" or "search for authenticity,"[7] both calling attention to roots in Romantic expressivism of the late eighteenth century. Reinforced by an all-embracing consumption ethic, the reigning cultural mood at present encourages people to try to make, or remake, themselves by changing life-styles and to cultivate cultural identities by aligning themselves with others of a similar persuasion. This inward turn privileges the view, as the philosopher Charles Taylor writes, that "each of us has his or her own way of realizing one's own humanity, and that it is important to find and live out one's own, as against surrendering to the conformity with a model imposed from outside, by society, or the previous generation, or religious or political authority."[8] An individual's own self discovery and self actualization is what matters, particularly in the religious and spiritual realms. This holds throughout the country, but is especially pronounced in the Pacific region, where so much of the counterculture of the late 1960s and early 1970s originated and shaped popular attitudes and outlook.

For the actual practice of religion, the implications are considerable. In the context of advanced modernity religion becomes largely a personal and voluntary matter. One "chooses" a faith or spirituality (or none) on the basis of "preferences" or "needs" or "convenience." Inherited religion, or that which one received from his or her parents, becomes less important than that which one claims for one's self. In this milieu an individual must assume responsibility for cultivating faith or spirituality. Congregations and other religious collectivities become, in effect, "affinity groups." They are options for an individual who selects them, or a set of spiritual teachings and practices, on the basis of how well they mesh with one's own personal and family interests. Such affinities obviously vary in strength of commitment; in instances where they are strong, people often develop enduring communal bonds. People can, and do, switch from one community to another as their life-situations change.

For religious organizations, this means greater competition with one another for followings. Especially given the Pacific region's secularity, organizational innovation is essential. The greater the challenge, the more religions are forced to become entrepreneurial. David Machacek in his chapter calls attention to organizational innovation—to nondenominational churches, "new paradigm" churches, multi-congregational churches, megachurches, and niche churches—all of which now flourish within the region. And in earlier times there were other innovations that marked the Pacific region as avant-garde—Aimee Semple McPherson's flamboyant, charismatic preaching that helped to shape the modern Pentecostal movement and Robert Schuller's drive-in church, to cite two well-known examples.

Traditional churches must also compete with other "spiritual suppliers," such as New Age bookstores, discussion groups, lectures on spirituality, home churches, retreat centers, corporate consultants on spirituality, and of course the Internet.[9] The notion of religious competition and need for creative innovation is sometimes resisted by traditional religious groups in some places within the United States, but in this pluralist and ever-changing region it is generally assumed that such efforts are essential to institutional survival.

Spiritual Geography

A theme that gets little explicit attention in this collection is that of spiritual geography, although its importance for the region generally comes up here and there in the chapters. "Spiritual geography" refers to a way of organizing reality in relation to the sacred that privileges the centrality of nature and its capacity to inspire—often referred to as "nature religion." Because nature religion does not, perhaps cannot, institutionalize well, it is difficult to define its expressions with any precision. Yet the depth of its sacred qualities and symbolic significance shouldn't be overlooked, especially considering that in many important ways as a theme it intersects with the argument about the region's modern consciousness.

The region has its own distinctive spiritual geography dominated by mountains and valleys, oceans and deserts, towering pinnacles and deep caves. Its high mountain peaks and open vistas inspire solitude, reverence, awe, and the pursuit of harmony—themes perennially important to metaphysical religions. Mystics and contemplatives are attracted to the region's natural beauty, seeking to become attuned with nature and its flow; convinced that it holds the secrets to overcoming personal pain and hardship, they believe nature fosters "positive thinking," or an optimism with respect to healing, health, and visionary expansion.

Nature worship likewise draws upon religious and spiritual vocabularies—Julia "Butterfly" Hill speaks of the "majestic cathedral of the redwoods" and of forests as "the holiest of holy temples"—for describing how it inspires a sense of the unity and connectedness of all living things. Connecting with nature is seen as a way of connecting with a mysterious but purposeful universe. Presumably it was the overwhelming beauty and majesty of the natural landscape that led a Presbyterian minister in 1893 to describe California as having "a contended indifferentism" toward organized religion. Even so, however, he chose not to dismiss the setting as secular, noting that "God is acknowledged and believed in and believed to govern, good-naturedly withal."[10] Goodness prevails—on the part both of Nature and its people!

Important is the fact that attention to nature in California, and to some extent in Hawaii and Nevada, on the part of non-Native Americans came roughly at the same time that interest in metaphysical religion flourished in New England. A direct lineage extends from Ralph Waldo Emerson, who published *Nature* in 1836, to John Muir's hikes at Yosemite and the founding of the Sierra Club in the late 1800s, and right on down to the more recent environmentalist movements, concerns about animal rights, and interests in neo-paganism, earth-based spirituality, and Native-American spiritualities.

Not to be overlooked too are the many sacred sites. Pilgrimages to these sites, as Tamar Frankiel emphasizes, activate memories of a person's spiritual nature and realization of the divine potential or "higher self" within one. Nature religion is thus closely intertwined with self-discovery and self-transformation, and thus two themes very prominent in the Pacific region's spiritual culture become conflated. Modern religious consciousness as it arose in this part of the world encompasses not just a broad acceptance of the plurality of competing organized religions, but recognition that there are many differing epistemologies, or ways of knowing and relating to the sacred—and nature is one such important way.

Of course, nature has its harshness and unpredictability: earthquakes, fires, mudslides, and volcanic eruptions result in fear and an impulse to try to control and master. Given these wretched and largely uncontrollable events we might say that residents of this region live on the edge, never far removed from the primal forces. This too engenders spiritual awareness. Facing the wildness of nature is not altogether dissimilar to visiting the pilgrimage site in Nevada where the first atomic bomb was tested, or on a much lesser scale, playing the odds at the casino. They all confront one with risk, and thus amount to existential moments. Risk-taking forces upon one a spiritual response, perhaps even a leap of faith.

Multilayered Spirituality

A third theme follows naturally from the other two: Eclectic styles of religion and spirituality flourish within the region. Partly this is because of the openness toward diversity and the fact that people within religious communities feel free to absorb aspects of other traditions in their spiritual lives. But it also reflects a legacy born out of a particular history of migrations, conquests, and mixes of faith traditions that have come to co-exist in a particular area. Hawaii is a good example. Here many Christians are relatively at ease drawing upon elements from Native Hawaiian spirituality as well as Asian values and beliefs. Some 40 years ago a commentator wrote:

> Hawaii is neither a single religious community nor a plural society of several separate religious communities, but a society in which religions meet, interpenetrate, and change. An alert and trained visitor soon becomes aware of the great diversity....Here is an Episcopal church with its cross, flanked on each side by a Japanese Shinto shrine, each with a Japanese torii gateway. There he finds a little Chinese shrine to the fishing god in the living room of a small house, sandwiched between a Roman Catholic church and a Protestant Episcopal church. At the Pacific war memorial Cemetery he sees a Buddhist wheel on many gravestones in the place of the cross which is on most of the others.[11]

Such a high level of blending probably could not have occurred without the underlying spiritual framework of *pono* and *kapu* described by George J. Tanabe, Jr. Traditional Hawaiian spirituality dating back to the early Polynesians emphasized the maintenance of harmony and righteousness, and reinforced those ideals with taboos forbidding anything disrupting that equilibrium. Christian, Mormon, Buddhist, and other religious formulations of moral order and threats to moral order here continue to be cast in keeping with these foundational spiritual principles. Despite distinctive and competing visions of the public role of religion, the complex multilayered spirituality that follows sustains a sense of social unity amidst all its diversity.

Nevada has a similar culture of openness and borrowing from other traditions. Over the years Christians there have absorbed, selectively, Native-American spiritual teachings and practices. One commentator argues, in fact, that throughout the twentieth century Native-American religion has remained as a "potent undercurrent of mainstream religion" in that state, and predicts this will be even more so in the century ahead.[12] As with Hawaii, its native culture provides a substratum on which considerable mixing and matching of spiritual themes rests.

Much the same can be said for California, of course. But its greater size and pluralism make it impossible to point to any single spiritual undercurrent. On the part of European-Americans, there is, however, a strong yearning to explore primitive spirituality. It is as if there is a profound ambivalence arising out of centuries of dualistic thinking that divides the world—that is, the white world— between a primitive "them" and a modern "us."

Repackaged New Age spiritualities touching upon this quest for wholeness today flourish, both inside and outside traditional religious communities. This influence is far greater than often realized, even within the churches. "The New Age phenomenon surrounds conventional religion like a cultural fog, almost completely lacking in large-scale organization but giving the fringes of faith a mysterious appearance" writes the sociologist William Sims Bainbridge, describing a situation quite applicable to many Californians involved in religious communities.[13]

Nor can we overlook the long and painful history of conquest and contested claims to the land throughout the region, and its aftermath of tension and anger. Tensions continue to arise between Native Americans and others who would single out particular practices from their traditions and introduce them into the mainstream spiritual marketplace. It is still remembered that Mormons sought to carve out a new state named Deseret back in the mid-1880s in much of what is now California and Nevada. Emotions still occasionally get charged over the history of encounters between natives and American colonists in Hawaii; and of course this is even more the case between Mexicans and European-Americans with disputes over the lands in the Southwest. Considering that Mexico lost territory to the United States, the sociologist Milagros Pena points to the ambivalence and anger many Mexicans and other Latinos feel by posing the question: Are Mexican immigrants entering the United States, or did Anglo immigrants enter into the Southwest Latino/a homeland?[14] No matter the official or legal answers, people's identities and relation to the land are at stake.

But in a middle-class, consumption culture that privileges that which is new, even if it is little more than a repackaging of the old, the pursuit of spiritual growth and drawing off a variety of traditions is generally looked upon as a pleasant and positive experience. Spirituality, at least in its popular versions, is defined as something to be explored and tried out, and then finally judged subjectively as to its adequacy or appropriateness. Many phrases are used to describe the style of religiosity and spirituality that is so prominent in the region—privatized religion, invisible religion, spiritual seeking, religion a la carte, hybridity, mixing of the codes, and of course the frequently cited saying that one is "spiritual but not religious."

Some years ago the commentator Martin E. Marty proposed another phrase that seems especially well-suited to the region's highly secular and low-commitment religious sectors that make up about half the population—that is, the "religion of the highrise apartment and the long weekend." It captures something of the ethos of modernity as well as the ambiguity of deciding whether the region, and California in particular, is religious or secular, which was the issue posed at the beginning of this essay. Marty called attention to the fact that:

.....in a consumer society that assures great freedom, including the freedom to be nonreligious or utterly selective, many people find meaning without belonging, religions without community. They pick and choose among the offerings of the book store, the television set, the magazine rack, the dormitory, and the promptings of the heart. They are free to be eclectic, taking this from science and that from Zen, this from remembered Catholicism and that from hoped-for therapy, to form what Margaret Mead in one speech called a "mishmash of all the religions ever known."[15]

Perhaps not a mishmash of all religions ever known, but certainly many of them! Marty's notion of "remembered religion" is insightful: many people in the region can talk about their family's religious history or even their own religious past better than they can affirm what they themselves actually believe in the present moment. This does not mean they have no beliefs but instead that their beliefs and doubts, convictions and curiosities are all coupled together. Living faith and spirituality in a fluid environment is very much like that—at times confusing and complicated, yet at other times quite centered and convincing. Especially for the large constituencies in this region caught between religious extremism and a full-blown secularism, such fluidity is common.

This summary interpretation must be concluded by noting that Elden G. Ernst once said that California is "a highly particularized instance of religious life, it stretches our religious imagination and our conception of what it means to be religious."[16] That is certainly a fair statement. As judged by religious diversity, style, or innovative institutional forms, it is difficult to imagine any place in the country matching it. Required as he says, however, is an imagination, or the ability to see religious possibilities that extend beyond conventional ecclesiastical views. His statement meshes with Wallace Stegner's general characterization of California quoted earlier as "pretty much like the rest of the country, only more so." Thinking about religious and spiritual currents in a context of advanced modernity, it is possible to extend Stegner's characterization as follows: California is like Hawaii and Nevada, but "only more so." And all three states combined are like the country, but "only more so."

Endnotes

1. Robert Whitaker, "Is California Irreligious?" *Sunset Magazine* 16 (1906): 382-385.
2. Jacob Needleman, *The New Religions* (Garden City. N.Y.: Doubleday, 1970), 4.
3. Elden G. Ernst, "Religion in California," *Pacific Theological Review* 19 (Winter 1986), 46.
4. Mark A, Shibley, *Resurgent Evangelicalism in the United States* (Columbia: University of South Carolina Press, 1996), Part III.
5. Elden G. Ernst, "Religion in California," 46.
6. Reported in Richard B, Dierenfeld, "Religion in American Public Schools" (Washington, D.C.: Public Affairs Press, 1962).
7. The term "expressive individualism" comes from Robert Bellah and his colleagues, *Habits of the Heart: Individualism and Commitment in American Life* (Berkeley: University of California Press, 1985). "Search for authenticity" is discussed in Charles Taylor's book, *The Malaise of Modernity* (Toronto: Anansi, 1991).
8. Charles Taylor, *Varieties of Religion Today* (Cambridge: Harvard University Press, 2002), 83.
9. The Internet amplifies, more than it creates, the development of new religious styles and new attitudes toward religious institutions by encouraging people to explore other faiths and express their faiths in a personal way—which of course is very Californian. Internet users who most engage in online religious activities affirm some affinity with religious communities. See Wade Clark Roof and Nathalie Caron, "Shifting Boundaries: Religion in the United States," *Cambridge Companion to Modern American Culture* (Cambridge: Cambridge University Press, forthcoming).
10. This quote is reported in Elden G. Ernst's "Religion in California," 47.
11. Bernard L. Hormann, "Toward a Sociology of Religion in Hawaii," *Social Process in Hawaii* 25 (1961-62): 58.
12. Richard V. Francaviglia, *Believing in Place: A Spiritual Geography of the Great Basin* (Reno: University of Nevada, 2003), 116.
13. William Sims Bainbridge, *The Sociology of Religious Movements* (New York: Routledge, 1997), 390.
14. Milagros Pena, "Latina Empowerment, Border Realities, and Faith-Based Organizations," in Michele Dillon, ed., *Handbook of the Sociology of Religion* (Cambridge: Cambridge University Press, 2003), 400-411.
15. Martin E. Marty, "Interpreting American Pluralism" in Jackson W. Carroll, Douglas W. Johnson, and Martin E. Marty, *Religion in America: 1950 to the Present* (New York: Harper and Row, 1979), 83.
16. Elden G. Ernst, "Religion in California," 48.

APPENDIX

In order to provide the best possible empirical basis for understanding the place of religion in each of the religions of the United States, the Religion by Region project contracted to obtain data from three sources: the North American Religion Atlas (NARA); the 2001 American Religious Identification Survey (ARIS); and the 1992, 1996, and 2000 National Surveys of Religion and Politics (NSRP).

NARA For the project, the Polis Center of Indiana University-Purdue University at Indianapolis created an interactive Web site that made it possible to map general demographic and religious data at the national, regional, state-by-state, and county-by-county level. The demographic data were taken from the 2000 census. The primary source for the religious data (congregations, members, and adherents) was the 2000 Religious Congregations and Membership Survey (RCMC) compiled by the Glenmary Research Center. Because a number of religious groups did not participate in the 2000 RCMS—including most historically African-American Protestant denominations—this dataset was supplemented with data from other sources *for adherents only*. The latter included projections from 1990 RCMC reports, ARIS, and several custom estimates. For a fuller methodological account, go to *http://www.religionatlas.org*.

ARIS The American Religious Identification Survey (ARIS 2001), carried out under the auspices of the Graduate Center of the City University of New York by Barry A. Kosmin, Egon Mayer, and Ariela Keysar, replicates the methodology of the National Survey of Religious Identification (NSRI 1990). As in 1990, the ARIS sample is based on a series of national random digit dialing (RDD) surveys, utilizing ICR, International Communication Research Group in Media, Pennsylvania, national telephone omnibus services. In all, 50,284 U.S. households were successfully interviewed. Within a household, an adult respondent was chosen using the "last birthday method" of random selection. One of the distinguishing features of both ARIS 2001 and NSRI 1990 is that respondents were asked to describe themselves in terms of religion with an open-ended question: "What is your religion, if any?"[1] ARIS 2001 enhanced the topics covered by adding ques-

179

tions concerning religious beliefs and membership as well as religious switching and religious identification of spouses/partners. The ARIS findings have a high level of statistical significance for most large religious groups and key geographical units, such as states. ARIS 2001 detailed methodology can be found in the report on the American Religious Identification Survey 2001 at *www.gc.cuny. edu/studies/aris_index.htm.*

NSRP The National Surveys of Religion and Politics were conducted in 1992, 1996, and 2000 at the Bliss Center at the University of Akron under the direction of John C. Green, supported by grants from the Pew Charitable Trusts.

Together, these three surveys include more than 14,000 cases. Eight items were asked in all three surveys (partisanship, ideology, abortion, gay rights, help for minorities, environmental protection, welfare spending, and national health insurance). The responses on these items were pooled for all three years to produce enough cases for an analysis by region. These data must be viewed with some caution because they represent opinion over an entire decade rather than at one point in time. A more detailed account of how these data were compiled may be obtained from the Bliss Institute.

Endnote

1. In the 1990 NSRI survey, the question wording was: "What is your religion?" In the 2001 ARIS survey, the phrase, "...if any" was added to the question. A subsequent validity check based on cross-samples of 3,000 respondents carried out by ICR in 2002 found no statistical difference in the pattern of responses according to the two wordings.

BIBLIOGRAPHY

Abbott, Carl. *The Metropolitan Frontier: Cities in the Modern West.* Tucson: University of Arizona Press, 1993.

Coffman, Tom. *The Island Edge of America: A Political History of Hawaii.* Honolulu: University of Hawaii Press, 2003.

Davis, Mike. *City of Quartz: Excavating the Future in Los Angeles.* New York: Vintage Books, 1992.

Engh, Michael E. *Frontier Faiths: Church, Temple, and Synagogue in Los Angeles, 1846-1888.* Albuquerque: University of New Mexico Press, 1992.

Ernst, Elden G., with Douglas Firth Anderson. *Pilgrim Progression.* Santa Barbara, CA: Fithian Press, 1993.

Ernst, Eldon G. "Religion in California." *Pacific Theological Review* (Winter 1986).

Francaviglia, Richard V. *Believing in Place: A Spiritual Geography of the Great Basin.* Reno: University of Nevada, 2003.

Frankiel, Tamar (Sandra S.). *California's Spiritual Frontiers: Alternatives to Anglo-Protestantism 1850-1915.* Berkeley: University of California Press, 1988.

Hammond, Phillip E., and David W. Machacek. *Soka Gakkai in America: Accommodation and Conversion.* Oxford: Oxford University Press, 1999.

Marsden, George M. *Reforming Fundamentalism: Fuller Seminary and the New Evangelicalism.* Grand Rapids, MI: William B. Eerdmans Publishing, 1987.

Miller, Donald E. *Reinventing American Protestantism: Christianity in the New Millennium.* Berkeley: University of California Press, 1997.

Moore, Deborah Dash. *To the Golden Cities: Pursuing the American Jewish Dream in Miami and L.A.* New York: Free Press, 1994.

Mulholland, John F. *Hawaii's Religions.* Rutland, Vermont: Charles T. Tuttle Company, 1970.

Nugent, Walter. *Into the West: The Story of Its People*. New York: Alfred A. Knopf, 1999.

Numrich, Paul. *Old Wisdom in the New World: Americanization in Two Immigrant Theravada Buddhist Temples*. Knoxville: University of Tennessee Press, 1996.

Rischin, Moses, and John Livingston, eds. *Jews of the American West*. Detroit: Wayne State University Press, 1990.

Roof, Wade Clark. *A Generation of Seekers: The Journeys of the Baby Boom Generation*. San Francisco: Harper San Francisco, 1993.

Rothman, Hal. *Neon Metropolis: How Las Vegas Started the Twenty-First Century*. New York: Routledge, 2002.

Sandberg, Neil C. *Jewish Life in Los Angeles: A Window to Tomorrow*. Lanham, MD: University Press of America, 1986.

Starr, Kevin. *Americans and the California Dream*, 5 volumes. New York: Oxford University Press, 1973-1997.

_____. *Coast of Dreams: California on the Edge, 1990-2003*. New York: Alfred A. Knopf, 2004.

Szasz, Ferenc M. *Religion in the Modern American West*. Tuscon: University of Arizona Press, 2000.

Tong, Benson, and Regan A. Lutz, eds. *The Human Tradition in the American West*. Wilmington, DE: Scholarly Resources, 2002.

Voskuil, Dennis. *Mountains into Goldmines: Robert Schuller and the Gospel of Success*. Grand Rapids, MI: William B. Eerdmans Publishing, 1983.

Ward, Kenric F. *Saints in Babylon: Mormons and Las Vegas*. Bloomington, IN: 1st Books Library, 2002.

INDEX

Abbott, Carl, 83
abortion, 50, 52
Academy of Jewish Religion, 135
ACLU. *See* American Civil Liberties
Union
Acorn Sangha, 114
adherence. *See* religious adherence
Adventists, 33, 38
affinity groups, 172–73
Affleck, Ben, 128
African-American Muslims, 100–101
African-American Protestants, 53
African Americans, 26, *27,* 29, 30,
31, 32
African immigrant churches, 94, 95
African Methodist Episcopal Church,
44
African Methodist Episcopal Zion
Church, 44
African Methodists, 38
Agudath Israel America, 160
Aitken, Robert, 98
Alaska, 12
Alaskan Natives, 29, 30, 31, 32
Albanese, Catherine L., 83
Alliance for Traditional Marriage and
Values, 159
aloha'ina, 154–55
Aloha Ke Akua Christian ministry,
141
alternative religions: apocalypticism,
127–30; Buddhism, 120–22;

educational institutions, 134–35;
historical perspective, 110–15;
Native American issues, 130–34;
nature religion, 122–25; in the
Pacific region, 109; personalism,
115–18; public activism and,
118–20, 134–36; sacred ecology,
125–26
Aluli, Emmett, 154
Amat, Tadeo, 64
American Baptists, 35, 45
"American Buddhism," 98
American Civil Liberties Union
(ACLU), 69, 147, 148, 162, 163
American Dream, 9–10, 58, 84
American Holocaust (film), 130
Americanization, 92, 97
American Jewish College, 69
"Americanness," 90
American Red Cross, 95
American Religious Identification
Survey (ARIS), 15, 21, 32,
179–80
Americans and the California Dream
(Starr), 9–10
Americans United for the Separation
of Church and State, 69
Anabaptists, 49
Anderson, Douglas Firth, 41
Andrews, Lynn, 133–34
Angelus Temple, 71
Anglican Communion, 48

CONTRIBUTORS

Douglas Firth Anderson is professor of history at Northwestern College in Iowa. He holds a Ph.D. in American religious history from the Graduate Theological Union. He is the author of various articles on religious history in the American West and the co-author of *Pilgrim Progression: The Protestant Experience in California* (Fithian Press, 1993).

Tamar Frankiel is dean of students and professor of comparative religion at the Academy for Jewish Religion, California. She holds a Ph.D. in history of religions from the University of Chicago. She is author of *Gospel Hymns and Social Religion: The Rhetoric of Nineteenth Century Revivalism* (Temple University Press, 1978), *Christianity: A Way of Salvation* (HarperSanFrancisco, 1985), and *California's Spiritual Frontiers: Alternatives in Protestantism 1850-1910* (University of California Press, 1988).

Phillip E. Hammond is the D. Mackenzie Brown Professor Emeritus at the University of California, Santa Barbara. He holds a Ph.D. in sociology from Columbia University. His publications include *Religion and Personal Autonomy: The Third Disestablishment in America* (University of South Carolina Press, 1992), *Soka Gakkai in America: Accommodation and Conversion* (Oxford University Press, 1999, with David W. Machacek), *The Dynamics of Religious Organizations: The Extravasation of the Sacred and Other Essays* (Oxford University Press, 2000), and *Religion On Trial: How Supreme Court Trends Threaten the Freedom of Conscience in America* (AltaMira, 2004, with David W. Machacek and Eric Michael Mazur).

David W. Machacek is resident fellow at the Leonard E. Greenberg Center for the Study of Religion in Public Life and visiting assistant professor of public policy at Trinity College in Hartford, Connecticut. He holds a Ph.D. in religious studies from the University of California at Santa Barbara. He is co-author of *Soka Gakkai in America: Accommodation and Conversion* (Oxford University Press, 1999) and *Religion on Trial: How Supreme Court Trends Threaten the Freedom of Conscience in America* (AltaMira, 2004) and co-editor of *Global*

Citizens: the Soka Gakkai Buddhist Movement in the World (Oxford University Press, 2000) and *Sexuality and the World's Religions* (ABC-CLIO, 2003).

Wade Clark Roof is the J.F. Rowny Professor of Religion and Society and director of the Walter H. Capps Center for the Study of Ethics, Religion, and Public Life at the University of California at Santa Barbara. He received a Ph.D. in sociology from the University of North Carolina at Chapel Hill. Major writings include *American Mainline Religion: Its Changing Shape and Future* (Rutgers University Press, 1987 with William McKinney), *A Generation of Seekers: The Spiritual Journeys of the Baby Boom Generation* (HarperSanFrancisco, 1993), *Spiritual Marketplace: Baby Boomers and the Remaking of American Religion* (Princeton University Press, 1999). He is the editor of the two-volume encyclopedia, *Contemporary American Religion*.

Mark Silk is associate professor of religion in public life and founding director of the Leonard E. Greenberg Center for the Study of Religion in Public Life at Trinity College in Hartford, Connecticut. A former newspaper reporter and member of the editorial board at the *Atlanta Journal-Constitution*, he is author of *Spiritual Politics: Religion and Politics in America Since World War II* (Simon and Schuster, 1988) and *Unsecular Media: Making News of Religion in America* (University of Illinois Press, 1995). He is editor of *Religion in the News*, a magazine published by the Greenberg Center that examines how journalists handle religious subject matter.

George J. Tanabe, Jr. is professor of religion in the department of religion at the University of Hawaii. He holds a Ph.D. in East Asian languages and cultures from Columbia University. He is the author of *Myoe the Dreamkeeper: Fantasy and Knowledge in Early Kamakura Buddhism* (Harvard University Press, 1992), co-author of *Practically Religious: Worldly Benefits and the Common Religion of Japan* (University of Hawaii Press, 1998), editor of *Religions of Japan in Practice* (Princeton University Press, 1999), and co-editor of *Sources of Japanese Tradition* (Columbia University Press, 2001).